D0961843

The Microsoft Way

Other books written by the author

Steve Jobs and the NeXT Big Thing

Bulls in the China Shop, and Other Sino-American
Business Encounters

The Stubborn Earth: American Agriculturalists on
Chinese Soil, 1898–1937

Books edited by the author

Remapping China: Fissures in Historical Terrain (co-editor)

Technology and Society in Twentieth-Century America

Randall E. Stross

The Microsoft Way

**The Real
Story of How
the Company
Outsmarts Its
Competition**

♦♦ **Addison-Wesley Publishing Company, Inc.**

Reading, Massachusetts • Menlo Park, California • New York • Don Mills, Ontario • Harlow, England • Amsterdam • Bonn
Sydney • Singapore • Tokyo • Madrid • San Juan • Paris • Seoul • Milan • Mexico City • Taipei

Many of the designations used by manufacturers and sellers to distinguish their products are claimed as trademarks. Where those designations appear in this book and Addison-Wesley was aware of a trademark claim, the designations have been printed in initial capital letters (e.g., Windows).

Library of Congress Cataloging-in-Publication Data
Stross, Randall E.
    The Microsoft way: the real story of how the company outsmarts its competition / Randall E. Stross.
      p.   cm.
    Includes bibliographical references (p.   ) and index.
    ISBN 0-201-40949-6
    1. Microsoft Corporation—History.   2. Computer software industry—United States—History.   3. Competition—United States.   4. Gates, Bill, 1955–   . I. Title.
    HD9696.C64M536   1996
    338.7'610051'0973—dc20   96-25397
                                                                CIP

Copyright © 1996 by Randall E. Stross

All rights reserved. No part of this publication may be reproduced, stored in a retrieval system, or transmitted, in any form or by any means, electronic, mechanical, photocopying, recording, or otherwise, without the prior written permission of the publisher. Printed in the United States of America. Published simultaneously in Canada.

Jacket design by Robert Dietz
Text design by Jean Hammond
Set in 11-point ITC Garamond by Graphic World Inc.

23456789-MA-0099989796
Second printing, October 1996

Addison-Wesley books are available at special discounts for bulk purchases. For more information about how to make such purchases in the U.S., please contact the Corporate, Government, and Special Sales Department at Addison-Wesley Publishing Company, 1 Jacob Way, Reading, MA 01867, or call (800) 238-9682.

To my parents

Contents

The Microsoft Way

Camping with Henry and Bill

Consider this sign of the times: the April 1996 issue of *Wired* magazine supplied its readers with a helpful tourist guide to the World Wide Web entitled "On Hating Microsoft." Every site listed was dedicated to venting disgust, rage, and an assortment of other strong negative feelings about a certain software company and its chairman. A typical offering found on the Web at the "Bill Gates Fun Page" provided visitors with a photograph of Gates (two devil's horns added to the top of his head) and an array of weapons—knife, Uzi machine gun, cannon—that could be directed at him with a click of the mouse. Of course, anyone could devise a Web page, and to read too much cultural meaning into the appearance of such sites would be foolish. The Web was simply displaying an anti-Microsoft sentiment that has been in the air for years.

Essentially, we have two choices. On the one hand, we can accept a characterization of Gates as the antichrist, Microsoft as the evil empire, its software as junk, and the company's success as rooted in deceptions, outright lies, legal trickery, and brute-force marketing. On the other hand, we can take the company at its own word that it has benevolently ushered in the personal computer revolution and that its market success is the just reward for the service it has rendered the public.

Three years ago, I put aside both the company's own self-interested depiction of its story and the denunciations of its external critics. I sought my own answer to the question of how the company has arrived at its prominent position. By training, I am a historian, and my starting point was as an agnostic. I did not know whether I would conclude that the company deserved to be assailed as a monopoly delivering, if not evil, at least technological mediocrity, or whether its own benign explanations for its success made more sense. I had been drawn to the challenge of piercing myths in the computer industry in a previous book, in which I looked at the business adventures of Steve Jobs after he left Apple in 1985 and founded NeXT, Inc. Like the Wizard of Oz, Jobs's "brilliance" evaporated when I looked behind the curtain. I wondered if I would again find less than meets the eye if I peered behind the Microsoft curtain.

Research for this book was well underway before I knocked on Microsoft's door. The timing of my initial visit was not accidental: I wanted the company to know that the book's feasibility did not hinge on the company's cooperation. But when I jiggled its doorknob, expecting to find it securely locked, to my surprise the door gave way and in I went. I became the first historian granted access to Microsoft's archives, which include an extensive collection of videotapes of internal talks given by company executives, as well as internal correspondence, memos, "post-mortem" assessments of products, e-mail printouts, and other documents that have not been made public. The company also permitted me to interview anyone I sought and provided a "No Escort Required" badge and unfettered access to offices and the company's library. Unlike other companies I had encountered in past research, the Microsoft executives understood that ultimately this access would be of value to the book and that readers would accept my findings, if the access was provided unconditionally. The company accepted without a peep my dictum that it held absolutely no right to review the results of my work before publication. With unimpeded access to the raw materials of the company's history, I began working to find a satisfactory answer to the question: What accounts for Microsoft's place in the cosmos?

In a nutshell, my conclusions tend to exonerate Microsoft of the most serious charges leveled against it. My position already may have raised the eyebrows of many prospective readers. To be frank, the congruence of an author's views and those of the company that has fully cooperated with the author's investigation is indeed circumstantially suspicious. Having read only this far, I'd be suspicious, too, of the supposed independence of thought that the author claims to have had. I am not happy to find myself in this position, especially because Gates is rich and his company powerful. It does not seem fair, in the grand scheme of things, that he and his company should be praised, to boot.

Knowing that people's opinions about Microsoft are highly charged—and, outside of Microsoft, seem to be mostly hostile—I realize that almost anything I say defensively from this point on could serve to further undermine my credibility. I am tempted to address the skeptical reader, insisting that my range of motion was indeed independent, explaining that I was not a naïf duped by my hosts, asserting that I cannot do anything but call it as I see it. However, I wager I would only be greeted with, "He doth protest too much."

All I can ask of those who may be ready to dismiss my opinion is a bit of forbearance. Permit me to lay out how I have come to regard Microsoft, the apparent apotheosis of crude, ruthless business power, as not just surprisingly benign, but also as a company whose methods, if emulated more broadly by other companies, would for the most part improve our collective interests as a society.

What most struck me about Microsoft as I examined its operations at close range was not the company's market share but the intense, pragmatic thoughtfulness that informed its decisions. I observed no scolding "THINK!" sign on the walls as in the IBM of yore, but "THINK" permeated Microsoft's bloodstream through and through. This was a company of smart people, managed well, constantly learning as it went. The way that smarts have been harnessed, the extent to which the company has, we might say, learned how to learn, is not visible from afar, nor is it visible in a snapshot taken at a given moment. Only when I looked at the company's records over a period of time did patterns emerge. I paid attention less to what Microsoft employees now said, retrospectively, that they had done in the past than to what employees were saying contemporaneously, a year, or several years, or many years back, and what actually happened subsequently. A historical perspective on the company's evolution provides a depth that reporting on this week's industry developments cannot capture.

Historical perspective also is helpful in explaining the phenomenon of the enormous hostility that Microsoft has generated in the course of its growth. Even though I concluded that most of the charges directed at Microsoft are groundless, the criticism and the emotions that surface with the mere mention of the company's name constitute a phenomenon that begs for examination itself. Stepping back and looking at a much bigger picture is helpful here. We live in a time of major technological change, with uncertain economic impact. We know that we are in the midst of a historically important transition, but where that transition is headed is far from clear. Anxiety about the future needs to rest on something, and I suggest that Gates and Microsoft have been the handy, cathartic target for a host of free-floating, rarely articulated concerns about where we are going.

When journalists reporting on Gates require historical garnish, they casually describe him as the Rockefeller, the Edison, or the Ford of our times. The comparison with Henry Ford most intrigues me, especially because Microsoft's publicity blitz for the release of Windows 95 reached unparalleled heights. The campaign itself became a news story and generated still more publicity, pushing Microsoft into the nooks and crannies that had somehow managed to escape its penetration. The release of Gates's *The Road Ahead*, with a publisher teaming its own publicity resources with those of Microsoft, took Gates and his company to still greater heights and to the top of bestseller lists. Searching back through time from Bill Gates, who was the last business figure whose iconic face, every utterance, and company was so broadly disseminated throughout society if not Henry Ford?

Some observers have drawn a parallel between the similar roles Ford and Gates played in the earliest years of their respective industries. Each succeeded by making the inventions of others broadly affordable. However, Ford and Gates are really of most interest for what is revealed about the public in their respective eras. Surely the fact that both men's worldwide success was first achieved, and closely chronicled, in the United States, is important. American culture venerates business success like no other and confers a presumption of great wisdom on the winners. Contemporary culture seems smitten with celebrities and inducts business figures such as Gates into the same gallery of larger-than-life icons. Remember that Ford, too, not only engineered tremendous publicity for himself—like Gates, Ford was that most beguiling public figure, the Shy Person—but he also had a receptive public.

The business success of Ford Motor Company's early years is still remembered. However, public memory seems capable of honoring only a single contributor, like Henry Ford, and casts aside his irreplaceable partner, the icy James Couzens, with whom Ford would later have a falling out. Posterity also has been averse to remembering the dark side of Henry Ford: his self-presumed omniscience; his paranoia, verging on dementia, with its anti-Semitic obsessions; and his reluctance to release his hold on the company that bore his name, bringing it to the verge of collapse.

Ford was famous for his disdain for studying the past ("history is more or less bunk"). Gates, too, has been impatient with "looking in the rear-view mirror," the phrase he and others at Microsoft use dismissively; to him, it's a "a waste of time, basically." Even on the occasion of Microsoft's twentieth anniversary in 1995, he wrote that "the future is what matters, which is why I don't look back too often." And yet he has looked back all the time—frequently, insistently, systematically. He cites historical examples whenever he discusses future strategy. He uses a historical perspective when he notes that in the commercial history of computing, no company that was the leader in one era succeeded in maintaining its position in the next one, and when he worries that Microsoft's place in the personal computer era may "disqualify" it from maintaining its place in the coming network-centered era. Gates's historical sensibility saturates his analysis of the present and the future, but he simply does not label it as such.

To his credit as a student of history, Gates regards Henry Ford as a cautionary example rather than a role model. Unlike Ford, Gates has been willing to delegate operational power to subordinates, a point that even his critics have conceded as a strength of the company. Comparing Gates, 41 years old in 1996, with Henry Ford, who died at the age of 84 in 1947 and whose failings were most evident in the latter decades of his life, may be a bit premature. However, a comparison perhaps is not so premature if you consider that Gates already had twenty years of experience heading Microsoft by the time he turned 40, the same age at which Henry Ford incorporated the Ford Motor Company.

Like Ford Motor in its earliest years, Gates's Microsoft has secured attention disproportionate to its size if measured by sales. Microsoft is what might be called the smallest big company in the world. If you look at its $5.9 billion annual revenue, the company resembles a tiny field mouse, not an 800-pound gorilla. It was ranked only 219th in 1996 on the *Fortune 500*, which was a lower rank than Quaker Oats, among others (GM was first, with revenues of $169 billion).

Microsoft's 18,000 employees were dwarfed by GM's 709,000. Where the diminutive Microsoft is outsized is in market capitalization. In March 1996, the value of Microsoft's shares totaled $60 billion, ranking it ninth out of all industrial corporations in the United States.

Microsoft's market capitalization was partly explained by the high profitability of its business. Gates now looks back with amazement at the era when he and Paul Allen started the company. They thought the pharmaceutical industry offered a glorious high-margin model that, like software, involved assets that were primarily intellectual property and a workforce of "high-IQ people" that had to be kept happy. As events turned out, their software company went on to pass even the pharmaceutical companies in profit margins. Yet, contrary to public impression, Microsoft in recent years has not produced the highest profits within the personal computer industry. In 1996 rankings, Intel's earnings were exactly double those of Microsoft—$3.6 billion versus $1.8 billion, ranking seventh in highest profits of all corporations versus Microsoft's position of 29th. If its profits were broken out separately, the printer division of Hewlett-Packard, with estimated annual revenue of $16 billion, would also be more profitable than Microsoft. The amount of press attention thus is not consistently linked to size; Microsoft and its chairman receive attention that exceeds all personal computer companies combined.

If the torrent of words about Gates, and recently *from* Gates, that has washed over us seems to be unending, a similar torrent issued from Detroit in Ford's era. To gauge just how much press coverage Ford enjoyed, David Lewis's masterful study *The Public Image of Henry Ford*, focusing only on Ford's interaction with the press and the public, runs 500 oversized pages with small typeface. One way in which Ford captured reporters' attention was by speaking wildly on all manner of topics. In 1928, for example, in a single but not unexceptional interview, he told reporters that the army and navy should enforce Prohibition; that a "Master Mind" sent messages to the earth; that the younger generation was too intelligent for war; and that fruit, starch, and protein should not be eaten at the same time. He also found time to offer opinions about airplanes, rubber plants, farming, and textiles. This, clearly enough, is not Gates's style. In fact, when speaking publicly, Gates has always been reticent to venture very far from the home turf of his company or the personal computer industry, and the example of Henry Ford suggests that we should be grateful for that.

One of Ford's publicity-generating practices was to invite reporters along on ostensibly private camping trips that he took annually between 1918 and 1924 along with fellow industrial magnates Thomas Edison, John Burroughs, and Harvey Firestone. In contrast, when Gates and his friend Warren Buffett have traveled together, such as their journey by train through China in September 1995, they have guarded their privacy closely. The pairing of the business giants in the past did not necessarily result in history-shaking discourse. Edward Bernays recalled in his memoir how he joined Edison and Ford for lunch in 1929, eagerly anticipating "learning something from their words of wisdom." A discussion of the virtues of Carter's liver pills occupied the entire luncheon.

The eagerness to acquire pearls of insight not from spokespeople or subordinates but from the famous businessperson himself causes the public to seize upon any book supposedly authored by the titan. Henry Ford shrewdly played to this hunger in 1922 when he published *My Life and Work*. It was a ghosted work, built on a few interviews and other supplemental materials but written in the first person. The *New York Times* at the time described the effect as resembling less that of a "written book than it is that of a man sitting near you at his ease and talking." Ford's ghost writer had done his job so well that he had "eliminated from the text of this book every trace of himself." The imprimatur of the celebrity was all that the public apparently cared about. Ford's autobiography, published in 1922, was one of seven books about Ford to appear that year and the next, yet none of the six other books achieved wide circulation. Of course, the influence of the two most uncomplimentary books was not helped by the Ford Motor Company's campaign to buy up copies, steal them from public libraries, and have its automobile dealers demonstrate in front of bookstores until the stores withdrew them. Only Ford's own book was translated into other languages (twelve of them) and sold worldwide, becoming a bestseller in many countries.

Now in Gates's time, just as in Ford's, we are given a book affecting a breezy, first-person intimacy. The ironic constancy of the ink-on-paper book as the communications vehicle of choice, even when the subject of Gates's book concerned the obsolescence of such pre-electronic media, did not elude the many reviewers of *The Road Ahead*. The technical glitches that many customers encountered with the book's accompanying CD-ROM only served to underscore the printed book's safe position, at least for the historical moment.

The Road Ahead was presented in a seamless first-person style, making it unclear which portions were the original contributions of Gates's principal co-author Nathan Myhrvold, which were those of the professional writer, and which were his own. Even the collaborators had collaborators. Once Myhrvold's thought pieces, which were originally supposed to form the core of the resulting book, disappeared into the maw of the committee beast, they emerged in unrecognizable form. The resulting primer was not a crystal pane through which the public could see the "inner" Bill Gates. However, the very notion of this kind of duality, implying a false public side and a true private one, perhaps should be abandoned. Will we be disappointed if Gates someday undertakes an autobiography without editorial assistance, and the resulting book does not cast much more light on Gates the person than did *The Road Ahead*? Why not instead accept that he is best observed in situ, managing the company whose identity is inseparable from his own? Perhaps we should focus on the thoughts of Chairman Bill not as isolated theory but as propounded, tested, and revised concepts put into practice.

To see Gates's company more clearly, we must first discard a static picture of it. Microsoft in 1996 is in important ways quite different from Microsoft in 1995, which in turn had changed in other significant, if little noticed, ways from the company in 1990. In fact, 1990 conveniently divides Microsoft's history into a "before" period, when the company's business success can be traced to a whopping dollop of luck, and an "after" period, when it cannot. The great stroke of luck that provided Microsoft with ten very good years came in 1980 when it signed a contract with IBM to provide the operating system software that would be used in the IBM Personal Computer, introduced the next year.

This is the best-known episode in Microsoft's history and in some cases even today it remains the entirety of what is still said about its history, so let's briefly touch on the highlights. A felicitous conjunction of events helped Microsoft land the contract. IBM could not come to terms with Digital Research, then the leading vendor of operating systems for microcomputers and IBM's natural first choice to supply the software. Microsoft, which itself did not have an operating system to offer, bought another, still smaller company's operating system software to adapt for the project. The contract that Microsoft persuaded IBM to accept worked greatly in Microsoft's favor. The terms permitted Microsoft to sell the operating system to other companies and to consumers, but IBM, effectively, could not. IBM's executives did not foresee—but then again, neither did Microsoft's executives fully foresee—the enormity of the revenue to be derived from selling what turned out to be tens of millions of copies of this software.

That a company then consisting of just a few dozen employees would get the best of a partnership with the IBM leviathan has undeniable intrinsic drama. The major myth that sprang up concerning the deal between Microsoft and IBM—that Digital Research would have gotten the deal if its founder had not been rude to IBM representatives who had come to call on the company—has long been removed. However, a lingering whiff of manipulation and deceit from this early chapter in Microsoft's history continues to taint the company's reputation. Even though IBM's attorneys were not tricked, they, like everyone else, simply did not guess that an entire industry would emerge based on hardware and software compatible with the IBM PC. Many today still view Microsoft as the company that Pulled A Fast One On IBM, reaping the bounty of IBM's fateful misstep.

We are prone to forget, however, that no matter how indispensable to its growth in the 1980s its role as supplier to IBM of operating system software may have been, Microsoft grew beyond this identity around 1990. In that spring, the company had yet to be taken seriously when it offered new products without the imprimatur of IBM. Windows, the follow-on to DOS, was still afflicted with serious memory management problems, and customers and industry analysts ignored the product. Instead, Microsoft's joint development project with IBM on OS/2 was regarded as DOS's successor, and Microsoft did not exert control over it.

Microsoft's business still focused on selling to computer hardware companies, not retail customers. Earlier it had ventured into the realm of practical software applications like word processing and spreadsheet software that resided on top of the operating system; and though successful in selling to Macintosh customers, these efforts had yet to do well in Microsoft's own home territory of IBM compatibles. Microsoft was embarrassed that it had introduced its first spreadsheet, Multiplan, three months before Lotus introduced 1-2-3, and yet Lotus, not Microsoft, had secured dominant market share. A best-selling application in any category eluded Microsoft. In 1990, Gates ruefully admitted the truth of a Microsoft employee's summary of Microsoft's limitations: "We make the world's best plumbing, but we never think about the toilet seat."

Judging by public appearances, Microsoft in the spring of 1990 was hapless in doing anything outside of its original plumbing franchise. Yet Microsoft's subsequent developments in its extremely successful post-DOS businesses—first Windows 3.0, then Windows applications, and then a suite of Windows applications bundled together—showed strengths that had hitherto remained hidden. Particularly intriguing in retrospect are Microsoft's ventures into domains that were farthest removed from its original plumbing business, for example, establishing its own internal research groups in computer science, building new lines of software products for home PCs, exploring yet-to-be-launched interactive television software, and then jumping into online services and the Internet markets.

How did Microsoft manage to evolve from a software company stuck selling plumbing software—operating systems and programming languages—to one in which no software domain seemed beyond its range? The answers are not found in a single moment in 1990—their roots are found earlier, and their refinement can be observed later. However, since 1990, Microsoft has compiled a striking record of expanding into new businesses without hiccupping. Luck cannot be pressed into service as the primary explanation, not again and again. Nor do the presumed advantages of being the dominating vendor of operating systems carry very far in the varied environments into which Microsoft has chosen to expand. To discover a better explanation, however, we must think of Microsoft as an evolving entity and discard the assumption that Microsoft is Microsoft is Microsoft.

This book looks out beyond operating systems wars, and beyond the most familiar software packages such as Word, Excel, and the Office suite. It instead focuses on the newer digital domains that not only have taken Microsoft rather far from its well-known origins, but also have spurred noisy alarms from competitors, regulators, and other critics. By choosing not to trudge once again past the familiar milestones of Gates's early life—the smart kid, the private school, the early entrepreneurial ventures—and those of the company's earliest history, we can jump ahead to the 1990s. In this period, Microsoft has become a far more formidable competitor than ever before.

We should also lift our gaze from the immediate headlines of product announcements and internecine industry battles and pose some historical questions about where Gates and Microsoft fit into a larger picture. How do business philosophy and plain luck each contribute to the accumulation of great wealth? How should infant industries be nurtured and large enterprises managed? How should private ambitions and public interests be balanced? For answers, we should search back not only to Ford's time but even further, to the mid-nineteenth century. Without adopting some historical perspective, we have no way of assessing present conditions as defined by today's newspaper, of distinguishing the truly new from the not so new, of seeing the affairs of the moment in a broader skein.

We are not accustomed to associating the story of corporate magnates with intellectual history, but in fact isn't that what we assemble when we inquire into the power of Gates and Microsoft? Or when we question what portion of the company's success is properly attributed to prior thought, conscious strategy, or deliberate decisions? Or when we look into the thinking not only of Gates and Microsoft managers, but also that of competitors, customers, retailers, government regulators, and op-ed editorialists? Or when we wonder how various groups today, like their counterparts in the past, regard the power of a single company in a new and strategically important industry? Historical actors standing at the intersection of business, technology, and society whose banners announce "The American Way" or "The American Way Threatened" and whose thinking has real, visible consequences for many people—this is the stuff of intellectual history that is also high drama.

I draw from three distinct sets of research materials: the internal records of Microsoft and supplemental interviews with Gates and other principals; outside observations of the company, which are also revealing of us just as public observations of Ford were enormously revealing of his times, too; and relevant primary documents drawn from earlier periods in American industrial history. This combination of internal, external, and historical sources has not been applied to Microsoft until now.

I have organized my discussion of Gates and Microsoft into clusters of chapters, beginning in Part One with an examination of the business practices that are at the root of Microsoft's expansion. The arcadian campus on which the company's software developers dwell, the methods Microsoft uses to seek and harness smarts, and the adaptive way in which Gates has led the company's strategists to guide the company's investments are the most salient practices that have made Microsoft successful. They deserve praise, even if they do not lend themselves readily to wide duplication. Most people think of Microsoft as consisting of Bill Gates and a legion of faceless drones. In fact, the company has many, many brainy people. Its cultivation of a cognitive elite—how unusual to dare speak of a "high IQ" workforce!—is particularly interesting because its importance to Microsoft and the public's uneasiness about Microsoft's power are connected, I shall argue. To talk about Microsoft and public antipathy is to lay bare our longstanding national ambivalence about intelligence.

Next, the book shifts to the origins of CD-ROMs and Microsoft's long struggle to win broad consumer acceptance of the medium. Intertwined with the story of CD-ROMs is the creation of a market for software to be used in the home. The development and marketing of Microsoft's own encyclopedia serves as a lens through which we can watch personal computers arrive in the home, gain acceptance, and ultimately displace print encyclopedias, which had been an extremely profitable business in a seemingly unassailable market position. How Microsoft came to dominate the consumer software market has not been accorded much attention to date. My narrative does not attempt to claim, however, that Microsoft's every expansionist venture has been successful. We shall also look at the history of personal finance software and how the small but feisty Intuit defended the commanding market share of its Quicken product against Microsoft's rival entry.

Part Two takes up the ancient history of the Information Highway, that is, pre-1995. The earlier history lets us see what we might call The Road Behind. By examining Microsoft's research activities, early work on interactive television, and development of the commercial online service that would eventually become Microsoft Network, we can trace a series of changes in Microsoft's strategic direction. The changes reflect a melding of business and technical considerations that would both hinder and help it compete in the Internet-centered landscape.

Part Three looks at the evolution of antitrust concerns since 1989, a time period during which Microsoft has been the much-reported center of attention. Microsoft's rivals have raised questions of monopoly that staff members of the Federal Trade Commission and the Justice Department have largely accepted. The questions give us an opportunity to measure present monopoly concerns against those raised in other industries in earlier American history, to venture some thoughts on how the software industry compares to other industries, and to examine how the competition has fared during Microsoft's recent expansion.

I have arrived at a revisionist view on most of the issues. Misplaced ideological fervor or simple unfamiliarity with the software industry seem to have animated the government. The only instance where I believe there was cause for genuine concern was Microsoft's proposed friendly acquisition of the indomitable Intuit, announced in the fall of 1994 and then, in the face of the Justice Department's opposition, withdrawn in the spring of 1995. The monopoly issues thus were ultimately rendered moot. (In retrospect, the episode turned out to be an embarrassment to Microsoft and a boon to Intuit, at least initially.) By revisiting the Intuit and Microsoft Network stories and watching Netscape and new competitors associated with the growth of the Internet enter the marketplace, we can gain a new vantage point from which to assess the proper role of government oversight of business.

Finally, in Part Four I venture some thoughts on Gates's wealth, our collective reaction to it, and the ways in which that wealth has perhaps unconsciously shaped our thinking about the company and its chief executive officer. I also discuss how society might want to see that fortune deployed for wider social benefit. For those who might regard such a discussion presumptuous, I offer some historical perspective: our forebears had no qualms about laying claim to the largest personal fortunes of their times on behalf of society. Ultimately Gates's greatest social impact is not likely to be through his company's products nor any future philanthropic distribution of his wealth. The most important legacy may instead lie in the degree to which Microsoft's internal corporate practices can serve as a model for other companies. Henry Ford's prior example is instructive in this regard, and to Henry Ford we shall return.

Whereas the author of an official history of a company might write in a pseudo-objective manner, presenting unadorned facts and little else, I take a more venturesome approach by offering analysis and opinion as we proceed. I share some of critic Sven Birkerts's concerns in *The Gutenberg Elegies* (1994) that the very developments that I so cheerfully chronicle—such as the incorporation of multimedia capabilities in personal computers and the popularity of online information services—have come at a price of diminishing the place of reading in the humanistic tradition and of elevating facts over wisdom. Unlike Birkerts, however, I have not personally maintained a monastic distance from the machines.

I must confess that, like Bill Gates, I have fond memories of growing up with my family's *World Book Encyclopedia* always at hand. In 1991, I became what I jokingly tell friends was *World Book*'s last customer when I bought a new set for my own two children on the eve of the CD-ROM epoch. Perhaps some lingering touchiness about the apparently poor timing of this investment leads me to withhold the full praise due to Microsoft's own impressive online encyclopedia, Encarta, and its CD-ROM brethren. They have features that the dowdy printed versions could never offer. However, our household purchased these new encyclopedias, too, and none is as easy to consult—hence, none *is* consulted as often—as the printed *World Book* with its "instant-on" feature that the others lack. I really do not regret the purchase. In fact, as readers will soon discover, I have chosen encyclopedias as the subject with which to attempt a defense of the fast-disappearing world in which words matter—and here I freely confess my self-interested lack of objectivity.

Part One

Microsoft Basics

Chapter 1

Sitting and Thinking

SOMETIMES, IN A SUMMER MORNING, having taken my accus-tomed bath, I sat in my sunny doorway from sunrise till noon, rapt in a revery, amidst the pines and hickories and sumachs, in undisturbed solitude and stillness, while the birds sang around or flitted noiseless through the house, un-til by the sun falling in at my west window, or the noise of some traveller's wagon on the distant highway, I was re-minded of the lapse of time. I grew in those seasons like corn in the night, and they were far better than any work of the hands would have been.

Henry David Thoreau, *Walden* (1854)

Microsoft employees bear virtually no likeness to the unhurried Thoreau who stood on the shores of Walden Pond so long ago, who could laugh at what he knew the townspeople would dismiss as "sheer idleness." Nonetheless, the sole responsibility of those who work in software development is to "sit and think." The phrase is Bill Gates's, used to characterize the work of most Microsoft employees. *Sit and think* (and code). An industry whose productive activity is so purely cerebral is no less difficult for contemporary public policy-makers to comprehend than Thoreau's solitary pursuit of "indolence" was for the urban critics of his day. Consider the environment within which the sitting and thinking at Microsoft takes place. Usually re-garded as backdrop, if it receives any notice at all, it is one of the es-sential, deliberately crafted components of the company's success.

In the early 1980s, there was nothing noteworthy about Microsoft's environs: the company occupied leased office space in Bellevue, a suburb east of Seattle. When Microsoft outgrew its original building, it added space in a second, but a freeway hampered movement between the two buildings. The buildings themselves were ordinary; their standard electrical and cooling systems could not accommodate offices filled with personal computers, and their design did not take full advantage of natural lighting. As the company bumped up against these limitations, an idea took hold of starting afresh with a new environment shaped to the company's priorities. The term "campus" appeared in the vocabulary of Gates and his facilities planners as they looked around for suitable land.

Microsoft considered some forty or so parcels before buying a heavily wooded site in Redmond, east of the Bellevue offices, and still farther removed from Seattle. Large downtown developers had eagerly courted Microsoft when word spread of the company's decision to decamp, but the company turned them away. In retrospect, relocating to Redmond could be viewed as flight from urban problems, which probably is not an exemplary action for other companies. At the time, however, Microsoft executives did not view the move farther out as flight for one overriding reason—the city did not have the undeveloped land on which the company could create a verdant campus.

Microsoft wanted an environment that would resemble the college campuses from which many of its software developers had been directly lifted. Carl Bates, the Microsoft facilities manager, explained the rationale for creating a verdurous campus by pointing to how the company expected much of its programmers; it would help "calm the engine down if people can be sitting there stressed out at their machine and look out and see something pleasing outside, rather than a sea of asphalt." Glades had to be scooped out from the pines in order to clear room for the first four buildings, but cutting was minimized in order to preserve as many trees as possible.

An arcadian feel remains today, ten years after the company moved to the campus and subsequently expanded far beyond the original plan. Carefully manicured lawns extend everywhere the trees do not. The mostly low-slung buildings with white facing and dark green windows and the lingering sheen of newness have made it an inviting target of parody. In Douglas Coupland's novel *Microserfs* (1994),

Microsoft's campus is preternaturally quiet; the lawn resembles Lego pads and is mowed every ten minutes; the absence of any disagreeable intruder makes the "Tupperware-sealed" campus resemble Biosphere 2. Gates gets the last laugh, however, because the campus that his company has occupied since 1986 has worked precisely as he intended: as a place removed from the rest of the world, designed from the ground up around the particular needs of those whose full-time responsibility was "sitting and thinking."

The original buildings were designed in the shape of an X (instead of a squat cube) to maximize the natural light inside. The cross shape created a much longer perimeter and thus gave direct sunlight to more offices. Large windows on the interior wall along the hallway permitted the sunlight to reach the offices on the other side of the corridor as well. Very few offices were buried so far in the interior as to be out of reach of outside light. Each office was private—fully enclosed, with a door, and intended to be occupied by one person only. Most other software companies placed desks in semi-enclosed cubicles, or in open-space bullpens, which were much less costly and made close supervision easy. Gates was more interested in fostering a sheltering privacy in which the best programmers thrived. He did not see how "private thinking and private discussion" could take place within nonenclosed offices.

To counterbalance the tendency toward atomization that private offices would create, Gates and his planners relied on both physical infrastructure (such as numerous cafeterias serving as a magnet for individuals to mix and talk, lured by un-cafeteria-like food at subsidized prices) and electronic infrastructure. Electronic mail at Microsoft had long predated the 1986 move to the Redmond campus, but it became even more integral as the company grew. The buildings themselves were intentionally small. Early in Microsoft's history, Gates had come to believe that the best software was created by groups of only a few developers. Therefore, Microsoft designed its campus architecture and amenities to reinforce a small-group identity, rather than a monolithic one. Better to have many smallish, two-story buildings that allowed the small groups of developers to encounter all their co-workers in the course of daily routine than to have the logistical efficiency of a single U.N.-headquarters-like hulk.

The architecture also reinforced the company's egalitarian atmosphere. Gates had removed almost all the physical vestiges of corporate pecking order. Virtually all offices had the same furnishings and the same dimensions: nine by twelve feet. Besides eliminating the contention for larger offices that could proclaim differences in status, the standard office also facilitated internal moves—important because the different groups within the company were moved about frequently as reorganizations pulled everyone hither and thither. For example, 200 people could leave their old offices one evening and be moved into their new offices by the time they arrived for work the next morning, with no need for remodeling—and no disruption to work. Only senior executives, vice-presidents and above, were given a bit more office space: two nine-by-twelve offices from which the separating wall had been removed.

In proportions and furnishings, Gates's own modest work space resembled the office of a dean at a small college. The message that he sought to convey was that the company would not permit time-wasting political struggles over offices; such struggles would only serve to detract from "sitting and thinking." Gates himself was impervious to the entreaties of his facilities managers, who wanted to furnish his office with what they thought were the proper accouterments for the chairman of the board. He refused to accept a reserved parking space for many years until he realized that without it he could not also keep leaving his office at the very last moment in order to drive to the airport. Many Silicon Valley companies also adopted a similar egalitarian spirit, and some carried it further. Intel chairman Andy Grove insisted on the same cramped cubicle assigned his engineers, and Intel executives rented subcompact cars (Ford Escorts were referred to as "Intel limousines").

For contrast, we could compare the Microsoft campus with the headquarters of once high-flying Wang Laboratories, in Lowell, Massachusetts, in the early 1980s. Chairman An Wang had his office at the top of one of the towers that dominated Wang's central facility. Access to the chairman was severely restricted, and the vertical design gave all who entered a truly physical sense of the hierarchy within. On the Microsoft campus, the design of its first buildings deliberately rebuked a totem pole of hierarchy. Microsoft's one-employee-per-office dictum created a stubborn problem, however, as new facilities could not be built quickly enough to house the influx of campus-based employees. To accommodate the growth, company planners reluctantly adopted designs for buildings larger than the original ones on the Microsoft campus.

Within six months of its move to the new campus, Microsoft had more employees than it had planned to accommodate on it—ever. Fortunately it had the cash and the nimbleness to purchase the parcels adjacent to the original land before speculators could box it in and demand a ransom for additional expansion. (Room for annexation was another luxury that urban sites could never have provided the company.) Soon, however, additional building was impossible due to zoning restrictions or an unacceptably high price in obliterating the greensward. The company then moved all the groups that were not directly involved in software development off campus.

Number of Employees	
1975	3
1980	40
1981	129
1985	910
1986	1,153
1987	1,816
1988	2,793
1989	4,037
1990	5,635
1991	8,226
1992	11,542
1993	14,430
1994	15,257
1995	17,801
1996	20,561

Gates had not purged all hierarchy from the company. He was not interested in returning to an egalitarian Eden so much as he wanted to extract the maximal yield from his most valuable employees. He implicitly defined two classes at Microsoft: product development groups—and everyone else. The product groups received the lion's share of stock options; their programmers' private offices were defended most vigorously in times of office-space shortage; the product groups were allowed to stay together on the Redmond campus as persistent crowding forced the company to relocate, group by group, all others to leased space elsewhere. To ease the pressure on the original campus, Microsoft finally was forced, in 1995, to open an annex for product groups about a mile away.

It is ironic that Microsoft software developers were so insistent that they be kept close together even as they refined the software that, among other things, was weaning the rest of us away from relying on physical presence for communication. Every product development group would tell the facilities managers that it was crucial that its offices remain close to other groups to facilitate consultation and serendipitous hallway encounters. In response, the facilities managers pointed out—in vain—that whenever they studied the patterns of actual face-to-face communication, they invariably discovered that developers never seemed to venture more than a few feet from their own offices. The daily cross-fertilization of ideas among groups was not evident. Nevertheless, the product groups continued to win their fight to defend their entrenched position on the main campus until their numbers reached the point that all could no longer remain.

Microsoft, the company, was as reluctant to relinquish the idea that its employees must be present in the flesh as developers were reluctant to abandon the idea that their kin should be no farther than arm's length away. A few renegade developers and others needled Microsoft management about the company's split personality. The company was telling the public to get connected; that the personal computer, with Microsoft software, removes the limitations of distance; that one can go *virtually* anywhere. Internally, too, the company did practice the new electronic religion, as e-mail had become the central means of internal communication, even between neighbors along office corridors. Yet the company was rigid when employees asked to work at home, connected to their groups by the same electronic links that were used on campus.

In 1994, an employee wrote to the company newsletter asking why the company continued to build more office space on and near campus instead of investigating electronic alternatives that could be much less costly, to the company and to the environment. If the company was serious about the vision of the future that it professed to its customers, the letter writer challenged, why not show the rest of the world how telecommuting can be done, and in so doing learn from and solve the social and technical problems that the transition would present? The company line was that telecommuting was not explicitly forbidden, but that most groups had jobs "requiring frequent interactions with others, whether in our hallways, offices, conference rooms, or cafeterias," and any proposal to shift to alternative work arrangements had to demonstrate convincingly that it would not "impede my group's goals," would not "add any incremental costs to the company," would not "isolate me from my group and prevent me from helping on inter-group issues," and so on.

Microsoft insisted that its employees could best contribute to the company with their full-time presence on campus. Perennial employee pleas to lift the company's prohibition of part-time or job-shared positions fell on deaf ears. In the question and answer period at the 1994 annual company meeting, Bill Gates put the company's reasoning this way: "We're trying to do a lot; getting it done quickly is really critical." Part-time or shared jobs did not seem to him "effective for the types of work we're trying to get done."

The company's demand for ongoing all-out contribution from each employee was made more palatable—or deviously engineered, in the view of Microsoft's critics—by dispensing strategic forms of largesse. The private offices, loaded with multiple PCs and software packages, gave developers all the "tools" they required. Employee benefit packages were comprehensive. Amenities were provided throughout the campus. Microsoft spent $8000 per employee annually on nonmandated benefits—a figure that the company did not hide from the beneficiaries. By the early 1990s, the company was spending over $715 annually per employee on beverages and food service subsidies alone. "Anything with caffeine is free," a Microsoft employee sardonically commented to *Newsweek* in 1994. However, the free drinks plentifully stocked in the many campus refrigerators were not selected for their immediate pharmacological return on investment—they were part of the campus atmosphere.

Without a doubt, Gates and Microsoft's senior executives have provided amenities that are intended to make employees more happy rather than less, and no complex formula is needed to reason that happy employees do tend to be more productive than unhappy ones. Many outside critics have detected a diabolical intention here to keep employees parked in their offices, day and night, in servitude to Gates's mission. And at times Microsoft employees wonder, too. For example, in a skit presented at a company meeting, senior executives mock-seriously tell a dubious new employee that the company does not frown on employees having outside lives—why, walking from one's car to the office front door was an "outside life," wasn't it?

If Gates is Mephistopheles, he is rather incompetent in his plotting (and his employees are not too bright—even Faust asked for more than free fruit juice). The campus, as shimmeringly beautiful and as well-stocked with food and libations as it is, falls short of a

Biosphere 2 self-sufficiency. Instead of providing a health club on campus, the company subsidizes an off-campus club. Nor does the company provide on-site childcare. At each annual all-company meeting, Gates or one of the other senior managers would face the same question about childcare from employees, and each year the requests were brushed aside. Gates and the other senior managers claimed that it was best to leave childcare to "the experts" and instead offered the palliatives of help in the form of childcare-provider referral services and at-home nursing services—for a fee—for those with sick children.

No to on-site childcare. Yes, however, to a variety of other benefits that placed Microsoft among the ranks of the most generous employers and did not operate directly to keep employees entombed in their offices: matching of employee charitable contributions; $5000 reimbursement for adoption expenses; health benefits for domestic partners; four weeks' paid infant-care leave, for men as well as women. Like other companies in the industry, Microsoft imposed no dress code to speak of. The last visible attempt to rein in sartorial anarchy occurred back in 1988 when Jon Shirley, then company president, announced that he and Gates preferred that Microsoft employees not walk barefoot when indoors. Shirley, Gates, and the other officers donned jackets and ties for formal occasions such as that meeting, but when Shirley retired (at the age of 52) in 1990 and his successor, a conventional corporate-type recruited from Boeing, was dismissed within two years, Gates and his three most trusted executives became the Office of the President and reverted to casual wear. After attending Gates's wedding ceremony in 1994, a Microsoft vice-president observed that a high percentage of invitees not only did not normally wear a coat and tie but actually had to purchase them for the occasion.

In 1995, the internal company newsletter published a letter from Ben Goetter, an employee in the Business Systems group, who declared it was time for Microsoft to shed the "sophomoric trappings of our so-called 'Corporate' Campus" and adopt the dress standards of mainstream business. Walk down any hallway, the disgusted author said, and you would find bare feet, sloppy tee shirts, disorderly offices. "Does not software—a body of rules abiding by a precise order and internal discipline—mandate an orderly and disciplined environment for its correct construction?" Sloppy clothes might mean sloppy code.

"Every untucked shirttail reflects an unchecked error condition," Goetter reasoned, calling on everyone in the company to "clean up our act."

Reaction to this manifesto fell into two camps, neither of which, interestingly, could be described as Dress Code Advocates. One group was so outraged by Goetter's suggestions that it failed to notice that the letter was intended as satire; their refutation of Mr. Clean was deadpan and earnest. The other group responded in the same spirit that had launched Goetter's letter and provided satirical affirmation. Sometimes it was difficult to determine to which group a responder belonged. One letter asked, "Maybe bringing back arm bands is in order? After we accomplish that, we can start sending out the office police to ensure that no one has spare scraps of paper lying around." The ruckus was not quieted until the newsletter ran a picture of Goetter, his hair falling well below his shoulders, seated in his office amidst a comforting display of disorder.

The most important employee benefit was perhaps the one that had made Microsoft a *financially* comfortable place to work: ownership of Microsoft stock among employees. The company promoted employee stock purchases with a 15 percent discount and offered stock options to some extent to all salaried employees who worked at the company for one year, and more generously to all of Microsoft's senior professionals: software developers, project managers, marketing personnel, and editors. Relying on appreciation in share prices as the main element of compensation, rather than salaries—which deliberately lagged behind those for comparable positions at rival companies—was a conscious decision by Gates: "We're using ownership as one of the things that ties us all together."

Microsoft may well have a larger percentage of employees who own stock than any other publicly traded company. It refuses to disclose the number, however. Having at its head one of the wealthiest persons in the country certainly makes Microsoft an incongruous candidate for induction into the Hall of Fame for ESOPs (Employee Stock Ownership Programs), redolent with the sweat of blue-collar trades and organized labor. But the fact remains that Microsoft's compensation policies did indeed directly benefit an astoundingly broad proportion of its workforce when the market raised the company's worth.

Like other high-tech companies who were unabashedly focused on growth, Microsoft did not pay a dividend to its shareholders; the return they received was purely appreciation in the trading value of the stock. Gates and the other senior officers pointed out to their employees with no little pride that they themselves waived salaries comparable to those of their peers at Microsoft's rivals. Executives were as dependent on the upward movement of Microsoft share prices for their own compensation as everyone else in the company. In 1994, Gates noted that in the previous year Microsoft had paid its top five executives $1.9 million combined in salaries and bonuses, whereas Larry Ellison, the head of database rival Oracle Corporation, was alone paid $5.7 million. Comparisons with Novell and Lotus also showed wide disparities, which Gates said "sort of shows our culture."

Gates could have also gone on to point out that many Microsoft employees had become quite wealthy thanks to their holdings of Microsoft stock, but he balked. As a benefit that unified Microsoft employees, stock ownership served well, but to delve into the vulgar details of what its ownership meant for specific groups of people was not palatable. Disclosure of the happy outcome that had befallen others would also convey, no matter what qualifications accompanied it, a tacit promise that similar returns awaited recipients of today's stock. Gates took care never to make that promise, always emphasizing the difficulties of repeating the past rate of appreciation and negotiating the always-present shoals of volatility.

Denied hard data, members of the public were free to see a millionaire whenever a Microsoft employee crossed their path or sat down in an adjacent seat on an airplane. Employees learned when traveling to expect a repetitive battery of questions from new business acquaintances about their date of hire and position, facts that fed estimates of their net worth.

What outsiders may not have realized was the way in which the stock option program has changed in several important aspects over the years. In the late 1980s, the company typically would grant a certain number of options—for 3000 shares, for example, to a programmer who joined the company fresh out of college in 1988—and the package would vest in increments over four and a half years. This led to a certain amount of turnover when all the options had been vested, even if the most promising programmers were given new option packages on the eve of the four-and-a-half-year milestone. Microsoft did not like to see anyone leave—in the company's view, a junior programmer or marketer, nurtured in the warm bosom of its small-group culture, would not fully realize his or her potential in such a short period of time. So, instead of granting a large block of options initially, the company cut back. The recruiting package of options on 3000 shares in 1988 was replaced by 1800 shares in 1991, and by 1994 had dropped to 1100 shares. At the same time, the company offered on a regular annual basis new packages of options, each package starting a separate clock for full vesting that extended further in time than the previous package had. This change served to eliminate the idea that one's financial stake in the company would be fully claimed at one identifiable point in the future.

Options, by their nature, are speculative. The "option" is the choice of buying shares in the future at a price set in the quarter in which the options are granted. Thus an option is the difference between the set price and the actual price of the stock when the option holder wants to cash in. If all goes well for the option holder, the purchase price will turn out to be artificially low because the market price of the stock rose after the options had been issued. If the stock price has fallen, however, the option holder has of course no incentive to purchase the shares at a price that has turned out to be artificially high; in such cases, the options are literally worthless. Microsoft managers can recall prospective employees who were too skittish, such as the Harvard MBA who looked at the lower salary and the uncertainty in valuing the option package and walked away from the job offer. They can also tell stories of more daring prospects, who left jobs that paid double or even triple what their initial Microsoft salary would be, betting—literally—that the option package would, in the end, more than make up the difference.

Furthermore, the gambles paid off for successive waves of new hires, each wave thinking when they were hired that the days of dramatic stock appreciation were over. Early Microsoft employees made fortunes when Gates permitted them to buy shares for a dollar a share before the company went public in 1986; those shares increased in value ninetyfold within a mere year. What we might call the Class of 1988 arrived on the Redmond campus with the feeling that the unique position these veterans had been in would never recur. And, for a while, the price of the stock did dip, and the options that were being vested were worthless. But the stock then resumed its ascent, and the Class of 1988 subsequently had no reason to feel left out. In a study prompted by institutional investors' concern that a wave of retirements like president Jon Shirley's would beset the company, a Wall Street firm estimated that no fewer than 2200 developers in Microsoft's Class of 1989 became millionaires in just two years.

Such leaps in personal fortunes from options on just 3000 shares of stock may seem unfathomable. Keep in mind, however, that a package of options originally on 3000 shares at a base price of $50 ($150,000 worth of stock), after a two-for-one stock split, becomes 6000 shares at an adjusted base price of $25 (adjusted to keep the total value of the package—$150,000—unchanged). When it splits again, the package is now 12,000 shares at $12.50 a share. On paper, each split nominally made no difference in the total value of the package. Into the 1990s, however, Microsoft's stock prices tended to return to their historical highs after splitting. If, after two splits, the market price of the stock returns to its old price of $50, the arithmetic goes like this: $50 (current market price of a share) minus $12.50 (later base price for each share in the option package) times 12,000 shares. In other words, the holder of the original options on 3000 shares now has a package worth nearly half a million dollars. And, if the stock were to lift up to $100 and the base price for the options remains $12.50, options on the 3000 shares become a seven-figure package, well worth forgoing a higher salary elsewhere.

The principal warning about this sort of calculation is that it assumes a saintly patience on the part of the employee. Knowing when to exercise the options is tricky: if you *never* cash in, the options remain an abstraction with no value; but if you do cash in, and the stock price subsequently continues to increase, you will be haunted by thoughts of what the options could have been worth if you had not exercised them prematurely. A rueful inside joke at Microsoft is "there are a lot of $100,000 snowmobiles around here"—purchased for $2000 with money from options before their value subsequently increased fiftyfold.

How many employees hold how much wealth is not ascertainable as long as the company adamantly refuses to supply the data. Microsoft regards this question as wholly private, and public discussion as hopelessly crass. Even though the company is reluctant to call attention to it, Microsoft is singular in that its campus is a place unlike any other workplace in the world, at any other time in history, when several *thousand* millionaires, multimillionaires, and multibillionaires (two) continue to clomp to work every day.

In 1992, the author of the Wall Street report on Microsoft millionaires predicted that though some employees would retire or strike off on other pursuits, most would remain, motivated by the pleasures of the work itself. The prediction proved accurate: the company continued to have much lower turnover than its software counterparts. It suffered attrition mostly in positions outside of software development. When senior managers or developers left Microsoft, they retired or launched their own business ventures, but instances of their joining the competition were extremely rare.

Was this fair-weather loyalty? Would Microsoft face the same difficulty in retaining key people as other companies when, for the first time, it experienced a downturn in sales or the value of its stock, or it faced a prospect of diminishing business opportunities? The past offered no such test of company loyalty. Perhaps the most recent brush with such a possibility was in 1993, when Microsoft's share prices were languishing at an apparent plateau. An employee asked at the annual company meeting, "It looks like we're doing all the right things and getting great results, so what's going on with the stock?" Gates and the senior officers answered by warning, as they always had, that the very size of the company meant that it was unlikely that the stock price would continue to grow in the near future as it had previously. Yet the plateau turned out to be temporary. The stock, defying Gates's predictions, doubled in value still again in the next year.

Of course the time will come when Microsoft stock cannot continue to multiply in value as it has so many times in the past ten years. It may even drop and stay stubbornly well below its historical high. Until that moment arrives, we cannot determine the portions of employee loyalty that are due to the intrinsic pleasures of the intellectual work itself, to the social and physical milieu in which the work takes place, and to the extrinsic rewards deriving from stock options. In the meantime, that so many employees who are already wealthy continue to work at Microsoft is strong testimony to the intrinsic components of motivation.

Outside observers, like me, who live in Silicon Valley can easily understand one reason that Microsoft has a low turnover rate, and it is because Microsoft is located in Seattle rather than in the Bay Area. Microsoft might never have become as successful without the remarkable continuity among its executives and managers. How could it have had such loyalty in the job-hopping culture of the Valley? If a Valley start-up is successful, its employees resemble nothing if not a bank-heist gang, only too eager to divide the money and scram, each in separate directions. Early on, Gates appreciated the advantages of being well away from the Valley. Later he could delight in Microsoft's low turnover rate and gloat that "those guys in the Valley can't keep secrets."

The competition for experienced software developers is not so much between Microsoft and its rivals as between Microsoft and the lure of working on one's own—or not working again, period. Over time, with thousands of his developers achieving a net worth that would permit them at any moment to walk away from their jobs, you would think Gates would be under pressure to provision the workplace with ever more amenities. The campus thus would provide not just the comforts of an ordinary home but the comforts of a millionaire's home. Yet Gates succeeded in retaining the services of his developers without increasing the company-provided comforts on the job.

In fact, the company launched a campaign in 1993 to eliminate all expenses that were deemed frills, a campaign that internally came to be called "Shrimp versus Weenies." The campaign was intended to reinstill a "small company" mentality in an organization that undeniably was now quite large, to reaffirm an ethos in which "every penny counts, every new head count is precious, and you feel personally accountable for the top line [revenue], the bottom line [profitability], and all the stuff in between." The traditional company culture had remained intact: informal dress, coach class and moderately priced hotels for business travel; no limos; no executive dining rooms; no-frills office furniture. Nevertheless, some employees had lost sight of this ethos; they were taking advantage of the company's generosity. The remedy was vigilance! Employees were reminded that Microsoft's success had to be earned, in the words of Mike Murray, the vice-president for human resources, "a day at a time"; eating "weenies instead of shrimp" would be the path to continued growth.

The campaign was not greeted with unanimous support. On the eve of the companywide mobilization, employee proposals for improving the work environment ran along the lines of "more volleyball courts" and "more parties." So there was naturally some resistance. Some employees protested that Murray's examples of needless waste—such as issuing commemorative tee shirts for less-than-important occasions—were too inconsequential. Others argued that "time is money" and whatever expenditures eased the work of developers was money well spent. This being a technically inclined group, much of the continuing debate pivoted on disputed calculations of projected savings. When an employee suggested that workers should turn off their computers when they left the office at the end of the day to save money, another denounced the allegedly faulty assumptions behind the suggestion. The economics of turning the switch off and on were analyzed in excruciating detail.

The campaign surprisingly drew spontaneous support from many employees whom one might have expected to rush to the battlements to protect their perquisites. After all, everyone knew that the company's treasury was flush with a multi-billion-dollar cash kitty, so the call for a more ascetic style was based on a philosophical abstraction not on immediate fiscal urgency. Employees who had worked for other employers spoke up the loudest: "We should appreciate what we have . . . because believe me, it is not the norm in the outside world," declared one. An accounting office employee was glad of the opportunity to vent her frustration at seeing employees submit requests for all manner of reimbursements, including speeding tickets received while in a company rental car, dog grooming, and gold jewelry: "I often sit at my desk and do a slow burn at the expenses that are being paid that I know upper management cannot possibly be aware of." Microsoft was known to this employee's outside friends as the place with "bottomless pockets." If employees did not cease expecting that the company owed them more than what was reasonable, it would soon enough become, she warned, the company with empty pockets. In summation, she said, "This is not Club Med!"

It remains a tricky challenge for Gates to provide an environment that is well suited for sitting and thinking, with the proper amount of comfort, the right tools, and freedom from distractions—yet not *too* comfortable. The founding culture, which centers on the intellectuality of its challenges, not on the enjoyment of its material rewards, might be lost. To date, measured by Microsoft employees' allegiance to their jobs, Gates has managed the tension remarkably well. Microsoft's environment is not a flashy kind of advantage and, in its particulars, cannot be readily copied by all employers. However, the basic principle—that the setting in which work is conducted is indeed important—is too often forgotten. For the flinty boss who insists on bottom-line payoff for amenities extended to employees, Microsoft's profitable example could help melt the resistance of the most hardened skeptic.

Chapter 2

Smarts

ERHAPS THE READER does not possess remarkable talents. You were never called a "genius"; perhaps you are nothing more than TOLERABLE in the schoolroom. What of that? The world is not governed to-day by the men who were so-called geniuses, thirty, forty, or fifty years ago. A great many of the most "precocious" youths have dropped out of memory, while some of the plodding, but untiring and persevering ones, are holding the reins of government or guiding the counsels of school and senate.

William M. Thayer, *Tact, Push, and Principle* (1882)

Select a year, at random, and we can pick examples of the quaint belief that intelligence can actually be *inimical* to business success. "Why I Never Hire Brilliant Men," an article that appeared in the *American Magazine* in 1924, offered simple rules that deliberately eliminated "the genius" from productive employment. True, the author concedes, these rules would have disqualified Edison and Lincoln, but he comforted himself with the thought that "Cromwell built the finest army in Europe out of dull but enthusiastic yeomen; and that the greatest organization in human history was twelve humble men, picked up along the shores of an inland lake." Anticipating his readers' curiosity, the article's author did not flinch: yes, I myself am mediocre, he declared, and I do not apologize—"business and life are built upon successful mediocrity, and victory comes to companies, not through the employment of brilliant men, but through knowing how to get the most out of ordinary folks."

Three decades later, William Whyte uncovered the same sentiment in the large corporations he investigated in *The Organization Man* (1956). Whyte, however, was repulsed by the unapologetic anti-intellectualism that he found among corporate recruiters and executives. For example, a Monsanto Chemical industrial film shows three young men in lab coats: "No geniuses here; just a bunch of average Americans working together." Whyte also told of visiting an electronics company whose laboratory had been "infiltrated" by a young, brilliant scientist. When the researcher chafed under the supervision of his director, the company felt it had to choose between the unquestioned smarts of the new hire and his duller supervisor, whose most important asset was simple company loyalty. The scientist was dismissed. From corporate brochures, Whyte also collected numerous instances of companies going out of their way to discourage the waywardly brilliant from even applying for a job, lest these companies find themselves in the uncomfortable position of hiring, and then dismissing, the intellectually outstanding oddity. Whyte's chapter was aptly titled "The Fight Against Genius."

For the historian Richard Hofstadter, whose seminal survey *Anti-Intellectualism in American Life* (1963) placed American business's antipathy toward the brilliant into a larger framework, suspicion of intellect was not wholly to be condemned. He saw it as a manifestation of American practicality found in all spheres of American life. Only when the practical outlook took the form of exclusivity and disparaged what Hofstadter termed "other aspects of human experience" did he feel it deserved criticism. Anti-intellectualism in American business was so entrenched that even this preeminent scholar could not resist partially rationalizing it, softening the edges, and shifting blame to the intellectuals themselves, whom he chided for long deriding business and its practitioners.

My own theory about why American society to this day is reluctant to renounce anti-intellectualism is because of its underlying promise that anyone, with the right dollops of luck and pluck—the combination that served Ragged Dick and other nineteenth-century Horatio Alger heroes so well—can indeed succeed in business. It's not effortlessly, mind you. The Broadway musical could be renamed *How*

To Succeed In Business? By Really Trying. The credo of unlimited opportunities for the ambitious assumes that self-styled intellectuals are not really intellectually superior—not where it counts.

American anti-intellectualism will never again be the same because of Bill Gates. Gates embodies what was supposed to be impossible—a practical intellectual. He consistently has sought out and hired the smartest individuals in the computer industry—he overturns daily the 1924 article's message and *always* hires the "brilliant" if he can. Microsoft's principal assets, in fact, are the collective craniums of Gates and his employees. The deliberate way in which Gates has fashioned an organization that prizes smart people is the single most important, and the most deliberately overlooked, aspect of Microsoft's success.

The most convenient way for outsiders to deny the importance of Microsoft's husbanding of intellectual assets has been to adopt, unthinkingly or not, the familiar ad hominem aspersions of America's fine anti-intellectual tradition. The vocabulary might change— "eggheads" in the 1950s, "nerds" in the 1970s—but the message is the same: brains are a liability, not an asset. The cartoonist Berkeley Breathed has relished savaging Gates in his drawings, portraying a caricature with an oversized head and pencil-thin neck. On national television in 1995, Breathed described Gates after seeing him in a line at a movie theater: "He looked like he probably needed help buying that ticket; he doesn't fit; he's the kid that we made fun of in school." Many others have drawn similarly unflattering physical descriptions— unimposing posture, or dirty glasses, or uncombed hair—combined with the surprise that this unlikely physical specimen would end up as the richest person in the land. The movie title "Revenge of the Nerds" offered headline writers a fruitful source of Microsoft-related headlines. (Even Microsoft employees used the "Revenge of the Nerds" phrase in skits and newsletters.)

The Microsoft model of a—what should it be called . . . *intelliocracy?*—is terrifying to contemplate from the outside because, for one thing, there's not much that lends itself to easy replication. The model requires Gates at the epicenter, and his formidable intelligence is the one part of Microsoft's story that its critics have never attacked. At most they have attempted to cast a sinister light on it, suggesting that hyper-intelligence is repellent, more machine than human.

Gates and his own employees are wont to use computer terms to refer to the mind. Gates describes unused mental capacity as "unused bandwidth," a waste that he has sought to remedy in his own case by posting maps on ceilings and joining friends for lunch at Burger King with issues of *Scientific American* and *The Economist.* Gates's ability to juggle a number of different threads of conversation simultaneously has drawn the description "massively parallel," naturally enough. Gates tends to ask many blistering questions of his subordinates; the answers enable him to update the vast "database" of his mind, in which he stores the "best idea" that he has encountered to date for thousands of different categories or tasks. His questions are a process of searching for better ideas that will replace the incumbents; when he discovers them, the database is then "updated."

However Gates's intelligence is characterized, the singularity of the intelligence itself is not disputed. And Microsoft's recruiting policies are designed with unapologetic single-mindedness to find others among the smartest. From the moment that Microsoft moved from Albuquerque to Seattle in 1979, when Gates had exhausted his supply of "smart friends" and had to identify and recruit "smart strangers," Microsoft has devised and refined techniques to hire the very brightest software developers, the programmers who form the heart of the company. In its quest, Microsoft offers no sop that every person is potentially able. Gates is blunt: "There is no way of getting around [the fact] that in terms of IQ, you've got to be very elitist in picking the people who deserve to write software; 95 percent of the people shouldn't write complex software." Strictly speaking, Gates was too generous to imply that even 5 percent of the population could meet his standards. In fact, Microsoft hires an almost infinitesimal sliver of the 120,000+ candidates who submit résumés each year.

Gates's preference for hiring freshly minted college graduates is well known. The origins of the company's preference can be traced back to the beginning of its Seattle era, when Gates saw that his approach to developing software could best be nurtured among "very young people, fairly inexperienced." Mindful of federal regulations that render any age-related preferences verboten, Microsoft's human resources department does its best to remove this same bias favoring youth. In the 1995 *Microsoft Employee Handbook,* company recruiters are instructed not to utter any statements in the presence of a candidate "regarding the need to hire 'bright, young people,' that Microsoft is a 'young company,' or any other statement implying age is an employment factor." Gates, however, could not always suppress his preference for youth over experience. By 1994, when the average age of Microsoft employees had risen to 31, he confessed a wish to increase the percentage of employees hired directly from college to the 80 percent it had been in Microsoft's earliest years. "Young people are more willing to learn, come up with new ideas," he averred. The number of annual college hires, however, remained, in absolute terms, extremely small: 150–175 new college graduates hired annually from 1988 to 1994. And these few did not come randomly from across the land. Microsoft devoted its most intensive recruiting efforts to a handful of "target schools" that were likely to produce the academic crème de la crème.

In 1993, Gates melodramatically told his software developers "there's not a single line of code here today that will have value, say, in four or five years time." That rapid perishability meant that Microsoft's new employees would need to possess not merely technical expertise but, more importantly, the capacity to acquire quickly whatever skills might be needed in the future. Microsoft could teach its employees in specific skill areas, but it could not instill intelligence and creativity—those, Gates said, were "reasonably innate."

The best programmers, in Gates's view, were people who were "super smart"—his shorthand for a number of attributes, including the capability of grasping new knowledge extremely quickly, in "real time"; of generating acute questions on the spot; of perceiving connections between disparate domains of knowledge; of possessing such familiarity with programming structures that a quick glance is sufficient for them to understand a long printout of code; of thinking obsessively about the code, even when driving and eating; of concentrating with special intensity (whether "smart people" have a knack for concentration, or the ability to concentrate makes them "smart," Gates had no opinion); and of having photographic recall of the code they had written. This last attribute is not unlike the ability of chess masters to memorize effortlessly every move of ten games. "Other people look at that recall in chess players, or in programmers, and they think it's like some freak show," Gates said. But good programmers possessed that kind of recall; Gates himself pointed to his own ability to recall "huge slabs" of code years after he had last tinkered with them.

Gates sought not merely good programmers; he wanted the best, and he applied his own model of technical intelligence in this enterprise. He did not place high value on previous programming experience, especially if it was in areas not at the leading edge. His self-confessed "bias" in hiring—"towards intelligence or smartness over anything else, even, in many cases experience"—led him to devalue programmers who had worked on mainframe computers, for example. He felt that the chances they could adapt to personal computers were poor. His model welcomed the inexperienced who came from the pure sciences, math and physics in particular. In Gates's view, people who had done well in these areas had passed a screening test for those with the highest IQ. Microsoft's experience showed that when these pure-science graduates were asked to apply their minds to computers, it was actually rather simple for them.

Brains were necessary, but alone they were insufficient. Microsoft sought a particular kind of a smart person—one who was also pragmatically inclined, verbally agile, and able to respond deftly when challenged. The combative nature of internal "discussions" reflected Microsoft's tendency to rank prospective smart candidates who were shy lower than those who were not. Once, a senior vice-president of a leading computer company who was being interviewed for a position at Microsoft told Gates that she would have to research the answers to some of his questions. He is said to have demanded of her, "Why don't you have an answer? Are you stupid?" This exchange appeared in the press and provided yet another example of why Microsoft acquired an image of a company with a macho culture hostile to those whose communication style did not match that of Gates and his coterie of almost exclusively male lieutenants. But the "Are you stupid?" remark obscures the real issue at the heart of Gates's displeasure, which was not lack of smarts, which hardly could be determined by Gates's question, but lack of another attribute that Gates sought: verbal facility.

Smart people were assigned to roles at Microsoft other than that of pure programmer, or in formal parlance, "software design engineer." Microsoft's software development groups had large numbers of program managers who were responsible for defining code specifications, serving as liaisons between the code writers and the marketers, and shepherding the different pieces of the product to completion and release. Microsoft's *product* managers—not to be confused with *program* managers—were responsible for still another area, marketing issues, and were sometimes based in the development groups instead of separately in marketing. They required both a familiarity with the world of the code pounder and the big-picture, bottom-line sensibilities of an MBA in order to judge the technical feasibility of adding features. Microsoft also viewed software testing as professionally separate from software design. Testers specialized in sleuthing, seeking out weaknesses in the software code, drawing on expertise that also depended on smarts. Add up all of the bodies that were nominally in software development but were not directly producing initial code, and their numbers outnumbered the programmers.

Examining the evolution and codification of Gates's directives for recruiting people for software development and allied tasks reveals that Microsoft's ranking system is based on an older view of intelligence, defined as logic skills. This view is at the epicenter of controversies in the cognitive sciences and public policy. Are not Microsoft's recruitment policies indeed appropriate for the software industry, where logical powers and programming ability are so tightly linked? Or, alternatively, does such a view of intelligence based on IQ as a proxy for programming ability reflect a foolish blindness to the multiplicity of forms of intelligence, to the outside factors that greatly influence individuals' abilities, to the cultural biases of test instruments, and so on?

Microsoft's emphasis on intelligence over industry experience can represent either the realization of a meritocratic ideal based on pure ability, or the repudiation of a meritocratic ideal based on the notion that any reasonably intelligent and well-educated person, with sufficient grit and determination, should be able to pursue any position he or she desires. For those who occupy the stratospheric thin air of the IQ hierarchy, Microsoft harbors no prejudice against those who lack professional programming, testing, or technical project management experience. For everyone else, Microsoft stands as elitist, its success coming as it has at the very time that corporate America was in the throes of great downsizing.

A person who was not among the very best that Microsoft would be interested in—and this is what was so radically disturbing to people with faith that "Success is merely a matter of will-power"— would *never* be able to make the grade. Stanley Kaplan cram courses may be able to boost SAT or GMAT scores, but none can boost raw IQ and problem-solving talent. Community college courses can turn a nonprogrammer into a C programmer, and additional study can turn a beginning programmer into an intermediate or advanced programmer. But Microsoft did not subscribe to the faith of the many souls who flocked to introductory programming courses, that each of us *inherently* has the ability to remake ourselves into whatever we want.

Gates was once asked if he thought that many years of experience helped to make programming easier. He did not answer the question but instead commented on the assumption behind it. He said that "after the first three or four years, it's pretty cast in concrete whether you're a good programmer or not." By "good," he was referring in an understated way to "world-class." Yes, experience could help in learning how to manage projects and handle people, but as far as optimizing code went, Gates could not think of any initially mediocre programmer at Microsoft who had become a late-blooming champion code warrior. You've either got it, or you don't, he said— and we Americans do *not* like to hear that message.

The rest of the software industry essentially agrees with Gates's "bias towards intelligence," but Gates has been more explicit about it than his counterparts have been. His company has pursued the very best more successfully than other companies, and his company has visibly reaped the rewards more dramatically than others, too. Gates will seem the villain to those who abhor the anti-egalitarian implications of the Intelligence-Above-All-Else model. Yet programmers who do not work for Microsoft—even those who, for sundry reasons, viscerally despise Microsoft—make observations identical to what Gates or his Microsoft legionaries would say: the best programmers are not marginally better than merely good ones. They are an order of magnitude better, measured by whatever standard: conceptual creativity, speed, ingenuity of design, or problem-solving ability. All else being equal, the company that recruits the largest number of these super-programmers, the alphas among alphas, is most likely to win the biggest sweepstakes.

In the software industry, a single programmer's intellectual resources, through commercial alchemy, can create entire markets where none had existed. Software can be likened to the movie industry. Compare the cumulative worldwide gross revenues of the studio that captures the services of the next Steven Spielberg compared to the rival who has to settle for a second-round draft pick. Differences separating the rewards generated by the top tier versus the second-best tier are geometric, not arithmetic.

Microsoft's rivals have also sought to capitalize on this same insight. Where, for example, would Lotus be today without the services of Ray Ozzie, the ingenious creator of Notes, the combination of database and communications program for large corporate networks? It was Ozzie's Notes, not the sickly spreadsheet-software business, that so bewitched IBM that, when it acquired Lotus in 1995, IBM valued the smaller company at an improbable $3.5 billion. Although many programmers would play smaller roles in realizing Ozzie's vision for Notes, he was literally indispensable: no Ozzie, no Notes. Lotus was lucky to have him. Indeed, Ozzie had felt so stifled working within Lotus that he resigned in 1985 less than two years after joining, and set up his own shop working on contract. Retaining Ozzie, even in that unusual business arrangement, meant a multi-billion-dollar difference in the buyout price Lotus received. Such are the stakes of bringing into own's own galaxy the stars among software developers.

Gates knew that attracting very good programmers made it easier to attract others of the same caliber. Stars sought to work wherever the best in their fields congregated. Gates in 1981 had recruited Charles Simonyi from Xerox PARC as one of the first "really bright guys I hired in software development." The presence of Simonyi, who can be regarded as the father of Microsoft Word, in turn helped to lure others. This was only one of many virtuous cycles that were the centerpiece of Gates's management philosophy. The converse was also true. If Microsoft were to lose its best programmers, others would begin thinking about leaving, too. Thus Microsoft had to pay ongoing attention to retention as well as recruitment.

Missing from Gates's directives to his lieutenants is any emphasis on close scrutiny of newly hired developers in a probationary period, however. Gates wanted the stringent evaluation to take place *before* hiring, knowing that morale suffers whenever an employee is dismissed, even if he or she was not performing well. In fact, the organization should dread a mediocre new employee more than a new hire who was an unmitigated disaster. "We're actually okay if the person doesn't come in to work," Gates explained to Microsoft managers in a 1993 company video outlining his hiring priorities, "but if you have somebody who's mediocre, who just sort of gets by on the job, then we're really in big trouble." The less-than-ideal employee is hard to dismiss if managers harbor even a flicker of empathy, and yet the employee occupies a seat that an exemplary contributor could be offered. Thus Gates admonished his recruiters not to settle for second best or a near fit, even if a continuing vacancy creates hardship on other members of the team; instead, wait for the perfect candidate.

The company's tight control on head count reinforced the pressure to resist settling for the merely satisfactory candidate. Watchful of signs that underlings were asking for "100 people to do something when it should be twenty," senior executive managers scrutinized requests from individual developer groups who sought expanded payrolls. The Microsoft credo was to employ fewer than the number of employees that the work calls for—"*n* minus one" was the company's formulation—even when the company was growing rapidly. The reluctance to add to head count underlined the message about talent: hire only the smartest because your group is never going to get all the bodies that you want.

Helping his managers hire "smart people" was the single accomplishment that Gates returned to again and again when asked to review the events of a given year. He did not want his company to forget that Microsoft's success in the past, and in the future, was inseparable from its success in hiring and retaining the best brains. Toward that end, Gates made himself available to interview prospective candidates brought to campus by managers who were well below those whom he officially supervised. Sometimes Gates would put on the hat of a Microsoft recruiter himself, ready to drop other matters and make a helpful call to a prospective star when Microsoft was in a "sell situation." He would weigh in when a group's own evaluations of a particular candidate's strengths and weaknesses were inconsistent, or when a candidate had passed muster but needed the nudge of the flattering attention from the chairman himself.

No software rival of Microsoft would dispute the basic tenets of cultivating the most able software developers. The difference between Microsoft and the others is in the degree to which Microsoft has so deliberately—and successfully—pursued it. Who else but Microsoft would maintain in 1995 its own internal "Strike Team in Recruiting," with a staff that phoned potential leads around the country from six in the morning until eight at night? Even with the 120,000 résumés the company received annually, Microsoft managers assumed the most desirable potential candidates were not even looking. It was up to Microsoft to seek out the very best who did not yet realize that Microsoft was interested in recruiting them. Merely taking the initiative to approach Microsoft about an opening almost lowered the person's attractiveness as a candidate.

In addition to scouring college campuses for young prospects, the company also remained vigilant for opportunities to recruit the best experienced hands from rival companies. "Direct sourcing" is what Mike Murray, Microsoft's vice-president for human resources, called the recruiting campaign that would fasten on a software company that was doing technically interesting work. Murray explained, "We might find the org chart at an XYZ software company and we'll just start dialing, we'll just start looking for people who want to talk to us." If the recruiters found five or six individuals willing to talk about a move, Microsoft flew one of its people to the city posthaste to conduct a battery of informational interviews, efficiently prospecting for the largest number of promising candidates using a single recruiter.

Microsoft acquired small software companies, not primarily for their customers or for their code, but for their in-house programming assets. When the best programmers in such companies were the main shareholders, it was often easiest to simply buy the company outright, in effect, providing the talent with the equivalent of a signing bonus. University faculties were also the targets of Microsoft recruiters. A memo from one of Gates's senior vice-presidents listed the fruits of his group's 1993 recruiting efforts: the CEO of one supercomputer company and two senior executives from another, two influential people from Apple, one Caltech graphics expert, and two math professors from Princeton.

Microsoft rivals have spent more energy in the 1990s complaining to the government and the media about the absence of a "level playing field" in the software industry than they have in mounting similarly extensive recruiting efforts. Gates's virtuous cycle seems, if anything, to have sped up, enabling Microsoft to recruit with increasing ease over time. Having conceded the pivotal importance of a small number of individuals in software development, what is the basis for condemning Microsoft's recruiting practices? If the playing field, tiresomely characterized by Microsoft's competitors as "uneven," should be perfectly level, how should that be achieved in personnel? If Microsoft's rivals have not been willing to zealously seek out and pay for the best minds, should Microsoft be penalized for its rivals' failure?

In 1990, Philippe Kahn, then CEO of Borland, called Gates to complain that Microsoft had hired away Borland's head of research, a violation of an agreement that Kahn and Gates had signed that forbade stealing each other's employees. Gates pointed out, accurately, that the agreement had expired. If such recruiting is unseemly aggressive, how exactly would we distinguish "overly aggressive" recruiting from "merely aggressive" recruiting? Is it unfair for Microsoft to send more college recruiters to campuses than either IBM or Hewlett-Packard, much larger companies that annually hire many more college graduates? Merely posing these question serves to expose the problem with the criticism that Microsoft somehow plays unfairly because it snatches the largest number of the smartest technical hires that it can.

We do not like to acknowledge the elitist notion of comparative intelligence ratings that are the foundation of the Microsoft recruiters' world-view. The company attempts to soften the hard facts with other gestures. It dispatches its employees to volunteer in local schools, or makes cash donations to educational programs, and hosts "Career Days" to bring inner-city high school students to the Microsoft campus for a day of encouraging speeches. An improved educational system may discover overlooked potential, but, by definition, only the same percentage of individuals can occupy the elite club of the 99th percentile and above.

If we recall the long history of antipathy toward intellectuals in American society in general, and in American business in particular, we may take a less harsh view of Microsoft and its unapologetic cultivation of the brightest. If we were not jealous of how Gates and his stock-owning employees have done so well financially and are hardly in need of alternative forms of compensation, perhaps our culture would take more positive notice. If we want to encourage other businesses—and students, their future employees—to value intellectual attainment too, we could point to Microsoft as a shining example of the rewards that come to the company that prizes the intellect.

Knowing of the public's unease about smarts, Microsoft has had to police itself to suppress any signs of arrogance concerning its reservoir of above-average minds. A single incautious statement instantly erases a year's worth of self-deprecating decorum. Gates usually has been vigilant, but he is queried so often about his own intelligence that he occasionally tires of the game in which he is supposed to speak humbly and instead says something that seems purposely provocative. When *Playboy* asked him in 1994, for example, what was the last thing that he had encountered that he did not understand, he replied, "The quantum theory of gravity."

Sometimes Microsoft should be forgiven for pointing to how highly it regards intelligence, for example, when the company has been placed on the defensive, charged with besting its opponents. In 1992, Frank Gaudette, who until his death the next year was one of Microsoft's most senior executives, told the *Washington Post* that Microsoft was successful because "we're smarter—you can take that as arrogant—it's not meant as arrogant." As self-serving as Gaudette's explanation is, it remains not far from wrong, especially considering how Microsoft has expanded into new areas in the past ten years. Gates was serious when he said in 1992, "Take our twenty best people away and I tell you that Microsoft would become an unimportant company." We—the public, our elected proxies, and the regulatory agencies who represent our collective interests—should look at Microsoft's record and appoint Gates to lead the worthy, long overdue cause of *anti*-anti-intellectualism. Otherwise, our advice to companies that value intelligence is what Gates, in defending the company's success, once mockingly proposed he should tell his employees: "Don't be so smart."

The faint praise our society is willing to grant Gates and his company for serving as avatars of intellectually based business success is understandable given our history. Undoubtedly playing a role, too, are the shrinking of U.S. manufacturing since the 1970s and the dislocation and unease that has followed. This may not seem to pertain to Microsoft, a new-era manufacturing company whose output of physical objects—primarily, discs and manuals stuffed in cardboard boxes—has never occupied the attention of more than a small part of its workforce. Yet that's precisely why our society is inclined to view Microsoft's success in unflattering ways, or to be unsettled by it in ways that are not clearly understood.

We know that the sectoral changes in the economy and the internationalization of manufacturing are permanent changes and that there can be no return to the past. We know that the services sector, for the most part, offers jobs to those with middling education that pay considerably less than those available when domestic manufacturing flourished. We know that the link between intellectual ability, associated with the number of years of formal education, and lifetime pay has become ever tighter. All of these changes mean greater insecurity for most. And we have nothing but amorphous economic forces on which to fasten blame . . . unless we take aim at the company that epitomizes the economy's shift to an information-based dynamic—a company that "manufactures" the ineffable, employs people with smarts possessed by only a sliver of the population, and is directed by a person who has become richer than Croesus at a time when wide swaths of the workforce have been downsized into employment that pays less—and has pushed us unwillingly into an uncertain post-manufacturing era. Microsoft is the handy villain, the corporate symbol of a future we did not ask for.

Chapter 3

The Model in Their Head

I CHARTED MY COURSE BY FIGURES, *nothing but figures. I never felt the need of scientific knowledge, have never felt it. A young man who wants to succeed in business does not require chemistry or physics. He can always hire scientists. No, he should study figures, figures, figures and apply them to his business.*

John D. Rockefeller

I CAN HIRE MATHEMATICIANS *at fifteen dollars a week,* but they can't hire me.

Thomas Alva Edison

Edison and Rockefeller constitute an unlikely pair. Rockefeller did not share Edison's inventive genius; and Edison, who essentially lost control of his own Edison General Electric, did not share Rockefeller's trust-building genius. When Edison died in 1931, he was moderately wealthy and immoderately popular. When John D., Senior, died in 1937, he was of course immoderately wealthy and not nearly as popular, notwithstanding the image-boosting philanthropies he had launched in the last decades of his life. Yet the two men held similar beliefs: that business and technical acumen were separate and that business talent was scarcer and hence more valuable. These older verities come to mind in examining Bill Gates's management philosophy because Microsoft's history to date effectively refutes the assumptions of Edison and Rockefeller.

Reporters repeatedly question Gates about his business philosophy out of an old desire to grasp the formula for business success. One of the earliest American business advice books, Edwin T. Freedley's *Practical Treatise On Business, Or How To Get, Save, Spend, Give, and Bequeath Money* (1853), tried and failed to extract pithy advice from John Jacob Astor, whose son assured the author that his father was "not known to have had any fundamental rule or favorite maxim." Gates's responses to such questions over the years have been consistent in tetchiness, in his disbelief that anyone would even think to characterize the business side as intellectually challenging, and in what he has said about Microsoft's own story. The emphasis that Rockefeller placed on "figures" would be misguided, in Gates's view. "If you're any good at math at all," Gates said in 1992, "you understand business—it's not its own deep, deep subject." Business required a mere 10 percent of his own "mental cycles." Business schools may choose to use Microsoft for case studies, but they will have to look elsewhere for any respectful words from a chief executive officer about the schools' own value. When Gates was groping for a way to drive home his point, he gestured to the shelves in his office and asked rhetorically if there were any business books to be found. "Oops," he said, with feigned surprise, "we didn't find any."

Academic business education and popular business books— these reflected other people's business models. Gates's own business cosmology began with several assumptions that conventional wisdom had failed to provide. To begin, he reasoned that unceasing, dramatic improvements in the microprocessor would fuel the growth of Microsoft and that of the larger PC industry. Gates credits Microsoft co-founder Paul Allen for showing him, in 1971, the business potential in exponentially improving semiconductor technology. "Exponential phenomena" are rare, Gates recalls asking Allen skeptically, "Are you serious?"

A few years earlier, in 1965, Gordon Moore, a founder of Fairchild Semiconductor and later of Intel, had quantified the rate in what came to be known as Moore's Law. Based on the rate at which the number of components placed on the most complex integrated circuit had increased since the first ones had been developed—plotted on semi-log graph paper, the data points formed a straight line—Moore predicted that over the next ten years the number of components would continue to double every twelve months. That meant in practical terms that every year the capability of a chip roughly would double without an increase in price or, alternatively, that you could produce a chip with undiminished capability for half the price. In 1975, Moore revisited his forecast and altered the projected pace of the doubling effect to every two years henceforth. The prediction turned out eerily to be right on the mark—improvements in the next twenty years proceeded in the uncannily predictable fashion that Moore had foreseen.

Such wondrous improvements meant not only decreased manufacturing costs, but also other happy effects as circuits were squeezed into ever smaller spaces: faster speeds, improved system reliability, less power consumption. Even measured against the development of other historically significant industrial technologies, the record of improvements in semiconductors stands out. Beginning with the first planar transistors in 1960, in only 35 years the semiconductor industry had reduced the cost of a transistor by *ten-million*-fold. From the vantage of the present, it's not difficult to nod and agree that such an astonishing development would probably create a few business opportunities. Earlier in this period, however, it does not seem to have been so obvious that semiconductor improvements would in turn create opportunities aplenty in commercial software development, aside from the software written internally or commissioned by the computer manufacturers.

The absence of software-only rivals when Gates and Allen formed Microsoft in 1975 is telling. At the time, Gates had to convince Allen that it would be best to concentrate on software and not adopt the hardware and software "total solution" model inherited from the preceding generations of mainframe and minicomputer makers. Even as late as 1981, Gates would describe his company's software-as-primary-product strategy as a "lonely" one that he likened to an astronomical debate: others might still think the computer world revolved around the much larger hardware companies, but Gates maintained that software contributed the real value. It was software around which the world would revolve. Although the microprocessor had yet to be invented when Moore first projected semiconductor improvements, Moore's Law would apply to microprocessors no less than it did to other semiconductor devices. Gates could see that the seemingly inexorable advances in semiconductor technology would make raw computing power ever cheaper, heading in the direction of free computing "cycles." It would take increasingly sophisticated software to keep those cycles occupied productively.

One of the remarkable aspects of the rapid expansion of supply of computing cycles foretold by Moore's Law was that supply did not lead to surfeit, as in other industries experiencing rapid technological improvements. For example, the technological success of radial tires had become a business disaster because radials lasted so long that customers purchased replacements much less frequently. In the computer industry, however, technical improvements did not sate customers' appetites. On the contrary, software developers could not keep pace with the hardware side of the business. To Gates that meant plentiful business opportunities for software developers—without imminent fear of oversupply.

Whether the software was to be given away or sold embroiled the earliest owners of personal computers in the hobbyist 1970s. Even today Gates is remembered as the precociously outspoken advocate for commercializing the distribution of software in order to encourage software developers to continue to invest their labor. Arrayed against him were individuals like Jim Warren, of the People's Computer Company, who wanted developers to regard what they did as "play," not as "work." In the thick of heated exchanges between Gates and the hobbyists, whom Gates had charged with "ripping off" software without payment, Warren wrote a manifesto in 1976 arguing that if software were free, or priced so inexpensively that paying for it was easier than duplicating it, the problem of "stolen" software would disappear. Warren praised Gary Kildall's plan to sell an operating system on floppy discs for "not much more than what it would cost to duplicate them."

Gates, as we know, won this battle. While hardware cycles progressively approached a state of free availability, software was commercialized with well-known happy consequences for Gates and his estate. Note, however, that those who seemingly lost also did well in the end. Although Kildall had planned to give away his operating system, he did not do so when it came time to release the software. Revenues from that product helped Kildall's company, Digital Research, grow far faster for a few years than Microsoft before Gates entered the operating system market, too. Even Warren, who had founded the earliest personal computer trade show, the West Coast Computer Faire, did not give away his own commercially successful creation. He cashed in his ownership of the Faire for $3 million in 1983.

Gates also saw another fundamental trend at work. He inelegantly called it a trend toward "softness" wherein the general-purpose personal computer, which could take on infinite roles or tasks because it was programmable, was displacing specialized gizmos. As the machines "remembered" a particular customer's preferences and adapted to a person's particular proclivities, they incorporated greater "softness."

Having both technical and business antennae, Gates understood the need for standards that many personal computer manufacturers would adopt so that software could run on machines produced by disparate companies—a feat that was impossible in the anarchy of the late 1970s. In a column he wrote for a computer hobbyist magazine in 1977, Gates lamented that personal computer manufacturers had not agreed on a single operating system, which would save software developers from having to create different flavors for different computer vendors. With no evident premonition that his own company would step into this role four years later, Gates seems to have hoped that the manufacturers would solve the problem among themselves: "Anyone who thinks it isn't too late to do something along these lines has my enthusiastic support." Today, amidst the wails about Microsoft's dominance in operating system software, only historical amnesia refashions that standardless anarchy of the late 1970s into the "good old days."

What Gates understood better than his peers—and what also drove his advocacy of commercializing software development—were the three principles on which a thriving software industry would rest: volume, volume, and volume. Only by achieving high volume could software developers overcome the problem of high fixed costs in developing sophisticated products. Gates preached to fellow software companies in 1981, "It's only through volume that you can offer reasonable software at a low price." Prices for software did not fall as fast as prices for semiconductors. Still, Microsoft could accurately say in 1994 that it could sell very profitably a product to individual customers for $100 that the company had directly invested $100 million to develop—thanks to volume that gave any single purchaser "leverage" of a million to one.

A software company would have great difficulty achieving high sales volume as long as it had to prepare separate versions of a particular program for individual brands of hardware. An operating system, however, could serve as an insulating layer of software. If a software application worked on top of the operating system, the underlying hardware variation from brand to brand would no longer be a concern. The software programmer only had to concentrate on making the application compatible with a single operating system; the hardware problems would be a headache only for the company that wrote the underlying operating system software. The wide adoption of a single operating system would unify into a single market the Balkanized principalities of proprietary machines and varying flavors of CP/M, the most popular operating system software for pre-IBM PC personal computers.

Despite his discernment of these basic features of the new opportunities—features that would become banally obvious to others later—Gates was not unerringly omniscient. His company had gotten its start by tailoring different versions of BASIC, a computer language that it sold to people who wanted to write programs. To this business he added of course an operating system business in 1981, but he was slow to appreciate the need to expand into a third domain: developing applications, the programs that would run on top of the operating system. In 1984, he berated himself for the oversight.

The most challenging questions that Gates and his employees faced were neither purely business nor purely technical. Experience had taught Thomas Edison to combine commercial and technical considerations. The "electric vote recorder," the first invention for which Edison received a patent, tallied votes quickly and was intended for use in legislatures. But when he approached a congressional committee about sales, the committee chairman told him, "Young man, that is just what we do *not* want." (It would infringe on the sacred institution of the filibuster.) His machine was never produced, and he resolved not to devote his attention to the invention of anything that lacked "commercial demand." When working later on an electric lighting system, Edison paid close attention to economic factors at every stage in what one historian has termed an "econotech-nical" approach. But Edison—strikingly unlike Gates—regarded the gift of the "econotechnical" blend as his alone and did not ask his managers to think the same way. For Gates, the combination of business and technical skills was not a personal monopoly. On the contrary, Microsoft's growth would accelerate to the degree that Gates's recruiting and management brought into the fold more individuals who were strong in both areas.

Edison is of particular interest when we seek some perspective on Microsoft's recruitment of talented individuals. Both Edison and Gates held their employees to stringent standards, but they differed in how they tested prospects. Microsoft's questions sought to find out how interviewees solved unfamiliar challenges, whereas Edison was most concerned with an employee's command of facts—facts of all kinds. Edison attracted considerable attention in 1921 when newspapers discovered that he was administering a self-devised "intelligence" test to job applicants. The test consisted of over 150 factual questions that read like a game of Trivial Pursuit (What is copra? What states bound West Virginia? Who wrote "Home Sweet Home"? Where do we get domestic sardines? . . .) His own employees were subjected to the same battery of questions, and those who failed to meet Edison's standards were summarily fired. Edison said he was most disappointed with the performance of college graduates on his test, so reporters asked random college students to pit their knowledge against Edison's questions and gleefully reported to the public the dismal results.

Even Albert Einstein, who happened to be visiting the United States at the time, was subjected to mock testing. When reporters asked one of Edison's questions—What is the speed of sound?—Einstein replied without apology that he did not know offhand but that the information was readily available in textbooks. The *New York Times,* with tongue firmly in cheek, ran the alarming headline: "Einstein . . . Fails On Edison Test." Elsewhere, in an editorial, the paper made clear that it did not agree with Edison that the questions successfully tested intelligence. As for Edison, the editorial opined, the testing brouhaha showed that though he was exceptional in his combining "inventive faculty and business sense," when he ventured into other domains such as this one, he succeeded only in demonstrating that "a really notable man can give a startlingly lifelike imitation of mediocrity and unenlightenment."

In contrast, Microsoft has sought out intelligence not through open-and-shut questions like Edison's but by watching how applicants confront questions chosen precisely to present unfamiliar challenges. The company credits Steve Ballmer, Gates's classmate from Harvard, with developing the early brain-teasers. Having finished his undergraduate degree, Ballmer had completed his first year of business school at Stanford when Gates persuaded him to join Microsoft in 1979 to be in charge of recruiting new employees to the company, sixteen at the time.

Ballmer, neither then nor now, presents an intellectual mien. Nothing in his public speeches or interviews suggests a contemplative temperament or wide reading interests. When addressing employees, his delivery is punctuated with a clenched fist pounded repeatedly into the other hand; his words often take the form of a loud, repetitive war chant ("Windows! Windows! Windows!"); he screamed so hard for so long at the 1991 company meeting that he needed throat surgery to repair the damage. And yet Ballmer, who seems best suited for—and the one who became, in fact—Microsoft's head cheerleader, also understood early on the importance of recruiting individuals who could derive the best—often hidden—solutions to tough problems.

In its early years, Microsoft's cultivation of intellectual gymnasts went virtually undetected. The face that the company presented to the public was anything but impressive. The sheet that the company used to introduce itself and its products to prospective customers was typed entirely in lowercase ("we are microsoft, a company of over one hundred people. . . ."), filled with egregious typographical errors ("we maintain the high standards of uality. . ."), and was prepared, the company bragged, by Microsoft's own software. Nor did Microsoft's management impress observers. In 1984, for example, *Fortune* chided the company for failing to develop the "management depth" it would need to turn its "temporary victories" into "long-term dominance."

Out of view, however, the company was putting into place practices that would form a culture that devised what Gates and others referred to as "heuristics," the term philosophers and computer scientists use for theoretical formulations that are speculative in nature and used as an interim guide to trial-and-error problem solving. Microsoft's executives were self-conscious about what is otherwise a casual process of constructing and revising mental models as we bump along solving problems in daily life, employing a "heuristic" approach without referring to it as such. They understood that the ability to devise—and revise—mental models was the most important intellectual asset the company could seek in prospective new employees. Hence, as Gates explained to a group of college students in 1986, his technique for interviewing job applicants was to ask about their past projects—how things had been done and how they could have been done better. Candidates who shrugged and said they didn't really know were not the type of person that Microsoft sought, one "who builds this model in their head of how things go on."

If you want a person who wields models comfortably and is unafraid of constructing very large ones, you can't do better than hiring and promoting an astrophysicist. At least that could be one reading of why Gates hired Nathan Myhrvold in 1986. Myhrvold would come to public attention many years later as one of the "other" co-authors with Gates of *The Road Ahead,* and his career is worth examining as it exemplifies the themes that would contribute to Microsoft's elevation to worldwide notice in the 1990s.

Myhrvold's story is first one of social mobility based on smarts. Born in 1959, he was brought up by a single parent, his mother. A schoolteacher in Santa Monica, California, she recalls that her son knew by the age of two he was going to be a scientist. Myhrvold proved a precocious student. He graduated from high school by the age of 14; from UCLA at 19, with a bachelor's degree in mathematics and a master's degree in geophysics and space physics; and from Princeton at 23, with a master's in mathematical economics and a Ph.D. in theoretical physics. Myhrvold's dissertation was on "Vistas in Curved Space-Time Quantum Field Theory." (He once summarized for a lay audience his primary research interest in the origin of the universe as that portion of time when the universe was "about 10 to the minus thirty-third of a centimeter up to about the size of a grapefruit—after that, it's all sort of history as far as I'm concerned.")

Although Myhrvold's path hardly seems, in retrospect, pointed in the direction of Redmond, Washington, a second theme in this story helps to connect the dots: Gates's early appreciation of the value of cranial over financial assets in acquiring small software companies. After completing his Ph.D., Myhrvold had moved to England to accept a postdoctoral fellowship at Cambridge, doing research under Stephen Hawking. In the summer following his first year, he was enticed to return to the United States—temporarily, he thought—by a small group of theoretical physicists and mathematicians, friends who had worked with Myhrvold on a programming project in their spare time when they all were at Princeton. They were starting their own little software company. Before he knew it, Myhrvold was the president and the company had set up in Berkeley. Their principal product became an operating system with certain features that Microsoft wanted, but between the time that Microsoft signed a letter of intent to purchase the company and the time when the deal would have closed, the need for those features evaporated. So too, Myhrvold figured, would Microsoft's interest in his company. But Gates went ahead and completed the deal. As events turned out, this group of hires—who also included Nathan Myhrvold's brother, Cameron, and David Weise, a programmer whose technical reputation would spread far outside the company—would rise to senior technical positions within Microsoft, bearing out the wisdom of Gates's fondness for acquiring smarts in bulk.

For his first four years at Microsoft, Nathan Myhrvold worked under Steve Ballmer, then in charge of the division that developed operating systems. Myhrvold's initial position—director of special projects—gave him the opportunity to become an internal technical pundit looking at nettlesome technical decisions that the company faced while plotting future directions for its operating systems, adapting to new microprocessor designs, and resolving other Big Think "architectural" issues. Myhrvold brought a number of talents to the task. He could grasp the technical details of disparate fields quickly. He could move smoothly between a bird's-eye vantage point down to worm-level technical details and back again. He could marshal his thoughts into closely argued briefs that were not only clear, but also sprinkled with humor. He was personable, fairly bursting with good spirits, peering out at the world beyond his wire rims with an approachable face and a voice that would climb excitedly in pitch whenever a topic caught his interest, which was often. He was the antithesis of the dour, introverted scientist.

It did not hurt that Myhrvold was also a prolific writer—in a six-month period in 1991, for example, he dispatched 99 substantive reports—and fast, dashing off 20-, 30-, 40-page or longer, single-spaced memos over a weekend. When he was not busy with assigned projects, he took on other topics that caught his interest. Soon he was cranking out hundreds of pages of technical reviews, strategic suggestions, competitive analyses, scouting reports on prospective acquisitions or hires, and sundry whimsical opinions (sample memo title: "Totally Insane Ideas"). Myhrvold, who had no formal training in computer science or engineering, was becoming the de facto helmsman piloting Microsoft's technical direction.

The larger the questions Myhrvold addressed, the less they concerned purely technical decisions and the more they mixed technical and business issues. With the rise within the ranks of a gadfly as technically adept and articulate as Myhrvold—and younger than Gates to boot—Gates might have felt his perch as the resident boy-prodigy threatened. Certainly, Thomas Edison felt uneasy about his dependence on *his* key technical advisor, Francis Upton, coincidentally a Princeton-trained physicist. Edison, notoriously weak in mathematics, had to rely on Upton to solve all equations. To compensate, Edison took advantage of any opportunities that permitted his unschooled instincts to outshine Upton's formal training. Edison once assigned Upton to calculate the cubic contents of a pear-shaped glass bulb. Upton had labored for an hour on the problem, painstakingly calculating the curve of the lines, when Edison interrupted and declared triumphantly that Upton should have simply filled the bulb with a liquid and then measured the liquid, an elegantly simple solution. Upton always praised his employer's unique talents and lamented that though he could answer questions very easily after they were asked, on his own he found "great trouble in framing any to answer." Edison knew what questions to pose.

The Gates-Myhrvold relationship did not resemble the asymmetry of the Edison-Upton one. To Gates's credit, his response on discovering Myhrvold's talents was to promote Myhrvold and increasingly draw on his advice. Myhrvold was a quick study, but so too was Gates, and if Myhrvold learned something that Gates did not already know, Gates unlike Edison was able to absorb it quickly, too.

In 1991, Myhrvold was placed in charge of all of Microsoft's research and advanced development work, and from there his responsibilities grew upward and outward, as Gates had him participate frequently in negotiations with prospective corporate partners. By 1995, Myhrvold had risen to the position of group vice-president and was a member of Microsoft's six-person Office of the President. The broadening of Myhrvold's horizons and the consequent fusion of business and technical issues found in the memos, electronic mail, and increasingly frequent conversations with Gates in person made Myhrvold an influential counsel in strategic planning.

Myhrvold recruited hundreds of others, many of whom, like him, lacked a conventional background for their positions but who brought a protean intelligence. This tells us much about how Microsoft has so greatly increased its capacity to move simultaneously on all conceivable software fronts, new as well as old. It is wrong to view Microsoft as a ferocious marketing machine—a characterization that implies that the company merely "buys" additional market share with lavish expenditures in marketing that its competitors cannot afford. Instead we should characterize Microsoft as a ferocious *learning* machine.

Microsoft customers have long known that the company has introduced first and second versions of new software with serious flaws. This pattern was so pronounced by 1990 that even Gates mused aloud that if the company did not change, customers would simply skip the first two versions. But the company was usually able to return to the marketplace with much improved versions of the botched software without encountering the scorn of its intended customers because it excelled at studying and rectifying its own mistakes. It could do that because of Gates's attachment to the notion of feedback loops. More than just the amplified squeal of a poorly adjusted microphone, feedback is a general concept in many fields of engineering that refers to a machine or system that deliberately channels part of the output back through the input in order to continually adjust the operations. An early example is James Watt's late eighteenth-century steam engine, in which two rotating balls provided feedback, closing off a valve when the engine attained a high speed.

An organization can be likened to an engine, designed in such a way that its output is fed back into the input so that the organization, like Watt's engine, automatically becomes self-regulating. At Microsoft, feedback loops went from the marketplace back to the company, from employees back to management, and from management back to employees. As time passed, Gates would discern the importance of these loops in ever-broadening domains—even in other companies that did not recognize them as such. Despite his professed lack of interest in management books, he frequently praised Alfred Sloan, Jr.'s, dry treatise-cum-memoir *My Years with General Motors*. In Gates's view, Sloan's rise to the top was a manifestation of GM's having "the right feedback loops to draw out its talent."

Gates paid close attention to installing circuits that would serve as conduits of feedback in his own company, and he dispensed feedback with the same unstinting abandon that his lieutenants showed in sending him product development, business trip, prospective hire, and sales reports. Such missives provided him with far more details than chief executive officers of other companies would want to bother with. For Gates, the usefulness of feedback—to him and to others—was an article of faith, and his lieutenants preached the religion with no less fervor.

At the 1994 annual meeting, for example, Steve Ballmer recalled the price that he had personally paid many years earlier, when he was assigned responsibility for Windows version 1.0. The incumbent manager handed him a schedule of expected milestones that everyone on the development team knew were unattainable, but no one told Ballmer. The team simply snickered when he spoke with innocent enthusiasm of how well the project was proceeding. Eventually discovering the discrepancy between the rosy schedule and reality, Ballmer vowed never to allow development problems to be suppressed—and he pointedly noted that the manager who had hid the depressing facts from him no longer worked for Microsoft. Ballmer told the company's employees:

If you have a problem you don't think is getting resolved, well, you are not only allowed to, you are encouraged to talk to your manager's manager, your manager's manager's manager, or whatever it takes to get that opinion heard. You are encouraged to use electronic mail if it is too intimidating or threatening to go see your manager. And there should be no retaliation of any kind associated with that act.

Gates, Mike Maples, and the other senior executives echoed the same sentiment: they did not like to be surprised; they wanted information to flow, down and up, whether good, bad, or indifferent.

One of Nathan Myhrvold's early internal memos, "Notes on Application Innovation" (1988), combined the concept of feedback and the usefulness of modeling into a plea for Microsoft developers to formally develop what Myhrvold spoke of as "User Modeling." It involved the more systematic collection of data on how computer users actually went about trying to accomplish whatever it was they had set out to do. The research would note not only keystrokes and menu choices, but also more subtle measures such as disc utilization, network traffic, and recourse to online help. Microsoft should no less intensively study the real-world use of competitors' products, Myhrvold suggested, to give developers another source of empirical data to use in improving Microsoft's products. And why not take advantage of the huge amount of information collected by Microsoft's technical support department, which already logged, at considerable expense, all the technical problems that were called in by customers? Most of the data, he said, would not surprise the developers, but the 10 percent that would reveal something unusual would be a fertile source of ideas for making dramatic "wins."

These ideas all came to pass. Microsoft's technical support group became ever more systematic in collecting data, and Microsoft's developers squeezed that data for all the insights that they could get, motivated not simply by logic but also by a pecuniary goad. Each group was "charged" internally for the full cost of the centralized support staff who handled telephone calls about problems with that group's products. The fewer calls received, the higher profitability the software development group could post. Immediate feedback was also built into Wizards, button-activated routines within the software that helped customers carry out elaborate formatting changes or accomplish other tasks, depending on responses to a few questions. Myhrvold had proposed such features in 1988 as "semi-automatic add-ins," arguing they "could be an enormously valuable thing to the poor guy who has to otherwise do all the work by hand."

The notion that Gates is lord of an "accidental empire" does not accord with the basic facts, which are summarized here. An era-defining new technology, the microprocessor, arrived in the 1970s, and its power increased at an exponential rate every two years. Gates and Allen understood earlier than others that one consequence of this technological development would be an expanding need for software that would run on small computers. Gates recruited smart people, put them to work on a campus well suited for intense concentration, and maintained their allegiance with stock options whose value made millionaires of mere foot soldiers in the product development groups. The organization, even as it grew large, was deliberately fashioned to perpetuate the identity of small groups, and communication, up and down, was frequent and voluminous. Gates and his subordinates consciously devised—and revised, as needed—strategic models that guided decision making, imparting ever-improving capabilities to the organization. Given these fundamentals, if any mystery lingers, it is simply why Microsoft's competitors were slow to catch on to the basics themselves.

Part Two

The Home

Chapter 4

Big Files

*T*HE SUMMATION OF HUMAN EXPERIENCE *is being expanded at a prodigious rate, and the means we use for threading through the consequent maze to the momentarily important item is the same as was used in the days of square-rigged ships.*

Vannevar Bush, Director of the U.S. Office of Scientific Research and Development, in the *Atlantic Monthly* (1945)

Machines as the handmaid of memory, helping humans store and recall knowledge, was the role that Vannevar Bush envisioned for machines. Two ideas in particular stood out in his proposal. First, the entire sum of human knowledge that had found expression in print—all books, magazines, newspapers, correspondence—can be converted into a storage form so small that a copy of the entire corpus could be installed in a desk-like machine from which an individual could easily summon and enlarge the desired information. Second, that same information can be indexed in multiple, nonliteral ways so that summoning and enlarging the desired information is quick and convenient. The principal means that Bush proposed to achieve his aim—an ultra-small form of microfilm—has not turned out to be the most practical path for document miniaturization in the personal computer age. Still, many of Bush's ideas anticipated later developments, from his invitation for readers to imagine the possibilities ("The *Encyclopaedia Britannica* could be reduced to the volume of a matchbox") and the corresponding dramatic drop in duplication costs, to his championing of "dry photography" for capturing images that resembles today's photocopying. Even though today's tools are more sophisticated than Bush had in mind, we still have not fully solved Bush's needle-in-the-haystack problem of information retrieval when the haystack is enormous. Proposing that everyone should have desktop access to identical copies of the entire haystack—reduced to smaller scale but fully intact and searchable—was a radical idea for the time.

From the vantage point of the present, the eventual realization of Bush's dream of instantaneous access to everything known seems to be taking the shape of a virtual library on the World Wide Web, which patrons will visit via network connections far faster than today's modems and telephone switching equipment can provide. An intermediate step that has helped move us toward that Promised Land was the introduction of the CD-ROM, the platter adapted from audio compact discs. When introduced in the United States in the fall of 1984, CD-ROMs offered room for a much larger haystack of information—550 megabytes—than had ever been available on the desktop before. (The discs, from day one, have been referred to as CD-ROMs, never Compact Disc–Read Only Memory.) When CD-ROMs were introduced, people were using personal computers as glorified calculators and typewriters, with which they typed, stored, processed, and printed their *own* data. CD-ROMs helped shift attention to the utility of data that someone else had collected and culled, which users could slice and dice into their own concoctions. Although the CD-ROM owed its birth to the music industry, you would not have guessed it from the first CD-ROMs—devoid of multimedia, they held text, and only text. One of the first discs to reach the market was a text-only encyclopedia adapted from the *Academic American Encyclopedia* and offered by Grolier (graphics and sound were absent due to technical problems unrelated to insufficient space—the encyclopedia occupied only a fifth of the CD-ROM). The adaptation was the creation of Gary Kildall, Gates's software rival who earlier had produced an operating system for pre-IBM personal computers that fell victim to Microsoft's later entry. And in 1985, Kildall once again got the jump on Gates in this newly opened area of CD-ROMs, but it was to prove a short-lived advantage.

If the game were simply one of who could place the first CD-ROM titles on shelves, Gates might have dispatched his developers to slap existing databases of information onto the discs as quickly as possible. But, in 1985, a CD-ROM business would have had no foundation on which to flourish. File standards and other technical specifications had yet to be agreed on, and CD-ROM drives were distressingly expensive. Initially priced at $2295, they still were $1000 or more at a time when the ostensibly similar audio CD players were only $150.

Though everyone knew that the price for CD-ROM drives would come down when high-volume production was attained, early purchasers were few and the virtuous cycle—increased sales leading to lower costs leading to increased sales—was not in sight. Consumers also were reluctant to pay high prices when virtually no CD-ROM titles were available, and software developers of course balked at developing titles as long as so few prospective purchasers owned CD-ROM drives, delaying another virtuous cycle of consumers and developers mutually increasing their respective numbers. Derived from his experience with the operating system for IBM-compatible personal computers, Gates's model envisioned a wondrous alchemy that produced software, consumers, and profits—as long as a clear standard was established that would allow software to run on disparate brands of machines. A CD-ROM business could not be built without completing the foundation of standards. Not surprisingly, Gates saw a role for Microsoft in the task.

The shrewd tactical decisions that followed the strategy were not carbon copies of the tactics employed to secure dominance of the operating system market. Acquiring the leading position in the nascent business of CD-ROMs was trickier, given that there was no single partner such as IBM, association with whom conferred a leadership role. *Perception* of leadership was more important than any tangible measure of market share, and Microsoft secured that perception by performing a nominally selfless service—sponsoring a conference for the entire CD-ROM industry in March 1986. It was the first such conference and was billed as ecumenical in spirit, with any and all interested parties welcome. By inviting Gary Kildall as a keynote speaker, Gates adroitly avoided any charges of partisanship; and by hosting the first gathering, Gates—whose company, after all, had not released a single CD-ROM title—would become the CD-ROM industry's paterfamilias, not Kildall, who had been working with optical technology for almost three years.

Suppose you gave a party for CD-ROMs and no one came? Though the conference had been publicized months in advance, advance interest was disappointing; until two weeks before the conference, fewer than 200 people had registered. A sudden surge of last-minute sign-ups, however, many from overseas, brought registration up to the planned capacity of 1000. The tardiest registrants had to be turned away. The fear of missing a party where everyone else was gathered had impelled the cautious ones to show up, too. Gates had expected to lose money on the event, but with sold-out registration, the conference broke even, another pleasant surprise. The event seemed to be going so well that, on the last day, Gates decided that what he had intended to be a one-time event would be held again the following year.

Gates also proved to be shrewd in recognizing at the time of the CD-ROM's appearance what he and the others at Microsoft did *not* know. He intuitively understood that to fully exploit the medium would require entirely new skill sets that had yet to be devised. Moreover, though he could see the technical possibilities in the medium, Gates was not certain that a profitable business could be built with CD-ROMs—but he was willing to spend a considerable sum of money to find out. At one point he confided to one of his subordinates that he was willing to lose $200 million to find out whether a market existed. He also understood that investing early—and making inevitable mistakes early—would be far cheaper than waiting until after a crowd of competitors had assembled. Learning would be even more expensive by the time everybody else had entered the game.

The entry of competitors was the only way to ensure a plentiful variety of CD-ROM titles and thereby set in motion the desired virtuous cycle: titles would entice buyers, who would then buy CD-ROM drives on which to play them, pushing the prices of the drives down, expanding the installed base, attracting more software developers, and so on, providing larger profits to the software vendors with each turn. Microsoft worked with a group of industry representatives from Sony, Philips, Digital, Apple, and others to accelerate the establishment of a single file format to help jump-start the industry. Microsoft also evangelized the religion of CD-ROM among hardware companies, persuading them to offer consumers not just add-on drives, but also personal computers with the drives already installed and configured. Microsoft wanted to convey the message that CD-ROM was not just a new technology but also a "platform," in computer industry parlance, a standard for which a new set of software titles could be sold. The message would not have been persuasive if Microsoft had not chartered a new internal business unit, the CD Consumer Group, to develop CD-ROM titles. Its establishment was evidence that Gates was doing, not just talking. As Tom Corddry, a manager in the group, recalls, when word spread that Microsoft was developing its own titles, other publishers took notice: "It was like following somebody around at Monte Carlo, seeing where he's putting his money."

Neither Gates nor his CD Consumer Group was sure of what titles should be offered first, but he encouraged the group to tackle hitherto impractical projects, thanks to the lifting of space constraints imposed by standard floppy discs. Now that CD-ROMs placed what Gates called "big files" within grasp, what, he wanted to know, could be done that had not been possible before? Frequently consulted yet unwieldy in conventional printed form, general-interest reference works were a natural choice.

A tiny San Francisco company called Cytation, founded in late 1984 by a former advertising executive, Tom Lopez, had gotten the earliest start in this area, licensing the *American Heritage Dictionary,* *Roget's Thesaurus,* the *Chicago Manual of Style, Bartlett's Quotations,* and the *World Almanac* for placement on a CD-ROM that Lopez entitled CD-Write. It caught the eye of Min Yee, the head of Microsoft Press. No one within Microsoft had experience developing a CD-ROM title and hardly anyone outside the company had such experience, either. When Yee persuaded Gates to purchase Cytation, it was Microsoft's first publicly disclosed acquisition. Tom Lopez was appointed head of a new CD-ROM division.

Microsoft revamped CD-Write, renamed it Microsoft Bookshelf, and brought it out as its first CD-ROM title. Eventually it would sell well, once a sizable number of computer users had acquired CD-ROM drives, but the technical difficulties and business uncertainties that hobbled the development of a CD-ROM software industry remained. Although Microsoft acquired Cytation in January 1986, the Microsoft version of Bookshelf was not ready for release until September 1987. Even when it finally came out, it was only the second general-interest

CD-ROM title on the market—it and Gary Kildall's encyclopedia constituted the entire catalog of available titles.

Microsoft looked behind, hoping to see others following its lead, but no other titles were slated for announcement that fall or the following spring. Carl Stork, one of Microsoft's lead hardware gurus, became concerned that if the dearth of titles persisted until the time of the third annual CD-ROM Conference in March 1988, the viability of CD-ROM would be questioned, retailers would withhold promotion, software developers would continue to sit on the sidelines, and the entire crusade would collapse. Lotus Development—which at that time was still larger than Microsoft—remained cautious, telling Microsoft that it had decided to wait and see how Bookshelf fared before committing to bringing out its own CD-ROM titles. Here, as in the better known case of its slow-footed development of programs for Windows, Lotus's absence was not for want of superior financial resources or invitations from Microsoft.

Stork proposed a quick-and-dirty solution to the problem. If Microsoft were to draw on public domain sources or backlist titles from its own Microsoft Press for content, thus circumventing licensing problems, it could push a number of CD-ROM titles out the door in short order. The titles that Stork suggested were not the most scintillating (Tax Bookshelf, World Fact Bookshelf, Government Access Bookshelf), but he was probably correct in claiming that Microsoft could shovel data onto six discs within six months—"6 in 6" was Stork's slogan. Gates, however, rejected this proposal for unappetizing shovelware. It would not have moved Microsoft closer to the overarching strategic goal that had made him so interested in CD-ROM in the first place. Here, it seemed, was the technological potential to do amazing visual and aural things that text-only software, lacking the spaciousness of "big files," had been unable to do. It was the multimedia additions, Gates believed, that would help fulfill his desideratum: the home as a market for software, distinct from that of the office.

Well ahead of rivals, Gates understood that creating a home market would require more than lower hardware prices for personal computers and an array of "productivity" programs similar to those used in the office. As an appliance that could entertain, educate, and inform, the personal computer would have to exceed the capabilities of other media entrenched in the home. Microsoft's principal competition would not be other software developers, but the television. With "big files" and sound and video cards, personal computers not only would be able to match television's sounds and images, but also could offer interactive capabilities and recall of viewer interests and preferences.

The idea that a smart PC eventually would supplant a dumb TV set would spread in the personal computer business in 1993 and 1994, but in 1985 Gates already was spelling out the reasons with remarkable clarity. When an interviewer for *Metropolitan Home* wanted Gates to comment on how personal computers would be used to turn home appliances on and off, Gates evinced little interest. He felt that such uses were a long way off; much sooner, he said, the personal computer would become the home's primary appliance for information, with as "rich" an image as the television—"rich" is the adjective that Gates and others in the industry use frequently and widely to describe images, information, text, and experience that are beyond the ordinary. And a personal computer was intrinsically better equipped to engage the viewer intellectually and permit control over the programs in ways that television could never provide. For illustrations, Gates often would describe how the educational programs would offer interactive self-quizzes, an emphasis that might be expected from an autodidact with a yen for competition. Thanks to CD-ROMs, Gates said, the new programs would be so compelling that "you're going to be involved, you're going to be quizzed, you're going to say, 'I'm a superstar, let me try this out.'" The programs would be so captivating that schoolchildren might become addicted, Gates suggested, but so be it: "If a kid is addicted to a personal computer, I think that's far better than watching TV because at least his mind is making choices."

Disclosing his view of the PC as the ultimate successor to the home TV set, Gates admitted that his ideas would undoubtedly seem farfetched and most of his listeners would remain skeptical. Nor did he predict that the ideas would come to pass quickly—in 1986, he said it might be eight or ten years before most homes would have personal computers with multimedia CD-ROMs. But he added, "Ten years is not [that] long a time." Gates could take an expansive view because he knew enough about the history of the technical work that had preceded the introduction of CD-ROMs to see that it had already taken ten years to accomplish only some of the things that had been demonstrated earlier in the laboratory. He knew also that the developers of

CD-ROMs' progenitor, the audio CD, had intentionally crippled the CD's capacity in order to secure the support of the music industry, and that the capacity of both CDs and CD-ROMs could—and thus eventually *would*—be increased by a factor of ten or more.

Most important, Gates saw in the mid-1980s that CD-ROMs were merely one manifestation of a much larger shift, from analog to digital forms of storing information. Vannevar Bush should not be faulted for failing to see in 1945 that this shift would separate his imagined solutions from those of the present, especially because the significance of that shift is often misunderstood even today. When speaking of information that has been converted into digital form, journalists today often attach the phrase "the language of 0s and 1s," which places undue emphasis on the limited vocabulary of a base 2 system. *Digital* simply means that the information is expressed in numerical digits only. This is more than a quibble. If we live in the age that we've come to call the "Digital Age," we should pay closer attention to what the age's namesake really refers to and why it has turned out to be so significant.

The microfilm that Bush had in mind in 1945 for information storage serves to illustrate the inherent limitations of a predigital medium: a book page captured on microfilm remained a proportionally perfect reproduction of the original, reduced on a scale of 20:1. It could be reduced further—Bush predicted that reduction could be improved to 10,000:1. But as long as the image was reproduced in proportion—an analog method—ultimately a point would be reached when it could not shrink further and still be usable.

Another shortcoming was that the microfilm image was necessarily mute, unable to provide additional information about its contents that would aid in searching. Today when the same page is scanned into a personal computer and the ink patterns are converted into numerical form, a number of possibilities open up that do not exist in analog form: easy translation, reproduction, compression, encryption, transmission, and transmutation into other media that have nothing to do with books. These and the other now-familiar conveniences of digital manipulation are possible because the original information was converted into symbolic representation—numerals. I can safely assume that the number 5 on my computer works in the same fashion that the number 5 on yours does, and any given 5 is interchangeable with anyone else's 5. In the analog world, the form in which information is stored is not interchangeable. The markings that indicate the number 5 on microfilm must be kept just so, in unvarying proportion, if they are to retain the intended meaning, and that severely limits any altering, mixing, or transporting of the original. The significance of digital expression is found in this flexibility and transportability, not in the particular format of 0s and 1s.

Gates understood well before others another decisive advantage of betting on the eventual triumph of digital over analog information storage: digital storage, reliant as it is on semiconductor technology, would enjoy the exponential improvements of Moore's Law. The analog world had no similar law at work that would swiftly, dramatically, and continuously increase the power and lower the cost of the technology used in microfilm readers, conventional television sets, VCRs, or other analog devices. Aside from a few specialized niches, analog has been or will be vanquished by digital, the outcome of an imbalance in respective rates of improvement that no one can redress. As clear as the general shift now appears, the particularities of its course were not so easily predicted in the 1980s. Thus we would be mistaken to regard, in hindsight, Gates's early investment in CD-ROMs as a means to create and enter a home software market as a low-risk proposition.

The attractiveness of the home market certainly was not visible to many at the time of the first CD-ROM conference. Most non-Microsoft attendees assumed that the deep pockets of business customers, not consumer purchases of CD-ROMs for home use, would make this technology an accepted standard, just as business customers' spending had supported new generations of chips from Intel. Business customers, it was thought, could use CD-ROMs as convenient repositories of financial and marketing data, but they had no need for glitzy multimedia. Jim Seymour, an industry columnist and consultant whose writings over the years have been consistently impervious to corporate hype, in this one instance erred on the side of dismissing too much of what Microsoft claimed lay ahead. Seymour allowed that a CD-ROM demonstration about whales that Microsoft put on at the first CD-ROM conference was a "dazzler." But the mix of text, pictures, diagrams, and haunting whale songs, as technically impressive as it was, did not change the hard fact that for business use, unadorned text was perfectly sufficient. Seymour said that the "Thomas Wolfe" rule— "You can't go home again to the world of plain text after you've seen what's possible with effective integration of sound, pictures, motion, and text"—simply did not apply to business users.

Jerry Pournelle, a science-fiction author and another influential columnist for personal computer magazines like *Byte,* did not foresee that CD-ROMs would succeed, either. He declared on his return from that first conference that he'd also been to the "last" CD-ROM conference. He contended that a newer product—one that, although it used a disc with storage capabilities similar to those of CD-ROM, would connect to a television set instead of a personal computer for display —would soon be introduced. So why would anyone buy CD-ROMs? Pournelle saw CD-ROM as a technology that was about to be rendered obsolete and was dependent on a PC that most homes had not purchased. He was not alone in predicting that CD-ROM would die a swift death, but the prediction proved wrong for the very reason that Gates had placed faith in a bright future for personal computers: PCs occupied an ideal intermediate position between smart but expensive computers and inexpensive but dumb household appliances. The PC was the least expensive, infinitely adaptable, multipurpose, programmable appliance yet devised. Strip the personal computer of its memory or its ability to be programmed by its owner and you lower the cost, but you also lose its limitless adaptability. A CD player connected to a dumb television set did not become a potent threat to a CD-ROM player connected to a smart personal computer. (Ten years later, the same issues would reappear when inexpensive Internet terminals were excitedly embraced as the personal computer's replacement, as we shall see in later chapters.)

In 1986, it was not easy to maintain faith that consumers would become the prime market for CD-ROMs as long as the price of the drives remained almost as expensive as an entire personal computer. In 1985, when Microsoft was planning for its initial CD-ROM conference, Gates reasoned that even though no mass market was in sight, the impressive sales of audio CD players—similar in mechanical and electronic guts to CD-ROM drives and manufactured by the same companies—would provide the volume that would lower prices for CD-ROM, too. Yet this did not come to pass as quickly as he hoped. Each year, Microsoft managers would have Gates declare at the annual

CD-ROM conference that the upcoming year would be the long-awaited one when prices would drop and CD-ROM would finally take off, and each year would come and go with the prediction left unfulfilled. (Eventually Gates became so disgusted with the ritual of declaring "This will be the year . . ." that he dropped it from his speech, and of course that was the long-awaited year.) CD-ROM drives, all of which were manufactured in Japan, remained scarce. Their price in the United States was affected by the yen's dramatic appreciation against the dollar, which coincided with these events. In 1988, the price of drives was still stuck at $800 to $1200. An analyst estimated that only about 170,000 drives were installed in the entire country—far too few to entice software publishers to start the virtuous cycle that would bring in more consumers.

In late 1988, IBM executives told Microsoft they wanted to try once again to crack the home personal computer market—the humiliating disaster of the PC Jr. had been the centerpiece of IBM's most recent foray. Gates suggested that the machine be equipped with an integrated CD-ROM drive and sound card—a true multimedia machine. Eager to restore the market's confidence in its ability to lead the industry, IBM accepted the suggestion and set about designing what the company thought would be a "killer" home machine. Priced at an attractive $1500, it was to be ready for the 1990 Christmas season. Gates assigned a team of Microsoft software engineers to work with IBM to ensure that Microsoft's operating system would work well with the multimedia additions.

Software issues turned out to be the least of the project's problems. The $1500 retail price for the machine proved unrealistic—remember that a CD-ROM drive alone still sold for more than half that. The Japanese supplier that convinced IBM it could deliver drives for only $200 each if given a sufficiently large purchase commitment proved unable to do so. The estimated retail price for the machine quickly climbed to $3000. The two IBM groups that shared responsibility for the project—one in Lexington, Kentucky, the other in Boca Raton, Florida—seemed preoccupied with inflicting harm on each other. Even in 1989 it became clear that the machine could not be ready for Christmas 1990. A successful outcome did not seem likely.

Gates had assigned Rob Glaser to be his principal multimedia advisor; Glaser had joined Microsoft in 1983 at the age of 21 and had come directly from Yale with a B.S. in computer science and a B.A. and an M.A. in economics. Glaser was most attracted to Microsoft by the intelligence he observed in the employees who interviewed him. Like Nathan Myhrvold and a number of others, he was given senior responsibility by Gates soon after joining the company, at an age when counterparts in other companies are barely starting their careers. When the collaboration with IBM seemed headed for disaster, Glaser suggested to Gates that Microsoft should launch what Glaser called a "virtual standard" for multimedia that could be used in all IBM-compatible personal computers, not just IBM's. Gates gave his approval.

Declaring a standard would have been meaningless without convincing computer manufacturers to modify their designs so that CD-ROM drives and sound cards would work properly with Microsoft's Windows operating system. Because Windows had not been designed to accommodate this new functionality, it required some inelegant modifications. In the absence of consumers clamoring for multimedia-ready machines, it was not easy to convince manufacturers to take a chance on that market, despite many years of predictions that its realization was imminent. Glaser likened the effort to throwing a party in which you invite a number of celebrities, each of whom you entice by mentioning that someone else was intending to come. He described the process this way: "Whitney Houston will come if Barry Manilow will be there, and Manilow will come if Ken Griffey will—and Griffey will come if Houston's there." So too, personal computer manufacturers had to be coaxed in a particular order that reflected the lattice of allies and rivals. It worked. Eight out of ten of the largest PC manufacturers were persuaded to join.

Each manufacturer who joined Microsoft's multimedia club had to contribute $250,000 to a marketing kitty that would raise the visibility of the multimedia-ready logo. Microsoft also contributed in-kind services to the kitty and assured the hardware vendors that it was doing its part to create consumer demand for the machines by readying multimedia software titles. But out of public view, Microsoft's campaign was hurt by its own internecine squabbling, not unlike what it had observed within IBM, but manifested in milder form. Troops who had been placed under Tom Lopez when Microsoft had acquired his company were so unhappy about his managerial and technical shortcomings that they openly revolted. Gates forced Lopez out of the company to put down the rebellion, but he was so disgusted by the in-fighting within Microsoft's multimedia group that he broke it up into pieces. He placed one subgroup, which would be responsible for writing hardware-related standards, in the group that developed operating systems, and another subgroup, which would be responsible for developing software titles, in the company's small consumer division.

The persistent bickering between the two groups would be of little historical interest if the tension had not exposed some interesting choices that Microsoft faced in trying to create a mass market for CD-ROMs. Examining the tension also can serve to dispell the notion that Microsoft is a monolith that hands down orders to each internal group from on high.

One source of disagreement concerned how Microsoft should define the minimal hardware configuration for the multimedia personal computer. If the minimum called for inexpensive but weak components, the considerable demands that multimedia software places on the machine to pull in data and display it or send it to speakers would be overwhelming. More powerful components might handle multimedia's demands technically, but the machine would be too expensive and would fail to sell in the volume needed to create a mass market. Tandy, the first personal computer manufacturer willing to commit to Microsoft's proposed multimedia specification and the manufacturer with the most success in selling IBM-compatible machines to a home market, persuaded Glaser, who headed the systems side of Microsoft's multimedia development, to power the bare-bones machine with Intel's 286 chip, not the more powerful and more expensive 386. Glaser, in turn, asked the Microsoft group responsible for software titles to accelerate its work on multimedia software. The titles group was not so enthused, however. They were close enough to the messy work in which the systems group was engaged to know that integrating multimedia into the operating system was proceeding painfully and was slowed by many technical glitches. Titles could not be developed without software development tools, and those had yet to be developed. And, in their view, no amount of ingenious tinkering would permit multimedia titles to run satisfactorily on an underpowered machine whose heart was a 286 chip.

Looking back on this internal split now, when Pentium chips with about ten times the processing power of the 286 are plentiful, it may be difficult to recall how woefully underpowered not only the 286 machines were, but also the 386 machines that were supposed to run the early versions of Windows, integrate CD-ROM, and provide satisfactory sound. Neither the hardware nor the systems software were then really up to the task, and it is a wonder that the performance problems in those earliest multimedia personal computers did not doom the entire campaign.

It is most remarkable that Apple did not exploit the tremendous technical advantages that the Macintosh enjoyed while the IBM-compatible world was fumbling to integrate multimedia pieces that the Mac accommodated easily. Junior managers as early as the late 1980s were pushing Apple's CEO, John Sculley, to make CD-ROM an integral part of the Mac. However, Apple's senior product engineers succeeded in delaying implementation, arguing that optical media that could write as well as read would soon render CD-ROM obsolete. Without consensus, Apple dithered, and the years passed. If Sculley had understood how multimedia could serve as the Trojan horse into the elusive home market, he would have overridden the endless internal objections and made CD-ROM a distinguishing advantage of the Mac. In delaying implementation during the years before sales of Windows took off, Sculley squandered the best chance for the Macintosh, not the Windows-equipped IBM-compatible, to become the dominant home computer.

To be fair, we should also remember that the strategic importance of the home market would only become widely apparent *after* multimedia became the technical innovation that excited home buyers in numbers that caused the personal computer industry to pay attention. That would not happen until the 1993 Christmas season. In the meantime, Microsoft's software rivals in the IBM-compatible camp were as slow as Apple in detecting the shift, and even when they decided to invest in developing CD-ROM titles, they continued to believe that the most promising prospective purchasers would be business users, not consumers. In 1989, Lotus's Jim Manzi boasted that a new division, Lotus One Source, provided corporate and financial statistics on CD-ROMs that Lotus's spreadsheet program 1-2-3 and its information retrieval program Agenda could extract. Manzi predicted that this combination would be the source of enormous growth for his company: "The big win is going to be owning the data interface to all the information that people use."

Wrong. The big win would instead be harnessing the appeal of CD-ROMs in the home market, which Lotus certainly did not. For Microsoft, where Gates had early intuited that CD-ROMs might be the key to unlocking sales to home consumers, the greatest challenge was to keep its eyes on the home market in the absence of confirming sales data. Like many companies that rehearsed their public pitch, Microsoft steeled itself for hostile questions from nonbelievers. "Microsoft has no real consumer experience. Do you think you are really equipped to understand the needs of the market?" asked a hypothetical questioner in a 1990 internal memo entitled "'Rude' Questions—with Draft Answers." Microsoft prepared a threefold answer. It did have some software titles—namely, Flight Simulator and the multipurpose program Works—that were directed at home purchasers. It was learning from Tandy. It *could* address consumer needs because multimedia personal computers were computers, not toys, and the company understood PCs "pretty well."

Microsoft posed another "rude" question for itself: Why would consumers be willing to spend the extra money on a multimedia-equipped machine? The answer: Because "we think people don't just want to either zap space invaders or become couch potatoes in their discretionary time." Multimedia encyclopedias, health guides, and travel planners were some of the future titles that would have broad appeal. This echoed Gates who, when noting the investments the company was making in this area, had said: "I better hope that passive entertainment isn't the ultimate at-home thing."

Ultimately it was faith that sustained confidence during the years before consumers embraced CD-ROM. Glaser and the other Microsoft managers who oversaw the long campaign drew what lessons they could from the history of consumer electronics, mindful that for every success (a videocassette recorder or a compact-disc player), there seemed to be a failure (the Videodisc or Quadrophonic Sound). They were also aware that VCRs and CDs enjoyed an advantage that a multimedia personal computer would not—programming that had been developed for another medium. In the case of the personal computer, such content could not be mechanically transferred to the new medium. But history offered some consolations. At the very beginning of the personal computer industry was a forgotten time when homes constituted a larger market than businesses. The untapped potential of a home market in the late 1980s seemed to be suggested in the discrepancy between the 20 million television sets and 25 million portable stereos sold in the United States in 1988—and the piddling total of 1.4 million personal computers sold in the same year. The closest equivalent to a mass-market home computer was the Nintendo video game machine, but without a keyboard, memory, additional processing power, and something akin to the CD-ROM for distributing a large volume of information or software, it could not offer the general-purpose capabilities that the personal computer could. The home seemed a natural destination for the multimedia-equipped personal computer, if only a program could be developed that would show off its capabilities so compellingly that buyers would overlook the technical headaches and take the leap.

Chapter 5

Britannica, Adieu

*T*HAT [AN ENCYCLOPEDIA ON A COMPUTER] *will be developed to the point where every purchaser will prefer to have some form of costly information storage and retrieval in place of a beautifully printed and illustrated set of books seems doubtful in the extreme.*

Otto V. St. Whitelock, former editorial director, Funk & Wagnalls, 1967

TODAY, THE MOST POPULAR ENCYCLOPEDIA in the world, Microsoft Encarta, comes on a CD. We sell over five times as many encyclopedias as World Book does, which is the second most popular encyclopedia.

Bill Gates, addressing Lakeside High School, 1995

Not so long ago, a household's encyclopedia resided on paper in bound volumes. The publisher was most likely an august name that was associated exclusively with encyclopedias (Encyclopaedia Britannica has been in the encyclopedia business since 1768). The encyclopedia was purchased from a salesperson who came to one's home, not at a computer store. How Microsoft entered the encyclopedia business without experience and seemingly overnight became by some measures the world's largest encyclopedia company is a thrilling business story. It includes overcoming numerous false starts in development, besting entrenched competition, overturning inherited business models for the industry, creating consumer demand for multimedia capabilities in home machines, and stimulating interest in other Microsoft titles targeted at the home—and it ends with depositing handsome profits in the company's coffers. As a business story, it exemplifies the shrewd blend of smarts and business acumen that are hallmarks of Microsoft. As a sign of the times, however, the same story also entails a cultural shift that is not to be altogether cheered.

The subtle shift has come into view only now, when the old-line printed encyclopedias are in desperate straits. Of course, Encyclopaedia Britannica's or World Book's traditional businesses were run by salesminded executives, not scholars dedicated to public service. The customers of the traditional encyclopedia mostly were parents, who fell prey to anxieties about the academic competition that their children soon would face and who often purchased the encyclopedia before their oldest children were old enough to use the books. But even when the printed encyclopedia seemed to exert no influence—in a household that never consulted the purchased books—its mere presence was important. While it gathered dust, it still authoritatively whispered to everyone who entered the room that knowledge resides in the world of text, a world whose dimensions are vast and deep. Whether we merely dip a toe into its ocean of text or gulp a stomachful, the encyclopedia is where we must seek out that which we do not know. Although the traditional encyclopedia text did have occasional breaks—a photograph here, a transparent diagram there—the ratio of text to illustration conveyed an unmistakable subliminal message: text is the primary container in which knowledge is to be found; the rest is ancillary.

Microsoft did not deliberately seek to destroy this primacy of text in the encyclopedia. The eclipse of text by the nontext media was the result of happenstance and tactical decisions that were made along the way. The first encyclopedia on CD-ROM—Gary Kildall and Grolier's—consisted of text only, and it was developed when personal computers still had difficulty handling illustrations, sound cards were all but unknown, and on-screen video clips were the stuff of dreams.

Perhaps Microsoft's first encyclopedia on CD-ROM would have been text only, too, if the company had quickly licensed rights to the contents of an existing encyclopedia. Min Yee approached the publisher of Microsoft's first choice, *Encyclopaedia Britannica,* in the summer of 1985, offering to pay a royalty for nonexclusive rights to use the encyclopedia's contents, with an advance and a minimum payment guaranteed. History might have been somewhat different if Britannica had responded positively to Microsoft's inquiry.

Britannica refused to negotiate with Microsoft lest it lose what its president called its "most valuable asset." Go ahead, he invited Microsoft's Yee, guess what that asset is. "The encyclopedia's contents?" Yee ventured. "No, it's my salespeople," was the reply. If the Britannica salespeople were to learn that a competitor was going to market a new encyclopedia with identical contents but in miniature form that could replace the printed volumes, they would desert immediately—they'd sell cars instead of encyclopedias. No salespeople would mean no sales. End of story.

This was not faulty reasoning. A CD-ROM version undoubtedly *would* diminish the sales of the traditional printed volumes, and the royalty payments received from the CD-ROM publisher undoubtedly would fall far short of replacing the revenue stream and lucrative profits that the company had enjoyed in the sales of the printed encyclopedia. The problem with this otherwise impeccable reasoning was that it assumed that Britannica actually could avoid diminishment of its existing sales by shunning offers from software publishers like Microsoft, guarding its franchise by deliberately ignoring the new information economy ushered in by the advent of the CD-ROM. With hindsight, we can see the fallacy in Britannica's thinking that consumers would continue to be willing to pay the premium that Britannica had traditionally exacted for the privilege of obtaining access to the encyclopedia's text.

Ten years later, the dramatic slide in Britannica's sales had pushed it to a state of bathos. Britannica finally relented and released its first CD-ROM package—priced at $995, an order of magnitude more expensive than other CD-ROM encyclopedias. But this was a timorous as well as belated response to the changes in the business and far too expensive to be a mass-market product. By then, the company was in dire financial straits and soon after was sold to a Swiss-led investor group. In 1996 it dismissed its sales force. Microsoft and the dawning of the CD-ROM presented a company like Britannica with an awful choice: it was damned if it replaced its premier product with technology that dramatically lowered production costs and thereby angered its sales staff—but it was damned too, as it found out painfully, if it did not co-operate in the development of the new medium.

Of course, even with rights to an existing encyclopedia's contents in hand, Min Yee's small group at Microsoft that Bill Gates had charged with looking into developing an encyclopedia naturally would have emphasized multimedia presentation above all else. At a software company, the illustrative graphics and audio supplements would not be mere garnish to text—they would be the main course, the place where Microsoft's *multimedia* encyclopedia could distinguish itself from the traditional printed form. How exactly the multimedia offerings should be deployed was hard to figure out without an existing body of text with which to work.

The years slipped by, and the encyclopedia's development group produced little. In 1988, three years after Yee had first approached and been turned down by Britannica, Microsoft's CD-ROM encyclopedia was still defined hazily. The current thinking had advanced to an ill-considered position that the encyclopedia should be organized thematically. Each year Microsoft would release a different disc—this year History, perhaps, next year The Arts—and purchasers would subscribe to the series like Book-of-the-Month Club members. Meanwhile, as long as the strategy remained cloudy, the actual coding had yet to start—but other software publishers now were jumping into the market.

When World Book, the other brand-name encyclopedia publisher, also turned Microsoft down, the software company did not consider for a moment developing text for an encyclopedia from scratch and hiring a large editorial staff to commission articles from distinguished authorities. To have undertaken such a venture, of course, would have been frightfully expensive, and the certainty of commercial success was not clear. Microsoft chose instead to continue working its way down a list of existing encyclopedia publishers until it found a willing licensor, which it finally did in the form of Funk and Wagnalls. This choice served to further diminish the relative importance of text in the multimedia encyclopedia. That Microsoft felt the need to negotiate the right to rewrite the contents of Funk & Wagnalls's articles tells us something about the regard it held for the quality of the original contents. Microsoft also knew that it could not market its own encyclopedia on the strength of popular recognition of the name Funk & Wagnalls; all the more reason to stress the non-text additions to the encyclopedia.

In 1989, as Microsoft received the tapes that contained the Funk & Wagnalls text, it discovered that its new partner had failed to clean up the tapes and remove internal codes as it had promised in its contract. Some Microsoft managers lobbied to reopen the question of who should supply the text for Microsoft's multimedia encyclopedia, and a delegation was dispatched to talk again to World Book. Peter Mollman, the president of World Book Publishing, listened to the pitch with some interest. Microsoft offered to invest $7 to $12 million over the next two years to develop a multimedia encyclopedia based on World Book's text, but World Book hardly was desperate for funds. Mollman mentioned in passing just how little World Book had to spend annually to update and maintain the source of its mainstream revenue. (Microsoft representatives were astounded to learn how small the figure required to sustain the franchise was, but they could have seen the same phenomenon within Microsoft, such as in the Word or Excel groups, where an astonishingly small team of a few dozen developers was needed to update mature programs that brought in hundreds of millions of dollars a year.) Mollman pointed out that World Book's commissioned salesforce of over 25,000 representatives remained a sticky problem, and he wondered how a truly multimedia encyclopedia could be compressed into one CD-ROM. Microsoft replied obligingly that it would keep an open mind about the question—perhaps multiple discs would be offered.

In a formal offer to create a partnership that Microsoft tendered to World Book after this meeting, Microsoft presented a number of ingenious arguments. A multimedia encyclopedia, Microsoft reasoned, would help World Book reach upper-income consumers who are reluctant to welcome a salesperson into their home. Here would be a way to use retail stores to distribute the encyclopedia without tarnishing the product image. Anticipating World Book's objection that the CD-ROM encyclopedia would hurt sales of its existing encyclopedia, Microsoft had two (weak) answers ready: Microsoft's research indicated that schools and libraries would continue to buy the print versions (tellingly, no mention is made of what percentage of current sales this market segment represented), and "several parents mentioned that they saw this product as a valuable addition to their regular encyclopedia and not a replacement for it."

The best part of the pitch to World Book, however, was the strategic reasoning, which shows Microsoft's acute awareness of how to secure and defend a dominant market position in a given category. It also shows the astute way in which the company used historical experience to inform strategy. "Early entrants on a new medium generate disproportionately high revenue *AND* create strong barriers to entry for competitors in the software industry," the proposal explained to World Book. The rule applied to anyone—such as Microsoft with Excel on the Macintosh, or Lotus with 1-2-3 on IBM personal computers. (The same phenomenon would work again in Microsoft's favor when Windows presented a new "medium." Microsoft acted quickly and Lotus chose not to, despite Microsoft's pleas that Lotus develop for Windows. On the new turf, Excel would secure the lead and hold off 1-2-3, which found itself in the unaccustomed position of challenger.) Microsoft told World Book that IBM was readying a personal computer that would be "optimized" for multimedia and would be released in late 1990. Survey research suggested that no less than 50 percent of purchasers of the new computer would buy a CD-ROM encyclopedia. Now, in 1989, was the time to join hands and prepare to sell to those early customers and secure a dominant position.

World Book demurred, and Microsoft returned to working with Funk & Wagnalls's text. What sort of multimedia enhancements it should build around the text remained a matter of fierce contention. More time was eaten up by elaborate reworking of possible screen designs and another year slipped by without much to show for it. As dismal as the rate of technical progress was, the business front was developing impressively. Gates, of course, had provided the original encouragement to his multimedia group to develop a CD-ROM encyclopedia—he saw it in 1985 as a "high-price, high-demand" kind of product, something that could become another Word or Excel. When the multimedia group got caught up in some less promising ideas—at one point, it had abandoned the general encyclopedia in favor of a Rock-'n-Roll Encyclopedia—Gates pulled the group back from certain disaster and suggested that it give more thought to the software tools it would need to create a true multimedia product.

Meanwhile, the business case that could be made to pursue this project was refined. A 1989 internal strategy memo pointed out that encyclopedias were a unique product in terms of the price that they commanded. Consumers were used to paying $5–$75 for a dictionary, or $5–$40 for an almanac, but $500–$1,500 for an encyclopedia. "No other broad-appeal content product in any category in any medium has a well-established single-user price point anywhere close to this." And unlike Microsoft, its competitors who were already in the encyclopedia business could not afford to disrupt their existing sales. If they decided to bring out a CD-ROM product, they would have to charge a high price because they could not afford to undercut the printed version of their own encyclopedia. Microsoft would have the flexibility to price its encyclopedia low enough to make it an impulse purchase and then concentrate on generating the bulk of the revenue from update sales, an option that a Britannica or World Book did not have.

This strategic hypothesis, composed in 1989, would turn out to eerily anticipate events in the mid-1990s. But on the way to realization, in 1990, Microsoft's board of directors demanded that the encyclopedia project be canceled, and as far as they knew, it was. Customarily a rubber-stamping body that did as Gates asked, the board would stir itself into a show of independence from time to time, and 1990 was one of those times. It was not happy that Gates had decided five years earlier to pour millions of dollars into developing CD-ROMs and trying to expand a home market. It asked, "What are you doing, Bill? Where was the return on this investment?" In their view, chasing a market that did not exist was an expensive distraction for the company. The board got its chance to direct the company back to basics when it was asked to approve Microsoft's minority investment in a British publisher of picture books, Dorling Kindersley, which Min Yee had proposed as a way of assuring Microsoft a steady flow of CD-ROM-ready content for future titles targeted for the home market. The board did not care much for Yee, a colorful character who, despite being a vice-president, was not imbued with sober corporate decorum. (Perhaps the board had heard of Yee's proposal for an early CD-ROM title "Sexualus" that Yee once described as covering sex "from A to Z, or even B to D, from bidets to de Sade.") Gates defended Yee's proposal to invest in Dorling Kindersley as a source of content for CD-

ROMs. The board reluctantly agreed to the purchase but only conditionally, telling Gates that if he were really serious about Dorling Kindersley, he should be willing to redeploy his troops to create titles based on this expensive investment and cease pouring additional dollars into work on the encyclopedia. Gates accepted these terms, and the encyclopedia project was halted. Thus Microsoft was unable to take advantage of a wonderful strategic opportunity to plant its flag in a promising new category of software applications.

The CD-ROM encyclopedia project would have slumbered indefinitely were it not revived, virtually single-handedly, by a young product manager, Craig Bartholomew. His job was to persuade computer manufacturers to bundle Microsoft's Bookshelf software—the dictionary, thesaurus, and other reference works on CD-ROM—with the personal computers that they sold. So many PC manufacturers told him that they really wanted to be able to include a Microsoft encyclopedia that he wrote a lengthy memo imploring his superiors to reconsider the earlier decision to shelve the encyclopedia project. The memo was passed upward until it reached Gates, who was persuaded to revisit the issue with the board of directors.

Here again the internal workings of Microsoft did not resemble the public image of the company as the robotic extension of Gates. Jon Shirley, company president and board member, disagreed vociferously with Gates on this issue. Microsoft was investing a fortune in Dorling Kindersley. To him, it was folly to also continue to invest in the CD-ROM rathole, an area from which the company had yet to see a dollar of profit. But Bartholomew's memo had provided Gates with a rejoinder to this familiar objection. The resuscitated encyclopedia would not take the built-from-scratch approach of the previous development work. It would instead use Bookshelf's framework and be a quickie. Plug in the Funk and Wagnalls text, add a few thousand illustrations and some audio, and quickly throw it out into the market as a placeholder. In the meantime, the company could be working on a multimedia encyclopedia as it should be done, built from the ground up around the nontext elements, using Dorling Kindersley material as the core of its content.

The development budget for this first, quickie encyclopedia would be modest because only a little new code would be needed. Dump content into the existing template, and presto, a CD-ROM encyclopedia would appear in a year. Recalling that approximately six years had elapsed since the company had first begun talking about a CD-ROM encyclopedia, the board of directors was persuaded that a quick-and-dirty approach could deliver the goods in just a year. Though Gates's position prevailed over Shirley's, the board was adamant that the budget for development be small.

Bartholomew, a soft-spoken man with a scholar's concern with details, became the program manager of the small group that would bring this encyclopedia to market. The business rationale that he composed in 1991 stands up well in retrospect. He foresaw the market appeal of a general-interest CD-ROM encyclopedia priced well below printed encyclopedias and erred only in being a shade too conservative in his forecasts.

The sales that Bartholomew forecast for the encyclopedia, eventually named Encarta, were not so obvious to others within Microsoft, however. Microsoft employees were always trying to transfer into the groups with the brightest prospects for expanding sales, and the politically savvy regarded the Multimedia Publishing group to which Encarta belonged as a place to avoid. The failure to develop an encyclopedia during the previous six years was well known within the company. Who could be sure that another six years would not be frittered away in unproductive efforts? The perception that the encyclopedia project was a quagmire that would end anyone's career aspirations became so widespread that one employee quipped that there would be "inter-galactic space travel" by the time Encarta shipped. Until October 1991, the Encarta full-time "staff" really consisted of a grand total of four and a half full-time positions.

Even within the multimedia group, support for Encarta was mixed, at best. Rob Glaser thought that the principal obstacle to enticing computer manufacturers to add multimedia features to their machines was the paucity of CD-ROM titles. He wanted Microsoft to devote its efforts to developing titles in categories that competitors had not covered already. Compton's had just brought out the first "multimedia" encyclopedia on CD-ROM. As a division of Britannica at the time, Compton's permitted Britannica to experiment with the new medium without immediately endangering its own encyclopedia franchise. But the experiment was still carried out timidly; the Compton's CD-ROM was initially priced at $895. To Glaser, thinking of the many other categories of CD-ROM titles for which no software publisher had brought out offerings, Microsoft was foolish to devote scarce development dollars and attention to a me-too product that would not advance the larger cause of making multimedia ubiquitous as soon as possible.

The project received a cool reception outside of Microsoft, too. When Bartholomew and others within the multimedia group tried to enlist experienced editors from the book and newspaper worlds, Microsoft was shunned—and perhaps this too contributed to the diminished place of text in the final product. In the eyes of experienced publishing professionals, a software company like Microsoft was hopelessly ignorant of the basics of publishing. What professional future could there be in a company that was so obviously a pathetic neophyte in publishing? Greg Riker, a senior manager who oversaw Bartholomew during Encarta's relaunching, laughed years later when reminded of the early difficulty of recruiting experienced editors and writers. In 1995, newspaper reporters called him daily looking for a position at Microsoft, complaining that their current employers were not "moving fast enough," or were not "where the action is." Such people had scorned Microsoft's entreaties to join the company five years earlier.

One experienced outsider who understood both the encyclopedia business and the potential in Microsoft's undertaking was Peter Mollman, the World Book president with whom Microsoft had unsuccessfully attempted to negotiate the rights to use the World Book text. Unhappy with the slow pace with which World Book was developing a multimedia version of its encyclopedia, Mollman decided to retire. Microsoft wasted not a moment in recruiting him, initially as a consultant in 1991, and then, with Bill Gates serving as recruiter, as a full-time employee in 1992.

Gates was too smart to unvaryingly apply a formula that valued youth over experience. Mollman not only had been the president of a company that was about to become a direct rival of Microsoft, but he had also been a publishing industry executive whose perspective on the electronic revolution went way back. Mollman would tell with pride how he had overseen the production of the first digitally composed book when he was an executive at Harper & Row—in 1967. To have someone like Mollman join the youngsters like Gates,

Bartholomew, and Riker made Microsoft all the more formidable. Now if another Microsoft employee with less industry experience doubted the profitability of the encyclopedia business, Mollman was on hand to explain that when Warren Buffett wrote out a check for $450 million to purchase World Book in 1985, he earned his investment back in about a year and a half! When Gates, the chronic worrier, became concerned that Encyclopaedia Britannica or World Book would crush Encarta, Mollman could explain with the detail only an insider possessed why this was impossible: both of the traditional encyclopedia companies were too afraid of alienating their salesforces. "It's a famous business-school principle, right?" Mollman concluded, "Nobody makes major changes until the disaster actually has happened—but not in anticipation."

When Mollman was at World Book, the company capped sales costs at 48 percent of revenue. Most of the costs consisted of commissions, which meant that the relative cost of supporting a commissioned salesforce was actually not different from the "cost" a software company like Microsoft paid when it had retail stores sell its software. The software publisher only netted about half of the retail price, too. So if the cost of distributing their respective products to customers took a similar bite out of the retail price for an encyclopedia, how could Microsoft greatly underprice World Book and Britannica? Two primary reasons stand out.

Microsoft could underprice the competition primarily because the manufacturing cost of a compact disc was almost nominal, then less than two dollars, whereas the cost of printing and binding a multivolume encyclopedia ran about $110 to $130 a set. The electronic medium also offered tremendous savings in permitting editorial changes without significantly increasing costs. Changes made during the annual updating of a printed encyclopedia required expensive repagination and the juggling of material to accommodate additions without enlarging the particular volume. Mollman said that as much as half of the $3.5 million that World Book spent on updating its encyclopedia annually went to pruning older material—the task was called "space patrol"—and reformatting pages to make room for new text. As long as World Book could sell customers a set for $649 for a vinyl binding, or $899 for leather—with the help of that reliable guilt-tickling pitch, "Aren't your kids worth $2 a day?"—there was plenty of room to cover these high manufacturing costs, commissions, and the other expenses, and still have a tidy net profit of about 5 percent. But this business model was not well suited for the entrance of a competitor who could manufacture the equivalent of a complete set for about 2 percent of the cost of the old method.

The other reason that Encarta could dramatically underprice the printed competition was the different editorial model that emerged, without conscious decision, but with cultural as well as economic consequences. When Mollman was at World Book, his company maintained a full-time editorial staff of 35; when Encarta was developed, Bartholomew had a full-time editorial staff of 1 (with about 20–25 freelancers). The comparison, at first glance, may not seem wholly fair. After all, Microsoft had licensed a supposedly complete encyclopedic text for use in Encarta. Why would it need to maintain a large editorial staff? In fact, initially, it was contractually prohibited from changing the articles it licensed from Funk & Wagnalls. But, then again, World Book at that time was not in the encyclopedia-creating business itself, either. It was in maintenance mode and probably had no more need of a large editorial staff in the early 1990s than did Microsoft. In both cases, outside consultants, not in-house employees, wrote most of the new articles. The World Book staff was present to ensure the highest quality and retain the respect of educator and librarian reviewers. If someone questioned the date of Mao Zedong's birth, to mention one example at World Book, a regiment of staffers was on hand to spend several days tracking down the answer. In other words, the considerable expense of maintaining a large editorial staff at World Book was a testimony to the primacy of the encyclopedia's text.

Encarta's development, on the other hand, was organized around assembling a multiplicity of parts. Because the text was purchased from an outside house and was the only portion that had previously appeared in an encyclopedia, it received the least amount of attention. Illustrations, sounds, video snippets—these were the elements that would not only distinguish the encyclopedia from its dowdy print-based ancestors, but also posed tricky technical problems that had to be solved and trade-offs that had to be addressed.

Video versus audio was one of the issues that received much attention. Video clips were a temptation, but they could not be played on a personal computer as well as they could be displayed on a television screen. If you ran the video in a window that was the full size of the computer monitor, a CD-ROM turned out to be not such a capacious storage medium after all. If you devoted a disc entirely to storing uncompressed data for full-screen, 30-frames-a-second video, the video clip would run for about 12 seconds, even if the data could be transferred from disc to PC sufficiently fast, which was not realistic. Going to a reduced-size video clip instead of a full-screen display greatly reduced the quantity of digital data that was required, but it still gobbled up valuable real estate on the compact disc. Instead of trying to pack in as many video clips as possible, the Encarta team concentrated instead on audio clips, which required much less space to store. With 2000 different clips, sounds could be provided in a wide range of categories, offering a consistency that would have been impossible to deliver with video. This was the kind of deliberation that preoccupied the development team, along with questions about the arrangement of menus and buttons and other features that the user would directly encounter. What was missing was a preoccupation with what had once been the heart of an encyclopedia, the text.

The "editorial" work that occupied the team from the fall of 1991 to the fall of 1992 was devoted primarily to the features that had once been ancillary: identifying, digitizing, and writing captions for 1000 illustrations, 800 maps, and 5200 photographs; creating a separate timeline, atlas, and learning game; and capturing, creating or licensing, and then digitizing, eight hours of sound. The one full-time editor was busy primarily with checking the 11,000 captions that had to be written for the project. Over $2 million was spent on personnel costs alone, representing an investment of over 30 person-years. A majority of that cost, however, was for contractors who acquired and prepared these once-supplementary materials and attachments. That they would turn out not to be supplementary would be revealed when the first version of Encarta was released and Walt Mossberg, the personal computer columnist for the *Wall Street Journal*, pounced on the fact that Encarta offered only a small number of video clips. Such reactions by reviewers meant that more video would have to be served up for the next version, no matter how logical the original argument that limited disc space should not be given over to jerky, unsatisfying video clips. Reviewers expected a self-described *multimedia* encyclopedia to put on a dazzling multimedia show, whether the technology was ready or not.

This expectation also fundamentally changed the way that the public would think about encyclopedias in general, a development that was anticipated by an exchange early in Encarta's development, in July 1991, when Gates held one of the periodic meetings with Bartholomew to go over development progress. Rob Glaser was present and took a shot at Encarta: "How are you ever going to compete with somebody who's got Britannica on the box?" This was a dig at Encarta's lowly Funk & Wagnalls text and the fact that Compton's encyclopedia on CD-ROM, by virtue of its parent company, could claim the lofty parentage of Britannica. Bartholomew's retort: "How is anybody going to compete with Microsoft on the box?" At the time it was bluster, but events would actually support Bartholomew's seemingly outlandish claim. Such was the enormity of the shift in how the public would judge encyclopedias.

Even Bartholomew, Gates, and the other Encarta champions among Microsoft executives would not immediately realize just how significantly Encarta would change the very rules of the encyclopedia game. In the fall of 1993, after Encarta's initial release, Gates asked Peter Mollman to look into the possibility of purchasing World Book, a possibility to which Mollman and another manager coincidentally had also recently given some thought—all continuing to feel that the Funk & Wagnalls provenance of Encarta's text was a handicap. Mollman's inside sources had reported that World Book's sales had been sliding downward in recent years—from 330,000 sets in 1988 to perhaps fewer than 150,000 sets in 1992. At Mollman's urging, Gates spoke to his friend Warren Buffett about a possible sale, but they did not arrive at a satisfactory arrangement. Encarta's sales, at this early point, had not yet taken off—we will look at the marketing of Encarta in the next chapter—so the impact of Encarta on World Book's business was not yet visible. Encarta's prospects were so unclear that even after Encarta had been on the market for six months, the new head of the Consumer Division, Patty Stonesifer, wondered aloud why Microsoft was even in the encyclopedia business. Bartholomew presented Gates with the following argument: rather than spend $400 million or so to buy World Book, why not spend $7 million to rewrite the text of Encarta over three years, removing the inadequacies of the

Funk & Wagnalls text by dint of Microsoft's own efforts and requiring much less money? This argument won the day. In retrospect, a more radical argument could have been made that once Encarta became commercially successful, the quality of the text would become all but irrelevant in the minds of prospective purchasers.

I admire the Encarta group and their boss, and their approach to overcoming the entrenched, seemingly unassailable competition when Microsoft entered the entirely new domain of the encyclopedia business. The product that they brought into being was pioneering in many aspects and, with the technical improvements of the 1996 version of Encarta, could offer a sensual feast of 29 video clips, 83 animation sequences, and over 8000 pictures. Encarta also would show us another advantage in the new medium that the printed encyclopedias could never provide—the ability to use online services to repeatedly and seamlessly update the encyclopedia with topical news events almost as fast as they occur. Nor has the text been ignored: by 1996, the Encarta editorial team was much enlarged and included five editors recruited from World Book, two from Britannica, and one from Grolier's.

Still, when thinking about this segment of Microsoft's history, I can't help but recall Neil Postman's brilliant and disturbing polemic *Amusing Ourselves to Death* (1985). Postman decries the invasion of "entertainment values" in public discourse in this country, and though he did not foresee digitally animated encyclopedias, his analysis seems pertinent here. He recalls that in 1854 a typical Lincoln-Douglas debate could extend for seven hours, and the audience would listen attentively for the entirety. I doubt that today much of an audience would stand still for one hour, let alone seven, of unadorned debate. The audience of that bygone time could follow the threads of the debate because that historical moment belonged to what Postman calls the Age of Exposition, when public discourse was still shaped by "the typographic mind." The Age of Show Business that displaces the Age of Exposition is a long process, involving radio, movies, television. (Postman gained few friends when he attacked *Sesame Street* for its contribution to the decline of education, as it too succumbed to the imperatives of an entertainment-obsessed culture.) The displacement of traditional printed encyclopedias by multimedia CD-ROMs would only be, at most, one small, and late, chapter in this process.

Postman's perspective is helpful in rebutting a possible objection to my lament about text's loss of primacy in Encarta. I can hear the objection already: Why insist on an either/or choice in an encyclopedia, text or nontext elements? Leaving aside the business issues, at least theoretically why can't the full unabridged glory of *Encyclopaedia Britannica*'s 44 million words of text be wedded to the fabulous illustrations, photographs, sounds, and video that Encarta shows off? Today such a combination would not fit on a single CD-ROM, but the new DVD format for discs will provide fifteen times as much storage, and in any case the day will come when such enormous digital files will be easily accessed over very fast networks. Wouldn't marrying the best of the text world to the best of multimedia offer an ideal combination of both worlds? I do not believe it would. I'm fearful that reading is inherently more demanding than watching or listening, and we will gravitate toward the less-taxing features of such an encyclopedia. If illustrations or sounds provided in an encyclopedia are so plentiful as to be more than an occasional educational gew-gaw, they will steal the show.

Like Postman, I'm rather short on solutions, and I may very well be guilty of clinging to an idealized picture of how pre-multimedia printed encyclopedias in the past were actually used. Robert McHenry, *Encyclopaedia Britannica*'s editor-in-chief, recently admitted that "the dirty little secret of the encyclopedia industry is that we don't know whether or not people read what we publish." Britannica is at this moment desperately trying to make a belated transition to the new era of the electronic encyclopedia by marketing access to its text via online services. Britannica Online will expose exactly how often a text-only encyclopedia is consulted because payment will be tied to actual usage, not to the wisp of a parent's hope of future use.

Credit or blame Encarta for contributing to a new set of rules, which encompassed not only the encyclopedia business, but also, as we shall next see, the retail distribution of software of all kinds.

Chapter 6

Pitching Consumers

A *COMPUTER ON EVERY DESK and in Every Home,*
All Running Microsoft Software

Microsoft company slogan

Bill Gates has been openly proud of his company's slogan, inordinately so. After all, the pairing of "desk" and "home" lacks symmetry when you think about it—can't homes have desks, too? And the way Gates and others at Microsoft often shorten the slogan when speaking publicly, omitting the tag phrase ". . . All running Microsoft software," serves to soften the slogan. Because it makes no mention of the benefit that Microsoft was to derive from the spread of computers to every imaginable horizontal surface, the slogan takes on an almost altruistic sheen, divorced from commercial benefit. "A computer on every desk" then becomes a twentieth-century equivalent to Henri IV's sixteenth-century desire that no peasant in his kingdom would be so poor that "he is unable to have a chicken in his pot every Sunday."

For ambition, the Microsoft slogan certainly cannot be faulted. If *all* offices and *all* homes are to possess machines running the company's software, what other places are left for Microsoft's competitors to fight over? Farm fields, underground mines, boat decks? As for the slogan's implication that office and home markets were equal twins, in fact the two had been anything but equal in size in the early history of the personal computer software industry. Office sales overshadowed sales to home customers by a wide margin. The lag in household purchases of personal computers is what had spurred Gates in

1985 to launch the company's CD-ROM development efforts and what would become Encarta. For the home, the mainstays of the office software market—word processing, spreadsheets, databases—clearly would not suffice. Entirely new products and approaches were needed if the size of the consumer market was to approach that of its supposed twin, the office market. Microsoft tested and modified its working strategic model as the company learned what worked and what did not in this new realm.

The company first learned about the unfamiliar challenges that the home market posed in its Usability Lab, established in 1983. Susan Boeschen, hired to improve user training with software tutorials to be shipped with the company's regular products, secured funding to set up an internal laboratory to try out training materials. At this early date, the company was so technologically arrogant that it thought its customer training materials were all that needed improvement. The Lab started out as nothing more than a room in which outsiders with no technical background were invited to give the software a test spin. Observers would record all that transpired and were not allowed to intervene, no matter what the user did wrong.

Boeschen invited her bosses, who had no clear idea of what their new Usability Lab was, to observe some early test sessions. Steve Ballmer was on hand when a user, who wanted to move the screen's cursor down, pulled the computer's mouse to the edge of the table—then down the table leg. Ballmer ran out of the room aghast: "They don't understand!" Gates watched a woman do her best to follow the instruction to press "Print Screen." She found the Print Screen button on her keyboard without a problem, but instead of simply pressing once, she held the button down, causing the printer to dutifully pump out multiple copies and placing Gates in the same state of surprise as Ballmer. After these experiences, funding for Boeschen's lab was never a problem.

The Usability Lab would grow both in terms of equipment—two-way mirrors and video cameras and other technical accouterment—and in scope, testing the software itself as well as the training materials. By 1992, the Lab had become so well established and highly regarded that its anteroom was jammed with product managers waiting eagerly to put their programs to the test. Encarta's development came to a standstill until it got its turn in the Lab, and it only got underway seriously after it was completely redesigned based on the Lab's test results.

Unsophisticated personal computer users committed all manner of errors that developers never foresaw. The front lines of the computer industry—the technical support staff at Microsoft and other software companies—added the more colorful cases to industry lore, passed around via computer magazines, the Internet, or word of mouth. Perhaps some day historians will look back on these stories as mean-spirited, just as today some historians perceive a sinister subtext in equivalent tales told among electrical engineers in the late nineteenth-century. For example, a cartoon portrays an "Uncle Hayseed" who had placed a boot over an electric lamp after futile attempts to blow it out, or a story tells of a country bumpkin who shouted in the direction of a telephone, without taking down the ear tube, "Kitty, Come home! Mary's sick!" Yet Microsoft's senior executives and product teams whose mission was to crack the home market did not deride the difficulty that consumers had in using software. The consumer's problem was viewed as necessarily Microsoft's problem, too.

In 1988, Microsoft formally recognized the new challenges it faced in pitching traditional software applications to home consumers as well as office purchasers by enlarging the Usability Lab into a full-fledged business division, with Boeschen as its head. But it still had a long way to go: its very name, "Entry Business Unit," fell short of suggesting a consumer orientation. Its name was bestowed by Mike Maples, who had just arrived at Microsoft after a long career at IBM, where *its* Entry Business Unit had nothing to do with consumers. By the time that Encarta development was accelerating in the spring of 1992, the unit had been renamed more appropriately the Consumer Division. Its catalog of products already on the market remained small, however, and fell far short of what Microsoft would need to make good on the half of its slogan that targeted the home.

The Consumer Division also had little credibility within its own company. Without a significant stream of revenue, it was regarded derisively by other divisions as the unit that produced "toy" software and not where top developers or program managers should consider transferring. And though the division had Gates's personal encouragement, it was not exempted from the stringent profitability tests applied to all divisions of the company. Having a cash cow like Excel under the same Microsoft roof as the Consumer Division's fledgling Multimedia Beethoven: The Ninth Symphony might seem to have been a tremendous advantage to the Consumer Division. Indirectly, no doubt, it was a benefit because it allowed Microsoft to dabble in new directions without taking on debt. But when division heads had to turn in their monthly and quarterly financial reports, the Consumer Division had aggressively high profitability margins to meet, similar to those for more established products.

Susan Boeschen compared the cost of developing a new software product in her Consumer Division with that in other parts of the company and discovered that consumer software required just as great an investment to create. Once its new software was completed, the Consumer Division also discovered early that adequate marketing dollars would be difficult to secure from Microsoft's internal allocation: the company's formula for divvying up marketing funds was based on the product's revenue, not on the relative maturity of the market. A Multimedia Beethoven would receive for a marketing budget the same percentage of its revenues, which were nonexistent, as would Excel. The Consumer Division's marketing managers thus had little reason to offer prayers of thanks for their good fortune in having Excel and Word as older siblings to their newer consumer products. Invidious comparisons between older and younger always worked to the disadvantage of the younger ones, creating dynamics that made Microsoft something other than one big, happy family. The Consumer Division managers had to confront the challenge of somehow producing and marketing many more titles, with proportionately fewer dollars, if it were to hold its own with the rest of the company.

Even within the Consumer Division, there was no unity. The portion of the Consumer Division whose products originated in the earliest CD-ROM development—that is, the old crew brought in from professional fields outside of computer science or business and directed by the unbuttoned Min Yee—were regarded by the other Consumer Division employees who had been forced into this amalgamation as unschooled creative types who lacked a modicum of business sense and were destined for failure. There was no love lost between the group within the Consumer Division that handled a package like Works or Publisher, which in lineage was closer to Word and other Microsoft software intended to increase the customer's "productivity," and the group that was readying Encarta, which was hardly a "productivity application."

Encarta's CD-ROM format also challenged marketers who now had to persuade retailers to carry products in a format that had yet to take hold. Six months after Microsoft had launched with great fanfare in October 1991 the design for multimedia-capable personal computers, only a dismal 5000 or so machines that had been outfitted with the Microsoft-ordained standard for CD-ROM and sound had been sold.

Martin Leahy, a young Microsoft sales manager stationed on the East Coast, had been so smitten by CD-ROM when he saw Grandma and Me, a children's program published by a Microsoft competitor, that he was one of those rare few at Microsoft who then voluntarily requested a transfer into the Consumer Division in Redmond. Once Leahy had moved, he was charged with persuading retailers to carry Microsoft's CD-ROM programs, a task made even more difficult by retailers' memory of being convinced to stock up on CD-ROMs in anticipation of a wave of consumer demand that had yet to appear. In early 1992, no major software reseller was willing to carry a single Microsoft CD-ROM title.

Leahy attacked the problem by presenting the large resellers with a picture of a future in which traditional software prices would decline precipitously. The customer who presently bought four "productivity" software packages like Word and Excel, paying $1200, would be paying perhaps only $400 for the same group of software titles a few years hence. How would resellers be able to make up the difference? Leahy dangled hope in the form of the new format of CD-ROM software titles. He told retailers that Microsoft was betting that an individual customer would purchase perhaps 18 or 20 CD-ROM titles, a number fewer than the 60 audio CDs a typical customer might purchase over a lifetime, but many more titles than the basic four programs in a suite of traditional productivity software titles. This new business model predicted that the revenue derived from a customer's CD-ROM purchases thus could replace the revenue lost from the decline in the price of software in the traditional mainstream categories. Without the boost from the CD-ROM format, Leahy told them, retailers would be unable to stay in business.

CompUSA was the first of the major accounts to accept Microsoft's pitch, reasoning that there was money to be made selling multimedia add-on hardware such as speakers, too. Egghead Software remained resistant, however, despite numerous presentations by Leahy and Microsoft representatives. Previously Microsoft had convinced Egghead that its Bookshelf CD-ROM would sell as fast as Egghead could unload the discs off the truck. Egghead had taken on a huge quantity of inventory in preparation and spent a great deal on promotion in advance—but the promised buyers did not show. This time, in early 1992, Egghead said it would take on CD-ROM titles only if Microsoft paid in advance a colossal bill that Egghead presented for future "cooperative marketing." Each time Leahy revisited Egghead, he was presented with a choice: pay the bill or forgo Egghead's distribution. Having Egghead on board the CD-ROM Express was critical, and Leahy had all but decided to accede to Egghead's demands when a Microsoft colleague persuaded him to be just a bit more patient. It had turned into a game of chicken—who needed whom more? Meanwhile, some momentum in CD-ROM adoption was just beginning to appear. The number of multimedia machines jumped from 5000 in March 1992 to 40,000 in June. By December, it would jump still more, to 100,000. In retrospect, these numbers were tiny, but at the time retailers were eager for evidence of salvation from declining prices, and they seized on the upward movement as an indication that The Next Big Thing was finally arriving. Egghead decided it could not afford to miss out and switched from conditional to unconditional acceptance of Microsoft's CD-ROM software.

By late summer and early fall of 1992, Leahy's campaign to enlist retailers to carry CD-ROM titles was succeeding. In the course of two months, he flew 40,000 miles, visiting prospective accounts large and small. The hook that pulled in retailers was not any of the existing titles like Bookshelf or Cinemania, Microsoft's CD-ROM guide to videos. Rather, it was the imminent arrival of Encarta, which unlike the others would carry a juicily expensive price tag—suggested retail price of $395—that promised to revive the good old days before software suites and price declines put pressure on the profits to be made from selling Word or Excel. An encyclopedia was additionally tantalizing because the very category appeared to have extremely broad appeal. In September 1992, Leahy told his clients: in three weeks, we'll formally announce Encarta and shortly after you'll have it in hand, still in time for Christmas sales. In the meantime, now is the time to prepare your catalogs and advertising.

Unbeknownst to the marketing staff, however, Craig Bartholomew and his development team were experiencing one setback after another in the fevered rush to complete Encarta. The encyclopedia project had been revived with the promise that it would rely solely on the code that had already been prepared for Bookshelf, but tens of thousands of lines of additional code had been needed in order to endow Encarta with the needed functionality. Under extreme pressure, the development team committed a variety of software engineering mistakes, such as not taking time for "milestone" meetings to identify problems and to check how well the features fulfilled the original specifications. At Microsoft, after a program is shipped, the program manager prepares what is called a "post-mortem" analysis. That it is called "post-mortem" rather than "post-partum" suggests how unmercifully critical these documents are, wringing from the experience all that can be learned for improvement the next time. Bartholomew's post-mortem for Encarta would be a model of meticulous self-criticism, running more than 80 single-spaced pages. He later described the mad final push to complete Encarta as "so bad it's an indelible learning experience."

The more anticipation that Leahy and his counterparts generated among retailers for Encarta, the more pressure Bartholomew and his developers felt back at the Redmond campus. When the developers informed Leahy of last-minute hitches, he was forced to cool down the flames of interest that he had just worked so hard to fan. He told retailers to delay their advertising campaigns for a little bit longer. Egghead, the retailer that Leahy had struggled to enlist, had by then enthusiastically embraced Encarta as the centerpiece of its Christmas advertising. It had printed up four million advertising flyers with a prominent role reserved for this program that Microsoft had yet to officially announce. On October 12, 1992, the day that Egghead had to mail out the flyers, whether Microsoft was ready or not, Bartholomew publicly announced Encarta. Hope had triumphed over reason. Two days later, the Encarta team ruefully confronted the stubborn fact that their work was still months from completion and shifted the shipping date accordingly. This sequence of failing to meet the original deadline for the Christmas season, then announcing the product prematurely, and then postponing the release date until early 1993 caused Gates, in Bartholomew's laconic report of his meeting with the chairman, to be "very irate."

Irate, too, were those retailers like Egghead that had been so laboriously recruited to join Microsoft's Christmas parade for Encarta. The other CD-ROM titles that Microsoft proffered for the Christmas season—Cinemania, Beethoven, Bookshelf, and a newly developed title that came from the recent Dorling Kindersley deal, Musical Instruments—did sell well. In fact, the multimedia portion of the Consumer Division was able to meet the entire fiscal year's sales goals with just these titles. But not having Encarta in the line-up was deflating. The word-of-mouth buzz that had built in the fall now dissipated. From the Consumer Division's perspective, the only good thing to have come out of the fiasco was that the premature announcement had caused arch-competitor Compton to hurry its introduction of its new lower priced CD-ROM encyclopedia. The old one had a nominal retail price of $895; the new one cost $395—and it arrived on the market riddled with bugs. In early March 1993, Encarta was finally ready—or so it seemed until a last-minute problem appeared after the final version, the "Golden Master," had been shipped to the pressing plant. A proofreader found the line "Slayer Sucks Like A Vacuum"—a reference to a heavy-metal rock band—buried in the contents list. A contractor had sneaked the line into the program as a prank. The reference was deleted and another *final* final version was prepared and shipped. It was priced at $395, identical to Compton's, and well below the price of the leading printed encyclopedias. Yet after an initial spurt, sales fell and the expected boom did not appear.

A number of problems contributed to the depressed sales. One was that Encarta was introduced with a bare-bones marketing budget, which may come as a surprise to those who think of Microsoft as the 800-pound gorilla who flexes its marketing muscle ruthlessly and automatically on behalf of all the company's products. Another problem concerned the source of the encyclopedia's text, Funk & Wagnalls. Compton's and the other CD-ROM encyclopedia publishers mocked the "supermarket encyclopedia" on which Encarta relied. (To emphasize the point in its advertisements, Compton's showed Encarta in a supermarket shopping cart, nestled with kitty litter, generic beer, and paper towels.) Reviewers also were critical of Encarta's relative paucity of video clips and its slow display speed. Instead of establishing new rules for the encyclopedia business that would allow Microsoft to define the measures that the marketplace would use when comparing encyclopedias, Encarta placed Microsoft on the defensive, reacting to criticisms on others' terms.

High visibility also eluded Encarta when Microsoft spurned opportunities to bid for bundling deals in which Microsoft would accept a small payment from a computer manufacturer—perhaps only $5 or less a copy—for allowing the CD-ROM to ship with all the manufacturer's new personal computers. Virtually giving the program away made no sense to Encarta's marketers, but in the meantime, competitors were not so picky and signed the bundling deals that Microsoft had spurned. In August 1993, six months after Encarta had shipped, Microsoft estimated that its encyclopedia held a grand total of 3 percent of market share for CD-ROM encyclopedias.

The single most debilitating problem was a weakness in the model used for marketing Encarta to consumers. The model had not deviated sufficiently from the inherited wisdom of the past, when door-to-door sales agents sold encyclopedias for a premium. Though Encarta was sold in computer stores, not door-to-door, internal discussions in 1992 led to a proposal for commissioned salespeople to visit prospective customers at their homes, offering to sell a personal computer to those households that did not already own one, along with the Encarta CD-ROM. This novel arrangement was proposed as a "reverse bundle." Instead of getting a program with the computer, the customer would get a computer with the program—and for a price that was about the same as that paid for a conventional printed encyclopedia alone. This particular proposal was discarded before it was tried, but the mantras that Encarta's marketers had learned from their research on the printed encyclopedia business and which they repeated again and again in the early planning had been "encyclopedias are sold, not bought" and "he who gets there first makes the sale"—both phrases emphasizing the importance of salespeople making the pitch in person.

Even though Microsoft had dared to go up against an *Encyclopaedia Britannica* or a *World Book* on the strength of its ability to price its CD-ROM encyclopedia for impulse buying, Encarta's initial suggested retail price of $395 was far above what consumers would consider for an unplanned purchase. Bartholomew and the other members of the Encarta group were misled by focus groups that had been convened early on—too early, it would turn out—to estimate the price of a multimedia encyclopedia and had provided answers in the $1000-$2000 range, $500 being the lowest estimate. This data led the team to revise its original plans to offer Encarta for $295 and instead price it higher. At one point before Encarta was launched, Bartholomew wondered whether the price should be raised to $495, lest Microsoft leave money on the table that was its for the asking. These discussions led to the introductory price of $395, which the Encarta marketers had every reason to view as a moderate compromise between slightly lower and still higher alternatives. Because the competition was also priced at $395, Encarta's retail price did not appear to be an important point of differentiation, but appearances proved deceiving.

When Martin Leahy spoke to store managers during field visits after Encarta's release, he discovered that Compton's CD-ROM encyclopedia was selling extremely well—but not the $395 version, but rather the $129 "competitive upgrade." Strictly speaking, this version was only for customers who could demonstrate that they owned a previous version or a competitor's. But, in fact, because retailers had every incentive *not* to insist on proof of prior purchase, first-time customers were happily taking advantage of lax enforcement and the opportunity to acquire a multimedia encyclopedia for a fraction of its nominal retail price. Having seen this spectacle, Leahy returned to the Microsoft campus determined to persuade the others of the need to dramatically lower Encarta's price, too. His credo: "We need a $99 Encarta; a $99 Encarta; a $99 Encarta!"

In the summer of 1993, Bartholomew and the marketing staff deliberated over the pricing. The troops had been set to work on the revision as soon as the first version had shipped. Having learned from mistakes the first time, they prepared the new version, entitled Encarta 94, much more expeditiously—within seven months. With the first opportunity for the encyclopedia to be on store shelves for a holiday season approaching and the second version of Encarta about to be released, the pricing question took on additional urgency.

Some Consumer Division voices spoke out against Leahy's proposal. Encarta had been the most costly program to produce in the entire division, they pointed out; it was too early in the game to engage in a price war. Look at the history of Excel—Microsoft had harvested many years of profits before its net price fell when the concept of marketing a suite of programs began to displace the sales of individual programs. Unfortunately for the high-price advocates, the example of Excel was not particularly relevant. Consumers who might be interested in a CD-ROM encyclopedia did not automatically resemble Information Systems managers who purchased office software. And more recent Microsoft history offered countervailing support for those who argued that Encarta should carry a much lower price. Microsoft had promoted its new database program Access with an introductory price of only $99—and it had sold briskly. Bartholomew and the Encarta marketers spoke to Access managers about their experience and learned that their rationale—setting the price below the $100 threshold that triggers the irksome bureaucracy of purchase orders in many offices—did not apply to a product like Encarta that was destined for the home. But the idea of creating "heat in the channel" with a temptingly low price that would expire at a preannounced date seemed no less applicable to a consumer software title. Bartholomew moved into the low-price camp, too.

Leahy personally did not take much comfort in the example of Access. He knew from speaking to store managers that, before the discount offer expired, resellers had stocked up on so many of the inexpensively priced boxes of Access that they had no need to reorder the software for the entire following year. "If we lower the price of Encarta to $99," Leahy told all colleagues who would listen, "you realize, don't you, the price is never going up again, right?" But the math would still be compelling: if Microsoft sold four times as many units at $99 as it did at $395, the price change would be a wash; but if it sold eight times as many units, the company would in one stroke be able to lift its market share of retail sales in the category (excluding the bundling deals with computer manufacturers) from the 10 or 15 percent it seemed to be at the time to the 50 percent it sought. The group's decision was an apparent compromise—a holiday promotion, from September to December, would offer Encarta at $99, and the old price of $395 would be restored after December 31. It was supposedly only a temporary price reduction, but Leahy was happy nevertheless. He had the $99 price for which he had lobbied, and he knew that the prices were no more reversible than a ratchet—the old $395 price would now be a relic of history.

Bartholomew took bets among top managers about holiday sales for 1993. Charlotte Guyman, the director of marketing for the Consumer Division at the time, guessed 20,000 units; Peter Mollman, about 65,000; Leahy and Bartholomew predicted 90,000 or so units. Everyone, even the most optimistic ones, underestimated sales, which turned out to be 120,000+ units, or more than 65 percent of market share. Net monthly receipts for Encarta had gone from about $500,000 in August to $5.4 million in December, more than 400 percent of its assigned sales quota. A graph of the dramatic lift showed the proverbial "hockey stick" effect, pointed gradually, then sharply, up. Arguing for a low price, Leahy held that anything better than a fourfold increase in the number of units sold would result in higher profits. Privately he had believed Encarta could enjoy an eightfold increase in sales; it turned out to be a 24-fold increase. The only dispiriting news was that Microsoft's manufacturing was caught unprepared, and many stores ran out of product. At the end of December, there were back-orders for another 60,000 units, which, if a sufficient number of copies had been made, would have boosted sales for that quarter still 50 percent higher.

The giddy success Encarta enjoyed that holiday season, of course, came only after enduring years of costly development and disappointments. Finally the product was ready, at the right price, at a time when sales of CD-ROM software and CD-ROM drives were mutually reinforcing. The 1993 season not only heralded stirring sales for Encarta, it also marked the point at which the Consumer Division became the fastest growing unit under the Microsoft roof. It was then that the concept of lowering development costs by cranking out multiple titles with a similar template was revived, an idea that had originally brought the CD-ROM encyclopedia back to life in 1991.

Although Encarta had ended up requiring huge investments, in violation of the charter to reuse the Bookshelf template, other Consumer Division titles employed the concept. Microsoft's Dinosaurs had cost almost a million dollars to develop. However, the Consumer Division's "titles factory" produced succeeding titles in the same series—Dangerous Creatures and Ancient Lands—for somewhat less, reusing design elements, compression techniques, and other knowledge learned from the first project. Gates had made consistency in design across the entire product line a high priority for the Consumer Division. Patty Stonesifer, who headed the division after Susan Boeschen retired in 1993, continued to press a related point by directing all Consumer Division developers to employ common code, developed within the unit and elsewhere in the company, in order to speed development and lower costs.

Unlike the developers of traditional Microsoft software, the Consumer Division rewrote the inherited rules in order to prepare the maximum number of titles in the maximum number of areas for the minimum cost. They faced a marketplace in which thousands of CD-ROM titles would be vying for the attention of prospective customers. The development and marketing of an Excel or Word had little relevance—the CD-ROM world was moving quickly from a state of virtually no titles to one of a glut, not unlike the traditional book publishing industry in which 40,000 new titles arrive every year. Adapting to these new circumstances, when the development team completed the first title in a Consumer Division series, they would split into two teams for the second and third titles. Those two teams would then become four teams for the next title. Each mitotic expansion served to create multiple lines of development and spread experience. Stonesifer was urging her division to aim for a title-a-week pace of new releases. By mid-1994, the company boasted 54 consumer products in 27 languages; by the end of 1995, it had over 100.

One of the basic marketing questions that the Consumer Division faced as its growth accelerated was whether to create a separate brand identity for the consumer titles, lest the Microsoft name, with its association with dull operating system or office software, hurt its appeal to consumers. Charlotte Guyman was among the contingent that advocated a name wholly separate from Microsoft, such as "Lifeware," that would provide as much distance as possible from what Guyman saw as the company's "techno-nerdy" image. She and other managers were convinced otherwise, however, by research indicating that Microsoft's name turned out to be an asset.

Consumers seemed to need a signal that a particular software title was intended for fun at home, not for work at the office. "Microsoft Home," the subbrand that was subsequently introduced formally in December 1993, is interesting because it did not follow the classic consumer-products model of Procter & Gamble. The P&G marketing formula calls for building brand identity around products. Consumers who buy Tide are probably not even aware of the company that manufactures it. Microsoft sought to make its corporate name more visible so that consumers, when faced with a bewildering array of CD-ROM titles (as well as risks of setup and software-hardware compatibility problems), would place their trust in the familiar brand. The guiding rationale drew less from the old merchandising of the industrial era of Procter & Gamble than it did from the newer merchandising of the entertainment era of, say, Disney.

Microsoft planned to reap a number of dividends from its "Microsoft Home" brand strategy. Instead of being split among the many separate products, advertising dollars could be directed at strengthening popular recognition of the overall brand. Other marketing programs reinforced the message among consumers that Microsoft was the name to remember. Microsoft supported "Family Technology Nights" that offered discounted software to parents at evening "seminars" held at schools, workshops for school administrators and principals, the National Parent Teacher Association's art contest "Reflections," software gifts to 50 children's museums and public libraries, and American Library Association traveling exhibits. Surveys that Microsoft later commissioned revealed that its home customers exhibited a high degree of what marketers call "cross-ownership," where consumers had purchased titles in dissimilar categories, for example, Encarta and Cinemania. The evidence confirmed the Consumer Division's supposition that if a consumer had had a good experience with one Microsoft Home title, he or she would likely purchase additional Microsoft titles.

The same evidence could also be read as confirmation of a paradox. The more competition as additional CD-ROM titles hit the market, the greater the clamor and noise for a consumer's attention; the more noise, the greater the consumer's anxiety about making the right choice—and the more Microsoft benefited, as the most readily recognized name in the pack. Microsoft was in a better position when a consumer faced twelve CD-ROM titles about dinosaurs compared to only three on the subject. Admittedly this advantage would not endure if Microsoft damaged its reputation by turning out poor quality CD-ROM titles. But the quality issue did not pose problems because, if anything, the Microsoft Home titles improved over time, as Microsoft sought out and took to heart the lessons it learned as development and marketing proceeded.

As the market matured, Microsoft's smaller but impressive competitor, Broderbund, showed the power of using product names to build an identifiable brand. In 1995 Microsoft pragmatically dismantled the "Microsoft Home" strategy, replacing it with product names that could serve as an easily identifiable umbrella over a family of related subproducts. Instead of banishing the Encarta product name from advertising and promotion in favor of the "Microsoft Home" banner, Encarta became a brand name that covered a growing line of reference titles. Microsoft's return to a Procter & Gamble model was solidified by its decision to deliberately recruit and learn from more P&G managers.

Consumer software became a major commercial force of its own, no longer the weak sibling of business software, when nontraditional stores like Wal-Mart and Target began to sell—and soon sell in large quantities—software produced by Microsoft's Consumer Division. The campaign to enlist the mass discounters had begun in 1990, when consumer titles might retail for $199—so expensive that the boxes had to be placed in locked glass cases, out of reach of shoplifters, but also out of convenient reach of legitimate purchasers who wanted to look the box over without having to find a salesperson. When retail prices dropped below $100, the boxes were released from protective custody and placed on ordinary shelves, and new store chains signed on to carry the software. Soon, Microsoft's Consumer Division was selling most of its product units through mass discounters, consumer electronics stores, and warehouse clubs. The Encarta development team knew that Wal-Mart *alone* had placed an order for 70,000 units of Encarta '95 that depended on meeting a September 1994 deadline.

With a heavily promoted consumer brand identity, with the industry's most comprehensive coverage of consumer software categories, and with the financial resources to invest in securing shelf space, Microsoft was in the best position of any company in 1994 when retailers were beset by too many software titles to accommodate any but a small portion. Whose software titles would a Price/Costco warehouse club be most inclined to stock—a new software start-up with only a title or two to its name or Microsoft?

Even the more traditional software-only store chains were forced, by declining median retail prices and changing economics in the industry, to discard their staff of evaluators who once had determined which titles would be carried. At one point, for example, Egghead had had a Product Evaluation Group, a staff of 25 people at its corporate headquarters, working exclusively on screening new software titles that publishers submitted for Egghead distribution. By 1994, the group was gone. With the proliferation of CD-ROM publishing, there were too many titles to be evaluated, and maintaining such a staff was simply too expensive. Instead Egghead relied on the product category and the publisher's track record, an obvious advantage for well-established Microsoft. Even in 1993, Microsoft's head start was evident when the company's annual report to shareholders could boast that Microsoft CD-ROM titles accounted for four of the top ten places in national sales.

For those who see something sinister in Microsoft's commanding position in this relatively new domain of consumer software, the particular way that Microsoft has gone about producing titles deserves some consideration. When home software finally did take off, some of the most fortunate beneficiaries were software companies that offered violent (Mortal Kombat), or violent *and* prurient (Night Trap) titles. Microsoft pulled off the feat while deliberately eschewing the "low road." Other titles that Microsoft produced expressly for children—such as Creative Artist and Fine Writer—were aimed at customers' higher faculties, too. When Bill Gates is overheard, as he is periodically, saying something that indicates a lust for profits and power that knows no bounds, we should remember his praiseworthy record. In fact, he demonstrated with Microsoft's first CD-ROM titles that he did not pursue *all* tempting business opportunities.

That Microsoft could succeed in the consumer software business was anything but foreordained when it began this quest in earnest in the mid-1980s. Most striking is not what the company had learned from developing operating systems and office applications but what the company did not know, realized it did not know, and set about learning. If we can distill from this portion of Microsoft's history a lesson that other companies could apply, it might be the ethos of learning, an ethos that companies of any size can embrace. As we shall see next, even a very small company could deploy smarts with great effect.

Chapter 7

David and Goliath

LITTLE STROKES fell great Oaks.

Benjamin Franklin, "The Way of Wealth" (1757)

Though Microsoft was early to recognize the profitable opportunities latent in the home market, the company was not necessarily the first to commercially realize that potential. Nor were the executives at all of its competitors as incompetent as those at Lotus, WordPerfect, and other large software publishers. The story of Microsoft's initial encounters with the feisty Bay Area software company Intuit, which specializes in personal finance software, reminds us that Gates's Microsoft is fallible, too.

Intuit's co-founder Scott Cook, like Gates, has served as his company's head continuously since its founding. He came to home software not from other precincts of the software industry but from Procter & Gamble. Cook, who is a few years older than Gates, would call himself in a self-deprecating way a "former fat salesman." (He had been a product manager for the Crisco line.) He took pains never to describe his software company, which was located near Stanford University, *as* a software company. He preferred instead to speak of it as a company that provided "solutions" to customer problems that pertained to finance. In addition to offering software solutions, helping customers write checks, balance checkbooks, and pay bills, the company also offered nonsoftware solutions such as special checks and forms, which proved to be an even more lucrative and recurring source of profits. For Cook, the model of success from which he took inspiration was not Microsoft or any other company in the computer industry, but rather his former employer, Procter & Gamble. P&G had developed a highly refined corporate culture to which Cook attributed the company's ability to remain "great for 100 years."

The timing of Cook's decision in 1983 to found Intuit was inauspicious. Cook had an idea for a consumer check-writing product, and he chose to advertise for a programmer on Stanford's campus. The first student he asked about a good location for posting his want-ad turned out to be interested in the position and became the company's co-founder. The program was released as Quicken in December 1984, when the category of personal finance software was already crowded—and a home software market had yet to appear. Unlike Microsoft's earliest days of cranking out versions of BASIC on contract for all manner of hardware manufacturers, Intuit necessarily faced the "in every home" challenge immediately. Cook's initial plan was to avoid the retail channel and have banks sell Quicken in their lobbies, which in retrospect is especially interesting now, given the convergence of software companies and banks in electronic banking. This earliest chapter involving Intuit, however, was decidedly low tech. A bank's sole connection to the software was provided in its lobby, where boxes of Quicken were displayed for sale. Banks proved to be maladroit when it came to selling software. By May 1985, despite the most stringent economies, Intuit had spent the $350,000 its founders had raised from savings, relatives, credit cards, and second mortgages. Intuit could not meet the payroll for its seven employees.

Intuit's employees seemed to be enduring a biblical sort of testing, one that Microsoft had been spared. Several of Intuit's employees jumped ship at this point, but new ones joined, accepted an equity stake in the company in lieu of salary for the time being, and turned out to be extremely well remunerated for having taken the risk. The company pulled back from the brink of insolvency with the release of a Quicken that could be used on Apple II computers (in addition to the original DOS version). Cook, who constituted the company's entire salesforce until 1989, convinced a number of banks to pay the company a $20,000 sign-up fee as an advance on sales. Some banks started to do well with the products and actually reordered.

Intuit showed itself to be adept in changing its business model to reflect the realities of the marketplace. In 1986, inspired by

Borland's success in its low pricing of software programming languages and utilities, Intuit slashed the retail price of Quicken from $100 to $50, a move that anticipated the price cuts that Microsoft adopted for the home software market, too. What Intuit gave up in revenue when a customer made the initial purchase was more than made up by what marketing professors call "aftermarket" sales. Even when its customer base was minuscule in 1986, Intuit received a steady weekly inflow of $8000 in cash from customers who purchased checks and other supplies—the revenue that helped the company through its fiscal crisis. By the end of fiscal year 1986, the company had generated about $750,000 in revenues, more than three times that of the previous year, and had about $150,000 in pretax earnings.

Intuit lore includes the story, passed down and embellished over the years, of an advertisement placed in a hobbyist magazine for Apple II owners in the fall of 1986. "End Financial Hassles," the ad's copy had invited, but company legend depicts it as a last-ditch investment—Cook staking the entire company treasury, $125,000, on the single ad. Legend attributes the salvation of the company to the tremendous consumer response to that single advertisement. In fact, Intuit was not in quite as dire straits as it had been the year before. The advertisement, and a boost from distribution by the two largest software wholesalers, helped propel the company's growth. Version 2 of Quicken, with more features, followed in 1987. Arriving in 1989, Version 3 permitted customers to manage credit card accounts, loans, and other assets, as well as bank accounts.

Many practices that Cook had his company adopt were ones that Microsoft learned on its own three or five years later, as its own consumer software efforts matured. After Quicken's Version 3 appeared, Intuit held itself to an annual cycle of updates, which placed relentless pressure on its developers but yielded steady upgrade revenue and a reinforced position as an innovator. Beginning in 1989, Intuit also experimented with advertising in magazines outside the computer industry, simultaneously marking and accelerating the diffusion of software throughout the culture. Airline magazines were an early venture. So too was *Golf* magazine, an experiment that did not turn out especially well. That magazine's readers, though possessing the right demographic characteristics as far as financial assets, apparently did not want to worry about their money when reading about golf.

More successful was a Quicken advertisement that appeared in the magazine for the American Association of Retired Persons. Intuit was also a software company pioneer in television advertising and in creating that dubious contribution to advertising's Hall of Fame, the infomercial shown to the captive audience of airline passengers.

To expand the distribution of its software in the retail channel, Intuit was well ahead of Microsoft in hiring people with retail merchandising experience. One of Intuit's early hires came from the video rental industry, where the science of shelf arrangements, end-of-aisle store displays, and other details of "merchandising" are critical. Intuit's first merchandising experiment was to convince retailers to place by the cash register a cardboard display—a cash register replica with pockets that would hold six boxes of Quicken. (Intuit picked six because it had noticed that most stores only stocked four copies; a six-unit display might impel a 50 percent increase in orders for store inventory.)

Intuit also pioneered in distributing software through mass merchant retailers like Wal-Mart and warehouse clubs like Price/Costco and Sam's Club. Initially the warehouse clubs were utterly uninterested in suggestions about how to display the software. When Intuit offered them market development funds to improve their merchandising, the clubs' first response was, "Thank you very much, we'll use the money to lower the price of your product." This was not Intuit's intention, and with time, the warehouse clubs became more receptive to suggestions about signage and other display aspects.

Intuit pursued alternative retail channels for its software without abandoning the traditional computer and software-only stores, which the company regarded with renewed respect after weathering a small crisis when Version 3 of Quicken was released. The company had notified its previous customers of the availability of the new version and had invited them to send their upgrade order directly to Intuit, which would mail the customers the new discs. The arrangement bypassed retail stores, but the volume of orders overwhelmed both Intuit's order fulfillment staff and the phone system. Cook later sent a contrite letter to Intuit's customers, extending his apologies and promising to make the necessary investments to prevent the snafus from recurring.

The episode convinced Cook and his employees that retail stores should continue to play an important role in off-loading the headaches associated with new releases. It was technically feasible to distribute upgrades to existing customers via the Internet or commercial online services, or even by mailing floppy discs directly. Despite the financial temptation to handle upgrades directly and retain 100 percent of the upgrade revenue (rather than giving up about half of the revenue to retail partners), Intuit still felt it was best to rely on the retailers and do whatever was needed to keep them happy.

Quicken customers who are unaware of this background have been puzzled by the letters they receive periodically from Intuit, inviting them to send in a check to the company to order an upgrade directly, when the offered "discounted price" is conspicuously higher than the price on Quicken boxes at the neighborhood software store. An irate letter to *Infoworld*'s "Gripe Line" in 1995 cited Intuit as guilty of forsaking its loyal customers by setting a price for a direct upgrade that was almost twice as much as could be had at a local store. Actually, the disparity in price was intended and the letter outlining the "upgrade offer" was merely a disguised form of advertising for the retail stores that Intuit supplied.

Intuit's executives *wanted* its existing customers to march down to the local software store to "save" money and *not* take Intuit up on its offer. The more customers who upgraded at stores, the fewer problems Intuit would face in staffing for spurts in its order fulfillment service. Such problems became more daunting as its installed base of customers continued to grow into the millions. And the retailers were pleased with the arrangement, not only for the sales of Quicken upgrades, but also for the impulse purchases that customers often made once they set foot in the store. One more benefit of this mode of distribution that the cheaper, more efficient electronic distribution of software will never be able to match was the creation of "heat" in the retail channel. The mountains of Quicken boxes stacked in stores when upgrades arrive are a visible testament to the product's importance that cannot fail to impress prospective customers who happen by. Existing Intuit customers who download an upgrade from a Web page or phone in their order to Intuit directly would remain invisible to prospective, still undecided new customers. Reconstituting the disparate and atomized customer base into a visible mass, a giant signboard for all to see, is a service that venerable retail stores are uniquely capable of providing.

Cook regarded customer satisfaction as Intuit's best form of advertising. He expected not only the company's developers but also its senior managers to learn what customers wanted by answering the technical support lines a few hours every month or by taking turns serving in Intuit's "Follow Me Home" program, in which new Quicken customers were asked before leaving the store whether an Intuit representative could accompany them when they opened the box, installed the software, and began using it. This form of research, observing through the eyes of real customers in situ, was an innovation that went well beyond what a usability lab like Microsoft's could do.

Cook, like Gates, understood the importance of securing a commanding market share, and he elected to remain focused on the single category of personal finance software before permitting any dilution of concentration. In 1989, for instance, senior managers urged Cook to acquire a company that produced income tax software, a logical complement to a personal finance package. Cook refused, arguing that the consolidation of Quicken's position demanded the company's full attention. Four years later, Intuit paid a considerably higher amount to acquire another company that produced tax packages, but then again, Intuit itself had grown in the intervening years and perhaps would not have been able to do so if it had made the acquisition prematurely.

Through the 1980s, Intuit enjoyed one other advantage that a number of other software companies lacked: Intuit did not have Microsoft as its competitor. In 1989, however, the hitherto separate histories of the two companies begin to appear in the same picture frame. Intuit then found itself as the temporary partner of the consumer group at Microsoft, which enlisted Intuit, along with two companies that produced tax software, to join Microsoft's own multipurpose Works in a bundling deal it offered to personal computer manufacturers. Intuit managers personally met with Microsoft counterparts, and the companies became mutually acquainted. Microsoft liked what it saw and offered to acquire the company; Intuit spurned the offer.

Intuit's marketing managers guessed that the company would soon face direct competition from Microsoft, and Windows would be the arena for the confrontation. Intuit's record for porting Quicken to other operating system formats had been, for the most part, successful. Besides an Apple II version, it had done a Mac version that had sold quite well. It also had been wiser than Lotus in electing *not* to place a large bet on the hapless OS/2. Its record had not been perfect, however. Tandy had persuaded Intuit to develop a Quicken version for Tandy's now-forgotten Deskmate environment. Like Windows, Deskmate ran on top of DOS. But unlike Windows, it was produced by a hardware company that needed to secure other hardware companies' support in order to achieve the volume that would make the software a viable standard. (One reason *consumers* chose to make Microsoft the standard bearer was because of Microsoft's ecumenical neutrality as a software company, distanced from hardware.) Intuit was paid for its development efforts on Tandy's behalf, but the work distracted the company and its developers. At one point, fully half of the company's development efforts were devoted to Deskmate, so Intuit was fortunate that this bet that never paid off was not as strategically costly as it might have been.

In 1989, Intuit executives knew that a new version of Windows would be out before long and would be sufficiently improved over the previous version to finally ignite market interest. Because Microsoft had demonstrated an interest in the personal finance category by offering to acquire Intuit and had failed in its acquisition bid, Intuit thought it highly likely that Microsoft would enter the category itself. At this early point, Intuit's managers regarded Microsoft as a formidable power and feared the prospect of direct competition. But their Microsoft counterparts did not reciprocate in conveying the same respect to its soon-to-be rival. A junior Microsoft product manager flew to California and offered Intuit the opportunity to license the Quicken name to Microsoft in exchange for a small royalty on a Windows version. The offer would have eviscerated Intuit's future, given the pittance it would have received as compensation for forsaking the Windows market. Many years later, the memory of the insult still lingers at Intuit. Remember that as dominant as Intuit was in personal finance software, the category was still small in 1989 and 1990. On the eve of the release of Quicken Version 3, the company still only had 50 employees. Its 1989 revenue of $19 million represented breathtaking growth from the brink of insolvency only four years earlier, but Microsoft was far larger, collecting $800 million in revenue and commanding 4000 employees at the same time. For Intuit to dismiss Microsoft's offers as insulting showed spunk.

Microsoft's Entry Business Unit had decided to enter the personal finance market one way or the other. If it could not acquire Intuit, it was more than ready to bring out its own software. And rather than entering the DOS and Mac markets, Microsoft would instead bring out a Windows product. The company assumed that Intuit, like so many other independent software vendors, would be cautious about moving to Windows, despite Microsoft's entreaties to develop for the platform. Microsoft calculated that it could get a good jump on the competition in personal finance software by betting on Windows well before Intuit would be willing to.

Microsoft turned out to be wrong. Intuit was able to deliver its Windows version of Quicken only six weeks after Microsoft introduced its new Windows product, Money. Microsoft's slight lead proved insignificant. This was partly due to the loyalty of Intuit's customers and store dealers. But it was also partly due to Intuit's sharp-elbowed aggressiveness in prematurely mailing its customers an announcement that the Windows version of Quicken was now available for purchase at local dealers. Intuit got a little ahead of itself, just as it had also done in 1988, when it notified customers that the first Macintosh version of Quicken was available—before the final debugging had been completed. In this case, however, the mailing that trumpeted the availability of Intuit's Windows product before it was actually on the shelves stopped Microsoft's Money dead in the water.

The incident brings to mind the charges raised against Microsoft for preannouncing products still in development, which of course the industry routinely does to let customers know what products are in the pipeline. In the case of Encarta, Egghead Software launched its advertising blitz before the product was ready for release, but that was because Egghead and Microsoft had not synchronized their timetables. Here, quite to the contrary, Intuit was mailing the early notifications on its own, a rather blatantly aggressive preannouncement. It was not especially nefarious, nor does it explain how Quicken would do so well in the Windows market. But Microsoft's critics seem to use a double standard that forbids treating similar behavior by other firms in the same way. We can learn from such comparisons to be more consistent. Intuit is an exemplary company, whose chief executive scrupulously avoids criticizing his competitors and who prefers to let the high quality of the company's products and devotion to customer service do the talking. Yet, in the trenches, Intuit is as aggressive as any other.

Intuit's previous customers on other platforms constituted a wonderful asset for Intuit at this moment. Microsoft had no such installed base in this category and had to entice customers who were perfectly happy with Quicken and willing to wait until the Windows version of Quicken finally showed up. Instead of being upset about the absence of product when Intuit made its Windows announcement, Intuit customers simply took the premature notice as indication of imminent arrival and held off buying Money. Intuit's cultivation of close relationships with its dealers paid large dividends. The dealers held the fort on Intuit's behalf, guiding customers away from the untested Money and inviting them to instead place their names on a waiting list, with the assurance that the store would call them the instant Quicken for Windows arrived. Intuit's fear that Money, arriving on shelves first, would suck up all the pent-up demand for a personal finance product for Windows was not borne out.

In its first two months, Microsoft Money sold only about 50,000 units, and from there it was straight downhill as Quicken captured the overwhelming share of consumer purchases. Like most first versions (not just of Microsoft products but any software company's initial forays into new categories), the first version of Money was technically no match for a more mature product that had been improved through several generations. Unlike Lotus, which was slow to respond to Microsoft's Excel for Windows, Intuit gave Microsoft no time to enjoy beating the incumbent leader to market with a Windows product. And in this case, Microsoft Money offered less, not more, than the Intuit equivalent. Microsoft had planned to offer electronic bill payment and investment tracking, as Quicken did, but it had to postpone those features for the next release because the technical work took longer than anticipated.

Money did have one small feature that Quicken lacked. Microsoft called it SmartFill. When the user was typing in the name of the payee on a check, the program would use the first letters typed as a guide to look up previous payees and, finding a similar name, would automatically fill in the rest of the letters. Quicken had a similar feature, but instead of automatically searching for similar names as soon as the first letters were entered, the program waited for the user to press the Tab key. The difference between the two programs' fill-in feature was minor, and it's unlikely that a new customer weighing Money against Quicken would regard the slight variation in this one feature as decisive. Yet Intuit was determined not to fall behind Microsoft in any respect, no matter how small. When its developers saw Microsoft's SmartFill, they realized that they, too, could eliminate the necessity of pressing the Tab key. They did a quick rewrite and sent out copies of Version 1.01 gratis to all of their Windows customers, adding to their reservoir of good-will.

Intuit looked to Microsoft to see what it needed to add, and Microsoft did likewise, of course. Later when we discuss antitrust issues, keep the dynamic nature of the Microsoft-Intuit competition in mind as it is emblematic of how competition in the industry leads to improvements. The practice of one company swiftly copying a functional innovation devised by another has been upheld by the courts as legal and is standard practice for the Intuits as well as the Microsofts. And we customers are the principal beneficiaries, not the companies, who end up, after all, ceaselessly matching what each other offers and casting about for still newer, yet-to-be-discovered improvements. Conversely, when consolidation of the two primary protagonists into a single company threatens to end this leapfrogging, consumers have the most to lose.

Microsoft could see quite clearly that it was now in the unenviable position of playing catch-up against a smart, focused opponent who would not stand still waiting for Money to become a competitive threat. Intuit would be fleet of foot, carrying out guerrilla raids right under Microsoft's nose. In the spring of 1992, when Microsoft readied its Windows 3.1 operating system upgrade for release, Intuit saw an opportunity to ride like a pilot fish with Microsoft, whose marketing might would be fully deployed. Guessing correctly that Microsoft would make it worthwhile for software retailers to devote most of their shelf space to the upcoming Windows release, Intuit created a special box for Quicken that advertised a special price of $19.99 for customers who were simultaneously purchasing Windows.

Intuit added an ingenious twist by limiting the number of boxes that would be available to all retailers. Each store battled to get as large an allocation as it could, which generated more "heat." The precious copies that a dealer secured were placed next to the Windows boxes, and out the door they flew. A disadvantage of Microsoft's cellular internal organization was that one part of Microsoft often had no idea what the other parts were up to. Thus, having arranged nothing comparable in tandem with the Windows marketers, the Microsoft Money group was embarrassed again. This would prove also to be especially costly because a Windows upgrade would not come around for another three years. This little moment in software marketing history is also illuminating because it underscores that Microsoft is anything but a monolith.

While Intuit smoothly replicated in the Windows world the commanding market share it held in the DOS and Macintosh worlds, Microsoft's Money group scrambled to recover from its clumsy beginning and reduce the market share gap with a strong second release. How best to do so was not clear. Intuit set the pace with its relentless annual releases. For Microsoft to countenance a schedule that had less frequent releases would be suicide. Yet the development team had not had the time to give much thought to Version 2 of Money when it was busily occupied getting Version 1 out the door. After the initial release, when the team could finally give the matter its attention, it faced a dismayingly short schedule if it were to match Intuit's next expected release in the fall. If Microsoft needed three months to plan the specifications, three months to build a prototype, and three months at the end of the development process to test the code, only three months were left in which to actually write the program. This sobering challenge sparked a reorganization within the group so that in the future there would always be a program manager responsible for looking beyond the immediate revision underway.

Microsoft's Money group was the first Consumer Division group to confront the new pressures imposed by the seasonal nature of consumer purchases. (Encarta's release was then still in the future.) In the category of personal finance software, some 80 percent of a year's sales would take place between October 1 and February 1. The next revision of Money absolutely could not miss the opportunity for a fall release. The one significant feature to add to Money's next release, electronic bill paying, was not an innovation. It was merely catch-up, but it was critical to the product if Microsoft were ever to convince customers that Money possessed the equivalent features of Quicken.

As Intuit knew, only a very small percentage of its customers—perhaps 1 or 2 percent then—actually used electronic bill paying, which it had brought out on DOS even before its Windows product had debuted. But it was a "checklist" feature that everyone seemed to pay attention to, as if customers had resolved to begin using a modem to pay bills tomorrow.

Intuit did not actually pay the bills for its Quicken customers. The technology needed to carry out the actual electronic bill payment for thousands—soon perhaps millions—of customers required a considerable investment and specialized skills. Therefore, Intuit used the services of an Ohio outfit named Checkfree, which used an IBM 3090 mainframe and a centralized banking clearinghouse to move funds from the accounts of Quicken customers to those of merchants that customers designated on their computer screen. Another, much smaller personal finance software vendor, MECA, also used Checkfree, and so too would Microsoft. The contract had been signed and the service would have commenced with Version 1 of Money if time had not been so short. As work began on Version 2, Microsoft's developers retrieved the unfinished bill paying code that had been temporarily cut out of Version 1. It was completed and polished in readiness for the announcement that electronic bill payment would be the centerpiece of the new release of Money.

On the eve of the release, Microsoft got in touch with Checkfree to confirm that everything was in order. Imagine Microsoft's surprise when it was told that everything was *not* in order: the original contract, it turned out, only covered Version 1. In the meantime, Intuit and MECA had arranged a newly exclusive arrangement with Checkfree that forbade Checkfree from contracting with Microsoft too. By now, Microsoft was completely out of time to devise a Plan B. If it wanted a timely release, it had to ship Money without electronic bill paying—without, in fact, any major addition of features. Instead of bringing out a strong follow-up to its weak Version 1, Microsoft now bumblingly introduced another weak version, permitting the features gap between Quicken and Money to widen still further.

Shutting out Microsoft from using the services of a third party, clearly, does not benefit software consumers as does, say, leapfrogging rivals by matching rivals' features and adding new ones. But business, by its nature, involves millions of partnerships, whose terms are

negotiated on an individual basis and thus often vary from one partner to another, depending on special considerations that could never
be foreseen or legislatively forbidden. Intuit's ploy was perfectly legal
and does not warrant condemnation. In fact, it did not draw public
criticism, which is testimony to the double standard—if Microsoft, not
Intuit, had secured an exclusive arrangement with Checkfree, the public outcry at Microsoft's temerity would have been deafening. Nor
should Intuit's muscular renegotiation of its contracts with suppliers
who service customer orders for checks and forms be denounced.
Nor its dispensing Market Development Funds to reward stores that
adhere to Intuit's requests to maintain a suggested minimum retail
price. These are all practices that Microsoft also employs—but, unlike Intuit and the other software companies that do the same,
Microsoft has been singled out for public criticism.

The Checkfree affair also reveals another similarity between
Intuit and Microsoft: the stoic reaction both companies maintained
when absorbing the blows dealt by the other. Microsoft's Money
group, which in the wake of being shut out of an arrangement with
Checkfree, had grounds to do some public grumbling, did not do so
and absorbed the setback in silence. And when other Microsoft rivals
publicly heaped charges of unethical conduct on Gates's company, it
would have been natural enough for Cook to throw in with the others. He did not, however. In 1993, for instance, when asked about the
criticism of Microsoft that others had raised, Cook replied that a
"mountain is being made of something that isn't even a molehill," and
he declared that, in all his dealings with the company, Microsoft had
never taken unfair advantage.

That the newly born Money had to compete against a mature
Quicken obscures how much alike Microsoft and Intuit really were. If
Microsoft's launch of Money in 1991 did not lead to instant success,
neither did Intuit's launch in 1992 of its first accounting program,
Quickbooks. Afterward, Cook would describe the principal advertisement that Intuit ran in *PC Magazine* to announce the product as
"probably the worst ad ever to run in the history of microcomputers."
The two-page spread in the most widely circulated computer magazine netted a grand total of four responses, a result that Cook laughingly suggested would have been exceeded if Intuit had simply run
two pages with just Intuit's 800 telephone number on them. Even

more disastrous, the first version of Quickbooks had bugs that destroyed user's data, which in a finance program is not a mere annoyance. Stomping out the bugs required six more months, but the subsequent story—of strong product, strong marketing, strong technical support—reads just like stories of many Microsoft products. The Intuit staff is smart and nimble, able to learn quickly from its mistakes, build strong successors in product lines, consolidate its position, and expose precious little of its flanks to competitors.

Both Microsoft and Intuit are headed by individuals whose respective success has not diminished their constant sense of vulnerability to competitive attack. The computer industry frequently invokes the line attributed to Intel's Andy Grove that "only the paranoid survive," but "paranoia" connotes a pathological delusion that is not intended here. A milder substitute—something that sits midway between "paranoia" and "alertness"—would serve well. Cook, like Gates, keeps himself in a state of acute receptivity to signs of incipient competitive threat. In the early 1990s, he not only had to weather a challenge from the number one software company, but also a separate one from the number two software company, Computer Associates.

If the name Computer Associates seems unfamiliar, it is because its primary focus had been serving mainframe and minicomputer markets. Not wanting to remain unknown to customers in the fastest growing segment of the computer industry, personal computers, Computer Associates hatched the idea of entering the Windows personal finance software market in 1993. Facing an entrenched market leader like Intuit that even Microsoft had been unable to dislodge, the company realized that it could not just offer a me-too product. So its Simply Money arrived with a splash, free to one and all, no limits on quantities. It was such a novel idea that the offer received coverage in many news programs. Here was a company willing to literally give away the razor just to be able to sell blades (checks, forms, and other supplies) and the next razor (the upgrade to Version 2).

Simply Money arrived in the summer, a bad time for Intuit and Microsoft, both of whom were planning on fall releases. Neither had new versions ready to answer this surprise entry. Computer Associates swiftly announced that a million customers had requested and received the new software. Industry analyst Jesse Berst expressed the worry of many observers when he suggested that Computer

Associates might capture millions of new customers who had not yet become accustomed to a particular software package like Quicken. Intuit would have to respond with price cuts that would cost it dearly. Scott Cook was indeed concerned, and though he did not reveal his alarm publicly, within the company he sounded a full alert.

Ultimately the entry of Computer Associates turned out to pose anything but a threat to either Intuit or to Microsoft. More than two million copies were distributed, yet when it came time for customers to pay in order to upgrade to the next version, they behaved no differently from those who had never tried out Simply Money. Intuit's internal research uncovered a comfortingly tiny percentage of households that actually continued to use the software; Intuit's 60+ percent share of the market remained undiminished. The next year, Cook allowed himself the luxury of a few disparaging public remarks about his competition, referring to the "fair pricing" of Computer Associates's free software. He argued that two costs are associated with software —the initial price in dollars and the subsequent price in time spent using the software, setting it up, and either entering data in it or moving data from another finance program. Computer Associates's giveaway program and Microsoft's ensuing price-cutting experiments (offering its own Money at a price well below that of Quicken) failed to produce the desired gains in market share because they could only produce savings of the first kind. They could not reduce—in fact, they risked increasing—the price customers paid in terms of time invested. Microsoft was in no position to complain, however, about this effect. It knew very well as market leader in other application categories that customers tended to be a loyal lot.

In many ways, then, Intuit's dominance in personal finance software resembled Microsoft's dominance in other categories of software, which suggests that the industry is subject to dynamics that cannot be ascribed simply to any allegedly shady business practices of one particular company in Redmond, Washington, and of its billionaire chairman. Intuit's success also refutes the notion that Microsoft could wield its size, derived from the revenues from its lucrative operating system software business, to enter markets and crush smaller rivals at will.

Intuit's and Microsoft's histories would subsequently become even more entwined, as we shall see later. But here we observe that the early portion of their rivalry marks a milestone for Microsoft's evolution from an operating system and business applications software vendor to an aspiring multidivisional powerhouse deeply interested in the consumer market as well as the business market. But even as the consumer software market passed into adolescence, it was already being overshadowed in public consciousness by the Internet, an "overnight" phenomenon many years in the making.

Part Three

The Highway

Chapter 8

Preparations

INTELLECT IN AMERICA is resented as a kind of excellence, as a claim to distinction, as a challenge to egalitarianism, as a quality which almost certainly deprives a man or woman of the common touch.

Richard Hofstadter (1963)

Of the possible stories that are important parts of Microsoft's strategic positioning, the one that has received the least attention is how the research group within Microsoft came into existence. Perhaps it is because critics find it difficult to paint the creation of new knowledge in sinister hues.

Stock analysts in the 1980s noticed that Microsoft, though not the largest software company, led the industry in percentage of revenues that it invested in research and development. Even when Microsoft's growth seemed to slow, research and development were protected. In 1986, for example, more than one-fourth of all new hires were assigned to R&D projects. This was a far greater portion than was assigned at Lotus Development and Ashton-Tate, then larger rivals that could more easily afford to divert revenues from ongoing operations into riskier new projects. Not only did Microsoft spend proportionately more on R&D, it also spent its money more astutely—the fruits of its emphasis on recruiting the right kind of smarts. The greater efficiency in R&D spending could be quantified: for every dollar spent from 1987 through 1990 to create or acquire products, Microsoft in 1991 received $4.80 in sales, compared to the $2.35 Lotus received.

As remarkable as Microsoft's harvest from its early R&D investment was, the very category R&D was a misnomer. Microsoft, like its software company counterparts, in those years invested exclusively in the development of new products, not in basic research—a lot of D but no R. But here is where Gates's interest in expanding Microsoft's reach into the home during the later 1980s would prove to be the crucial link between the old Microsoft, peddling the plumbing of an operating system to computer manufacturers, and the newer ubiquitous one, hawking software products for every conceivable use, including on the Internet.

The history of personal computers up until the late 1980s had been, in many ways, the story of moving ideas that had been proven on big computers over to little ones. When the personal computer industry began to devise unique innovations—there was no big-computer predecessor to the graphical screen of a Macintosh or a Windows machine—the storehouse of big-computer technology ready for adaptation no longer seemed an inexhaustible resource. In a speech given at the personal computer industry's 1990 Comdex conference, Gates gathered various ideas about the immediate future that had been percolating up through the company and attempted to wrap them into a coherent vision, which he dubbed "Information at Your Fingertips." Despite the efforts of the public relations staff, the phrase "Information at Your Fingertips" did not stick afterward, but Gates's speech did anticipate the reality of the World Wide Web, which had not yet been invented. He forecast that every kind of imaginable information would soon reside in digital form on networks—and would be easy to find via software that was radically easier to use than present software.

One of the subthemes of Gates's 1990 talk was "Home Computers Will Cause Markets to Explode." Because software for home use would "differ dramatically from the PC applications we use in the office today," new software technology would have to be invented to make online information readily accessible to nonexperts. Gates wrote in an internal memo: "Many of the changes that will take place in PCs can be anticipated (performance, memory, screens, motion video) . . . Other changes like linguistics, reasoning, voice recognition, or learning are harder to anticipate." To help the company learn, he thought Microsoft needed to work closely with Japan's consumer electronics giants like Sony and Matsushita and to strengthen its ties to the academic research community. But above all, he realized that Microsoft needed to undertake basic *research* that did not necessarily have an immediate payoff but would ensure that as the company brought personal computers into unfamiliar areas, requiring solutions to hitherto unsolved technical problems, its larder would remain properly stocked with the necessary scientific understanding.

When Gates decided in 1991 to establish a true research group, he did not require the consent of Microsoft's board, but he assembled a detailed rationale nevertheless. Gates put Nathan Myhrvold, the astrophysicist-programmer-entrepreneur who had joined Microsoft in 1986, to work on a memo that would explain the decision to the board. Gates once pointed out that Myhrvold, with a satchel filled with degrees, had worked for only three bosses: Stephen Hawking, the academic who held the Isaac Newton chair at Cambridge; Steve Ballmer, who had finished Harvard but not the Stanford MBA program and now headed Microsoft's operating systems division; and himself, Harvard's most famous nongraduate. Each boss had less formal education and a higher net worth than the preceding one. (No educator should let students derive a generalization from this happenstance!) The Gates-Myhrvold collaboration is interesting because it served as an experiment in applying high intellectual candle-power to business ends, without bowing to American culture's totemic Mr. Average, possessor of the "common touch."

Myhrvold's polymath capabilities were apparent enough in his unusual curriculum vitae, but there was nothing necessarily predictable about his rise from a technologist who was most familiar with graphics and operating systems to the position of grand strategist. The idea of forming a research group originated in technical work Myhrvold did deep in the bowels of the operating systems group, where an ongoing civil war raged over which of two models should be used in the next generation of operating systems. Myhrvold supported a minority position that appeared to conflict with the design recommended by Intel, the manufacturer of the chips on which the system would run. When the design decision was put up for a vote, on two occasions the Intel position prevailed. Myhrvold then organized a small group to conduct original research that would demonstrate the feasibility of the alternative approach. With the research, Myhrvold was able to convince the group to overturn their previous decision and adopt what was then an unorthodox design, but one that enabled the resulting operating system to be portable to non-Intel chips, too. Having research results in hand had proven helpful in settling the dispute.

When Myhrvold drafted the memo that called for spending $10 million annually for a permanent staff of full-time researchers, the scale of the proposed research group was quite different from a handful of people already on staff diverted to pursue an occasional ad hoc project. He argued that one reason Microsoft had to invest a significant sum was to convey the message of strong corporate commitment that the best researchers would demand as a condition of employment. Also, instead of dispersing researchers throughout the company, they had to be grouped together to create the right atmosphere. "A product group which is working on a deadline and is out to nuke the competition is just a lot different than a research group, no matter how driven and focused the researchers are."

Separating the researchers from the development groups raised the specter, however, of the ghosts of Xerox Palo Alto Research Center, IBM's Watson Research Center, and Apple's Advanced Technology group, all of which had become best known for their failure to translate brilliant research results into commercial benefits for their parent companies. In these cases, Myhrvold pointed out, general management issues rather than the research efforts, were to blame. Spectacular failures occur in other aspects of business, too—in marketing, advertising, finance—but instances of mismanagement do not prove that management must inherently act foolishly.

Xerox was the most well known sponsor of computer-related research that had failed to profit from the work of its own scientists. Xerox engaged in research that it had no business in—literally. Not only was Xerox attempting path-breaking research in pursuit of breakthroughs *and* shepherding the results quickly into commercial products, it also had to learn an entirely new business from scratch, which doomed the effort from the start. The results were the infamous fumbling-of-the-future at Xerox PARC and a multi-hundred-million-dollar write-off when Xerox purchased Computer Sciences Corporation. Microsoft was different. It was a software company that would work only on software-related research. The computer industry had no precedent for such a tight focus that matched the corporate sponsor's business. When IBM and Apple carried out software-related research, whether individually or collaboratively, commercialization of the results was hampered by the inattention or outright hostility of the companies' hardware divisions, which wielded decisive power because they brought in the majority of revenues. At Microsoft, software would not have to yield to a politically potent nonsoftware constituency.

When Microsoft publicly announced the establishment of a research-only group, Gates was critical of his own company's past record as well as the rest of the software industry when he said that Microsoft until that point "had gotten away without funding any internal or external research." There would have to be investment in the present if there were to be "incredible profits in the future." Praising Microsoft as the first in the software industry to invest in original research and no longer rely on "borrowing ideas as a stand-in for research," *Infoworld*'s Stewart Alsop issued a challenge to other software companies to launch similar initiatives. These invitations to invest in basic research were ignored. To the extent that Microsoft's enviable competitive position today can be credited to strategic moves enabled by research-related investments that began in 1991, could we not argue that Microsoft's rivals have only themselves to blame for their stinginess?

Retrospect also permits us to see how Microsoft's industry enemies were ready to attack, no matter what course the company chose. If it did not invest in research, it would have been criticized for lack of innovation. When it did invest in three linguistics specialists hired away from IBM, Microsoft was viewed as behaving just as unscrupulously as the United States government had in employing Hitler's rocket scientists in the late 1940s. Perhaps if other software companies had by then taken the lead in funding research, Microsoft's decision would not have excited such strong emotions. Its plan called for hiring 30 people the first year—hardly an earth-shaking number when Microsoft's head count at the end of that year would be almost 12,000. Nor was the $10 million planned for 1992 such a large sum when placed against the company's revenue of $2.8 billion for that fiscal year.

We might speculate that it was not the body count nor the dollars per se that outside critics regarded as significant—rather, it was the purity of intellectual enterprise to which these resources would be devoted. The addition of 30 sales representatives in the field would not have attracted a flicker of attention, but 30 full-time scientists was another matter. Because the world of science seems so remote for most Americans, the general public's overexcited imaginations conjured sinister, though necessarily vague, outcomes. Reality was innocuous and esoteric. Myhrvold envisioned that the research group would initially focus on the linguistics-related work in "natural language," which ideally would permit computer users to dispense entirely with a keyboard and talk naturally to the machines. Another target was "real-time kernel support for multimedia," that is, writing code for the innards of the operating system that would permit the streams of data from audio and video sources to process smoothly. "Hypertext and information structure," a subdomain in computer science that focused on how best to organize masses of data, was also of interest.

Both Gates and Myhrvold liked to say that they actually hoped that not all the research turned out well, because if it did, the research projects undertaken would not have been sufficiently venturesome and would not fulfill the charter to create entirely new knowledge. Whether successful or not, if Myhrvold's "Advanced Technology" group, as it was called, had remained focused on its original agenda, the group's influence on the company and Myhrvold's on the chairman would probably have been minor. But it was just as the Advanced Technology group was assembling its researchers that the history of technology seemed to have suddenly advanced to a microprocessor-based world of computers on the verge of connecting everything and everybody via the lingua franca of digital bits. In 1993, the information highway was the cover story of countless newsmagazines and Sunday supplements, but it was in 1992 that planning for the future highway began in earnest at Microsoft, which soon led to a greatly expanded charter for the researchers. If successful, the fruits of Microsoft's research would be measured by ordinary consumers, not computer scientists.

The precipitating event was Gates's trip to Japan to meet with the chairman of the consumer electronics giant Matsushita, which expressed an interest in working with Microsoft on home automation. When Gates returned, he asked Myhrvold what in Microsoft's cupboard would be pertinent. The answer was—nothing. But Myhrvold knew that Greg Riker (whom we encountered briefly in the story of Encarta's creation) had been outfitting his own home with some automation devices as a hobby, not as a formal project. Myhrvold gave Riker three weeks to prepare a presentation for Matsushita on Microsoft's home automation "strategy."

When Myhrvold asked what Riker wanted to call the new group that would be formed within Advanced Technology with Riker as its head, Riker said, "Advanced *Consumer* Technology." Thus was born a project that would soon grow far larger than the 24 people whom Riker initially recruited. It also immediately changed the character of Myhrvold's Advanced Technology group. Now, instead of being almost exclusively a group of researchers pursuing pure research for a better understanding of basic principles, Advanced Technology would also house the initial development of entirely new products for the unfolding digital world. Advanced Consumer Technology sat in the middle, between the mundane concerns of the Word developers working on their nth release on the one hand and the arcane agenda of the computer linguistics researchers on the other. Myhrvold distinguished the two kinds of activities for which Advanced Technology would now be responsible: "Research" was attempting to do something that no one other than you thinks is possible, and "advanced" development is doing something that others agree is theoretically possible but has not been built before.

Riker's home automation project fit neatly into this definition of advanced development. Fiddling with off-the-shelf microcontrollers that could control a home's TV, VCR, stereo—and, yes, the all-important toaster—the first developers in the Advanced Consumer Technology group worked on adapting existing technology to allow the various home appliances to communicate with each other without special wiring. The existing electrical wiring in a house could serve as one conduit for moving signals among appliances; the infrared used in television remote controls was another. The group constructed a prototype of a gizmo that would sit atop a television set, run a modified version of Windows, and permit easy programming of a VCR if a listing of upcoming programs somehow could be downloaded into the box. When Microsoft asked cable companies such as Tele-Communications Inc. and Time Warner whether they would be able to spare bandwidth in their cable systems to provide such listings, the cable companies said that one-way downloading was easy—in fact, the same cable could send information in the opposite direction, too. The idea that television sets could serve as the terminus of a two-way electronic connection was beguiling, and Advanced Consumer Technology's ambitions expanded as fast as such new technical possibilities revealed themselves. Advanced Technology's annual budget soon jumped to $150 million, far larger than the $10 million planned originally.

The expansion in charter, budget, and head count could be accomplished speedily because, organizationally, the decision-making process could not have been more streamlined. Anyone who wanted to embark on a new project had only to convince Myhrvold of its merits, and Myhrvold had only to convince Gates. So, essentially, the assent of only two people was necessary, and neither needed the technical esoterica to be translated. Microsoft employees regarded Gates's grasp of technical details as a major competitive advantage over rival software companies. Most rivals were headed by nontechnical chief executive officers who were trying to ride the "wave" of technological change all but blind, dependent on their technical staff yelling directions from the beach—Go left! Go right!

The Advanced Consumer Technology wing grew quickly for another reason. Myhrvold and Gates were convinced that Microsoft's brightest opportunities would be in entirely new domains that would open up as the Information Highway came into being, a conviction bolstered by Myhrvold's strategy memos that blended history, technology, business—and, occasionally, physics. For Myhrvold, predicting what the future would bring required understanding general principles, the "dynamics" that would shape the course of future events. Astronomy and predicting the future were similar in that in both cases "a good controlled experiment is hard to do." By necessity, then, he felt he had no choice but to look to the past to discern underlying dynamics.

Unlike Gates, Myhrvold had no problem with looking in the "rear-view mirror." Prior to the Information Highway mania, Myhrvold had rummaged around in the period when America's industrial age was dawning, and had derived the following conclusions. A few individuals saw the significance of an impending change in the dominant economic paradigm created by new technology before the majority caught on. Those who saw the opportunity first and could risk significant quantities of capital to be in an advantageous position for the shift became, then, the principal beneficiaries of the economic changes. Strong individuals who single-handedly controlled the levers of power in business organizations could move much more quickly than large, consensus-driven organizations, which were slowed by weak foresight, cumbersome decision making, or reluctance to discard the existing paradigm and take a chance on the new. The business rules that worked well in one era were not serviceable in the next, and in the absence of clear "rules of the road," it was individuals who forsook caution and plunged ahead who did the best in the transitional periods of uncertainty.

The advent of entirely new industries—the railroad, steel, oil, and motion picture industries, for example—all brought to the fore individuals who rode their early bets to fame and fortune. (Myhrvold, Gates, Ballmer, and sometimes, it seems, everyone else at Microsoft are much attached to the motif of placing "bets.") The winners would have many labels: "magnates," "tycoons," "industrialists," and of course, the unflattering "robber barons." In Myhrvold's mind, the stigma attached to robber barons reflected more than just the jealousy of those who had not had the foresight to anticipate technological and resulting economic change. It also represented the unfair way society used rules formulated later to judge retroactively a budding industry in the days before it had time to even take shape, never mind agree to any rules. Myhrvold told Gates that the age of digital information would resemble the early periods of the other industries, and consequently they should be prepared to encounter swashbucklers—and to expect to be accused of being robber barons, too. This prediction was prepared *before* John Malone and Rupert Murdoch knocked on Microsoft's door, and before Gates himself became the most sought-after quarry of Justice Department antitrust lawyers in Washington, D.C.

U.S. historians themselves no more unanimously agree about late nineteenth and early twentieth-century industrial history than they do about other fields. Revisionist interpretations of figures who formerly were viewed as the most villainous names of that era appear now in scholarship. Thus Myhrvold's interpretation of early industrial history cannot be dismissed out of hand, even if it seems blithely uncritical and not just a little self-serving. However, I do have cavils: the accused "robber barons" did not operate in a vacuum without rules—they flouted contemporary laws that were anything but ambiguous. Rather than offer blanket amnesty to all early industrialists, assuming that their canny willingness to bet heavily on new business opportunities is the only salient criterion for judgment, a more defensible line would be to note the critical ways in which Microsoft's rise to power does *not* resemble the patterns of a U.S. Steel or Standard Oil in the past. But Myhrvold's "Robber Barons of the Information Age" was an early, never-completed memo, a venture in speculative thought while visiting the attic of the past. His historical analysis grew more sophisticated the more thought he gave to possible parallels between the present and the past.

"Road Kill on the Information Highway," a lengthy memo that Myhrvold wrote in the fall of 1993, brilliantly combined an expert's familiarity with present technology and a more careful reading of past business to predict in detail how digital networks would create upheaval for many industries, personal computers included. In the best of Microsoft tradition, the paper was as hard on the home company as on anyone else. He began with apostasy: The "PC revolution" had not really been much of a revolution—word processing software had replaced typewriters and spreadsheet software had replaced the pads of multicolumned paper, but Myhrvold asked, "How radical can a revolution be if its rallying cry (at least implicitly) is 'Death to Columnar Pads!'?"

The real revolution would come when industries that had not yet experienced the vertigo-inducing pace of exponential change were caught up in the same whirlwind the personal computer industry had experienced from its inception. Telecommunication services; telecom equipment manufacturers; banks and financial services; brokerages; book, magazine, and newspaper publishers; television broadcasters; and Hollywood would all be affected. For each, Myhrvold spelled out the business implications of impending technical change, which would be enabled by another millionfold improvement in semiconductor technology that would follow the millionfold improvement of the preceding twenty years.

Not all industries were handed tickets to doom. For example, book publishing seemed to Myhrvold to be the best off among all print-based media (book authors of the world, rejoice!), and his reasoning offers a sample of the analytic technique used in the paper. Unlike most other media such as magazines and newspapers, books were not dependent on advertising and thus would be much less vulnerable to the diversion of advertising dollars when the information highway became a popular means of communication. Nor did readers of printed works derive much benefit if the contents of books were converted into digital form. Other than reference works, books did not need to have their contents mapped with computer-aided indexes. Furthermore, the tactile pleasures of entering a literary world from a printed page and following the author's trail from beginning to end would remain captivating. Newspapers, on the other hand, relied heavily on advertising revenue and thus faced a grave threat. Classified advertising, which provides 50 to 80 percent of many newspapers' revenue, could disappear because an online medium offered potentially a cheaper, faster way for sellers and buyers to find each other. Even if online services did not compete directly with newspapers' editorial content, they could greatly harm the source of revenue that paid the salaries of editors and reporters.

Why should Microsoft take an interest in the fate of these other industries? Myhrvold impishly predicted that "our own industry is also doomed, and will be one of the more significant carcasses by the side of the information highway." Personal computers would not literally disappear—mainframes and minicomputers had not disappeared, either. But like its older siblings, the personal computer would soon miss the greatest growth opportunities, which Myhrvold predicted would be found in products and services that were tied to the highway, not on office desktops. And the technical requirements for computers placed on the highway were different from those for personal computers. The new era would need machines that could handle video-on-demand, video telephony (or picture phones), 3-D games, and entirely new categories of software. Microsoft should not complacently assume that dominance in the PC age would lead to dominance in the information highway age. History, in the examples of the former heavyweight champions in the mainframe and minicomputer eras, showed the folly of such assumptions.

As Myhrvold refined his view of the big picture in subsequent memos, he concluded that Microsoft, in addition to its internal investments in Advanced Technology and elsewhere in the company, should look for external investment opportunities that would help position it for the age of the highway. In March 1994, Myhrvold presented Gates with a long list of reasons for breaking company tradition and more aggressively investing outside of the company. For starters, Myhrvold pointed to the embarrassingly large kitty of cash that the company was sitting on: $2.5 billion, and growing by $100 million a month. This showed, Myhrvold said, "how non-capital-intensive the software business is." Clearly, Microsoft was unable to find sufficient uses for that capital within its own campus. Microsoft needed to invest elsewhere to ensure that its software would not be shut out from a highway that had many different contributing components.

The business model that had served Microsoft so well in the past—hiring a few more smart people and putting them to work writing software—would not fit the new circumstances of a market that was fragmented into many separate, though interdependent, pieces. Again, Myhrvold's interest in history was influential. He worried that someone would attempt to compete with Microsoft "by doing what Sloan did for cars and create a General Motors equivalent (to our Ford, I guess) by accumulating our various competitors." GM was not a singular example, either—had not U.S. Steel and AT&T been built by acquisition-hungry empire builders? The only reason the pattern seemed not to have been repeated in the personal computer industry yet was that the "difficult" personalities of Microsoft's rivals had not yet figured out how to cooperate, and software companies by their nature did best when technical leadership was strong and coherent. The rise of a new industry based on an information highway, which would require the assemblage of many disparate parts, would better lend itself to empire builders. Myhrvold saw Microsoft as having two basic options: it could either "stay pure and take on the world," or it could defensively build a strong financial camp of its own partners.

We might say that 1993 was a watershed year for Microsoft in that for the first time, when the company looked to the future, its leading rivals were no longer the then much smaller software companies like a Lotus (compared to Microsoft's $3.8 billion in revenue in 1993, Lotus's was $981 million) or an even smaller Borland ($394 million). Instead its rivals were similarly sized cable-TV companies like TCI ($4.1 billion), much larger regional telephone companies like Bell

Atlantic ($12.9 billion), entertainment conglomerates like Time Warner ($14.5 billion), and even the giant that dwarfed everyone else, AT&T ($67 billion).

Myhrvold, the scientist, was thrust into a new role: Myhrvold, the negotiator. Media companies, cable companies, every Baby Bell, and every major Hollywood studio met with him to talk about the digital future and the possibilities of working with Microsoft. Michael Ovitz and his Creative Artists Agency, who a year earlier would not have had the slightest interest in spending time with computer geeks, now pressed Myhrvold and Gates about possible collaborative projects. Entertainment luminaries such as Robert DeNiro and Steve Martin had to have lunch with Microsoft's research head. Vice-president Al Gore, the person who claimed to have coined the phrase "information superhighway" back in 1978, also insisted on getting together.

As the parade of interested parties made its way to Redmond, the continuing centrality of software in the future, when disparate industries converged and computing became truly ubiquitous, was confirmed with the arrival of each new contingent. Myhrvold was not shy about counseling Gates to think big: Microsoft had the cash, the technical expertise, and a vision of new digital possibilities. History suggested that perhaps Microsoft was in an even better position to create an empire on the highway compared to the empire builders of a century ago. Microsoft's technical expertise could protect it from the fatal glitches to which rivals that were not steeped in the technology would be prey. "J.P. Morgan didn't really have to understand the process of steel-making very deeply to create U.S. Steel," Myhrvold reminded Gates, and Andrew Carnegie, who did know the technology, retired when the corporation was formed. "Would-be Morgans of the information highway may find that there are plenty of technical gotchas which give folks like us the edge."

Myhrvold also emphasized, edge or no, Microsoft would not be able to single-handedly create an empire on the highway, a place whose dynamics differed from those Microsoft had mastered in the era of desktop computing. Microsoft would have to enter into joint ventures and other partnerships in earnest. But it could not be indiscriminate in its haste. History had lessons to teach here, too. IBM, which seemed quite eager to enter into as many deals as possible, had recently reviewed its investment portfolio, Myhrvold had heard. The present value of IBM's $3.3 billion investment in joint ventures and other external investments during the course of the previous ten years was about $35 million. This was a pointed lesson in how *not* to go about expanding a web of technology partners.

John Malone's TCI, on the other hand, seemed to have developed an efficient partnering system without peer. It was said to have produced one deal every five days, year in, year out, for over a decade—and without a large staff to investigate prospective investments and negotiate the details. Myhrvold wanted Microsoft to study this lean model. As matters then stood, Microsoft would never be able to make a dent in its bulging cash reserves because a fresh $100 million in retained earnings was deposited in the corporate treasury each month. Yet it took far longer than a month to negotiate a $100 million deal. Opportunities of all sizes would present themselves, and of course it would take much longer to close ten $10 million deals than one $100 million whopper. But then again, if Microsoft were to restrict itself to a handful of giant deals, it would miss smaller companies and other ventures that might yield greater strategic value in the long run.

That Microsoft's chief scientist would be mulling over such questions tells us much about the inseparability of the business and technical issues. Microsoft's tradition, set by Gates, eschewed the notion that the business side could be handled by one set of executives, while the technical side would be handled by others. Everyone at the company was expected to keep both business and technical considerations in mind simultaneously. With the promotion of technical people who had been hired originally for their scientific and technical training and talents to positions of management, Microsoft's success as a company appears to refute the model of nontechnical management, with generic MBAs who worked effectively in any corporate environment. The Microsoft credo said that in a high-technology industry, managers, senior as well as junior, had to be steeped in the technology that was the basis of the business. How well Microsoft would succeed in the transition to network-centered computing in the greatly enlarged world of entertainment, publishing, telecommunications, consumer electronics, and other converging industries would to no small extent be determined by how well its technical elite understood and worked with representatives from industries formerly far afield from personal computing.

Aside from a historical sensibility, Myhrvold had another asset unrelated to his technical expertise: a sense of humor. When he took his family on a vacation to Montana in his newly purchased Hummer—the civilian version of the wide, strange-looking military jeep seen in the televised coverage of the Gulf War, and whose price, incidentally, is about $75,000 for a four-door model—he was asked at gas stations and roadside cafés "about how much 'mudding,' 'huntin', and 'haulin' I did, and had to confess that while I didn't actively pursue these endeavors, I did do quite a lot of e-mailin'." His response brought some dismay to the faces of his Montana hosts. He reflected in a letter to colleagues about his trip, "I'm sure that many of these folks went away wondering what sort of karmic snafu led to somebody like me having a Hummer." In fact, at that time Myhrvold was exploring interactive television as the next place for Microsoft to broaden its reach. That effort would place the technical cognoscenti into the unfamiliar terrain of popular culture. The go-anywhere Hummer works well as a metaphor in this picture.

Chapter 9

PCs Versus TVs

*T*HE MERCHANT CAN SIT IN HIS HOME *and by utilizing this unique telephone see the interior of his store and watch the conduct of his clerks during his absence. Deaf mutes can carry on a conversation in the sign language over the tele-vue and women can do their shopping by means of the in-strument. From this it is only a step to the time when a physi-cian will use the televue to scrutinize a patient's tongue at long distance and then prescribe the necessary medicine over the wire.*

E. M. Rotherie, "Seeing Through the Telephone" (1906)

IF A KID IS ADDICTED to a personal computer, I think that's far better than watching TV, because at least his mind is making choices. I'm not one of these people who hates TV, but I don't think it exercises your mind much. I don't happen to own one.

Bill Gates (1986)

In a culture infatuated with television, Bill Gates's famous preference for reading in place of watching television has been singular. His avoidance of television is a subject that interviewers have returned to repeatedly over the years. Apparently they refuse to believe Gates's heretical rejection of the central icon of popular culture. In 1985, he confessed to the public his sordid secret that he preferred to spend time thinking about how to instill artificial intelligence into computers—"how can we make these stupid machines learn"—and he believed that owning a television set would present a temptation to waste time. Watching educational videotapes, such as the late Richard Feynman's physics lectures, was an intellectually profitable way of using a television set, but when Gates went to purchase a VCR and a stripped-down television monitor without a tuner to pull in broadcast signals, he had a hard time finding a playback-only VCR.

The purity of his intention to keep television's pernicious influence out of his own home was accompanied by his wish to appear normal to the statistically average American who imbibed more than seven hours a day of television. Gates earnestly told a *Playboy* interviewer in 1994 that he watched television when he was away from his home, for example, in hotel rooms. His refusal to have a television set in his own home was not a religious code, never to be broken. It simply was a way to provide more time, as he put it, "to read." How else would he have the time to read the week's *Economist* cover to cover? He also knew that most Americans did not share this concern.

Thus how curious it is that the course of contemporary business history would bring Bill Gates, of all people, to the threshold of the television world—or perhaps it was television that came to the threshold of Microsoft. It was hard to tell who was where in the fevered cross-industry groping among players in 1992 and 1993. Microsoft saw the possibility of convergence—or direct competition—between personal computers and television sets when Greg Riker's home automation project stumbled on the likelihood that signals could be sent upstream from the home on a cable television network as well as down. If the signals that would move downstream into the home and back up were digital instead of the existing analog broadcast signals, what sort of home appliance should be attached to the network? Should it be the traditional television set with a set-top box added that would process the digital bitstream, or a personal computer—the box that was designed *precisely* to process digital bits?

In either case, a television or PC substitute that could handle dual-direction signals appeared to be a fundamentally different creature from the traditional television set. To Gates, an interactive network wired into the home opened up exciting possibilities for television to become something other than a mind-dulling, time-wasting scourge. Instead of remaining a boob tube, TV could be converted into an information appliance, a boon to the realization of "Information at Your Fingertips"—and the fulfillment of Rotherie's turn-of-the-century fantasies of the interactive "televue."

The prospect of interactive television also opened up new business vistas that did not necessarily have anything to do with education or public service. At the annual all-company Microsoft meeting in 1992, for example, Gates prepared a demonstration of how interactive television would lead to new business opportunities for his company. Opening with a Michael Jackson video on a computer screen, he jokingly apologized, "I can't say I'm an expert on this, but they tell me that's what TV's like." He then clicked on accompanying buttons to supposedly send e-mail to the artist, order a compact disc, purchase concert tickets, and display the text of the lyrics of whatever song was playing. An ordinary PC would not be able to provide these capabilities, but what should an enhanced PC that could play full-screen video be called? Gates did not want to call it a PC, fearing that the general public would jump to the conclusion that it was as hard to use as conventional personal computers. But to call it a TV would be inaccurate, too, because it would not convey the new machine's ability to store the user's preferences, to capture and resend videos, to perform any of the other new services. For want of a better term, Gates initially spoke of the yet-to-be-built machine as a "TV/PC."

Nathan Myhrvold had begun thinking about the possibilities of a TV-PC fusion—what he initially called the "Video PC"—as development work on high-definition television in the United States and Japan proceeded, hastening the shift from analog to digital. In September 1991, Myhrvold presented Gates with a long technical memo that laid out the necessary steps for bringing Video PCs into being. One of Myhrvold's key points was that the machines had to be connected to a high-speed network that provided point-to-point communication, meaning that any given machine could send signals both to and from any other machine. This is in contrast to the broadcast model (sending the same programs to all television sets) that cable companies perpetuated. Reviving the old images of the "televue," then, would not be inappropriate. The Video PC would actually have more in common, technically speaking, with a videophone than it would with a traditional television set because mass programs like movies would now be delivered individually. If thousands of users requested the same movie but at slightly different times, each household would need to receive its very own stream of video bits.

Measured in terms of the volume of bits transferred or the sophistication of digital switches needed to send data streams to the appropriate households, a future Video PC network would be enormously complex, and its various components would be difficult to harness harmoniously. In 1992, Myhrvold and Gates set out to recruit someone to head the development of interactive television software. The person they settled on, Craig Mundie, had a background in minicomputer design and most recently had worked for a minicomputer company that had switched to producing massively parallel supercomputers.

Supercomputing? What branch of computing could be more dissimilar to personal computing? Actually Mundie viewed his supercomputing experience as useful because it allowed him to think about stubborn computing problems without considering cost. With the relentless progress of Moore's Law permitting tomorrow's networks of personal computers to marshal the computing horsepower of supercomputers today, an outlook shaped by supercomputing allowed Microsoft to plan ambitiously for the future of personal computers. A city of individual households with Video PCs connected to giant central servers would resemble a supercomputer spread out over the urban landscape.

Myhrvold and Gates's recruitment of Mundie provides some additional insight into Microsoft's search for smarts. Mundie had been the CEO of Alliant, a company that he had co-founded in 1982 and had helped steer into massively parallel computing (in which hundreds or even thousands of microprocessors were harnessed in a single machine) before the company ran out of cash and filed for bankruptcy in 1992. Myhrvold was impressed with Mundie's technical command of his and his competitors' machines, even though his most recent responsibilities at Alliant had been those of an executive, not of the software developer who had once worked on parallelizing FORTRAN compilers. Myhrvold also was surprised and delighted that Mundie, even as CEO, liked to get his hands dirty and had recently ordered components out of *Computer Shopper* to assemble his own personal computer.

In personal manner, Myhrvold and Mundie did not resemble each other at all: the former had a ready laugh, a voice that swooped upward, and the wire-rim glasses that an academic might select; the latter had the frame of a football lineman and the gruff, no-nonsense look and deep bass voice of a football coach. But Mundie had the right combination of supercomputer technical expertise, ability to articulate business models, and willingness to explore unfamiliar computer technology on his own time. And though coming from a CEO position, he was willing to accept the subordinate role in exchange for the opportunity to direct Microsoft's interactive television group. Mundie was attracted to Gates's proposition that Advanced Consumer Technology would be treated like a start-up. Gates would serve as the financier, and Gates and Myhrvold would form a de facto board of directors. The financial failure of Mundie's previous company did not bother Gates. Later he would say that he wished more of his own managers had experienced and learned from failure, and the recruitment of a crash-and-burn veteran like Mundie had been deliberate. Gates wrote in 1995, "I would hire ten more like him if I could."

When Mundie arrived at Microsoft, he and Myhrvold rethought the company's initial assumptions for launching an interactive TV project. The personal computer as we had come to know it would simply not do, as neither its hardware nor its software had been conceived with the special demands of video and sound—what technologists called "continuous media"—in mind. That is why the earlier retrofitting of multimedia capabilities had proven to be so slow, painful, expensive, and unsatisfactory in result. When Mundie began work at Microsoft, nothing larger than a two-inch square of video could be put on a $3000 Windows multimedia machine, but an $89 Radio Shack television could handle continuous pictures and sound without a problem. To make a Video PC commercially appealing, the price of a multimedia-equipped PC somehow would have to be reduced by 80 percent. This price reduction could not be accomplished by incremental improvements to the current PC. It would require what Mundie called "technology discontinuity": entirely new software for the new hardware, which would be incompatible with the old. It would be difficult to convince existing customers to accept the notion that their software investments should be discarded. The commercial triumph of Windows, an unwieldy software layer placed on top of DOS, and the consequently marginal place of the Macintosh, was testament to the populace's general aversion to "technology discontinuity." But, if one company could orchestrate a successful break with the past, the rewards for playing the leading role and controlling the standards would be proportionately large.

The possibility that Microsoft might lead the way did not go unnoticed when public discussion of the information highway and interactive television began. In March 1993, the entertainment trade paper *Variety* co-sponsored a conference to give industry representatives an opportunity to sketch out the "Big Picture," as the conference was called. At the conference, Myhrvold's public demonstration of the interactive choices that could be matched with a music video playing on a Video PC, like the one that Gates had shown to Microsoft employees the previous year, alarmed some observers who feared the power of "Windows on TV." The seemingly innocuous clicks that would order concert tickets or call up music lyrics were seen as portents of "Microsoft's brave new world."

The concern about Windows was misplaced, however. By now Microsoft had already tried to move a stripped-down version of Windows, called Modular Windows, to consumer electronics devices that were not personal computers—and learned painfully that the concept was flawed. The effort had begun the year before when Microsoft worked with Tandy to create a product that resembled a CD-ROM player endowed with a small amount of memory and designed to be connected to a household television set. It was not intended as a substitute for a personal computer, but rather as a defensive move to prevent Sega and Nintendo from posing a threat to PCs with less expensive machines. It would be priced around $600 initially, and $300 as soon as volume sales pushed costs down. The two partners worked as fast as they could to have their "VIS [no poetry here: Video Information System] Multimedia Player" ready for Christmas 1992. The plan was to use this as the inaugural demonstration of Modular Windows, which could subsequently serve as the software foundation for the set-top box that General Instruments, then the leading manufacturer of such boxes, agreed to produce for interactive television.

The Modular Windows project went awry right from the beginning. To keep costs down, Tandy reduced the amount of memory that the machine would have, despite Microsoft's argument that software capable of anything interesting would require more memory. Rob Glaser, who directed Microsoft's half of the partnership, begged Tandy to hold off releasing the machine until more testing could be done. But Christmas was bearing down, and Tandy insisted that the machines be on the shelves in time for the holiday season. When the new machines were introduced into stores, industry reporters had great fun enumerating their many shortcomings. Software developers' initial hesitancy to bet on the machines' success hardened—and consumers shunned this new offering.

This seemingly embarrassing flop for Microsoft's first foray into consumer electronics worked out well for the company in a curious way. The experience freed the company to rethink its strategy and decide to work on the more radical "technology-discontinuity" that the Advanced Consumer Technology group pushed, instead of tinkering with Modular Windows 2.0. By the fall of 1993, Bill Gates was working hard to assure the public that whatever software would eventually be adopted for interactive television, the screens would *not* be Windows—in fact, he said, "I guarantee you that it is not going to look like a computer." This was a chastened voice speaking. He now knew that simplicity in use was essential in consumer electronics and was not an attribute associated with Windows. To illustrate this, Microsoft's creative services group produced a humorous video in the form of a futuristic newsreel on the "digital *SU*-perhighway." It reviewed the "history" of the late twentieth century, when Bethlehem Steel had become Bethlehem Entertainment and Chrysler had changed its name to Chrysler Studios. The narrator mockingly intoned in the earnest baritone of a television announcer of the 1950s: "Say, Mom, Windows for Radio means more enjoyment and greater ease of use for the whole family!"

Most parts of Microsoft would probably not yet have been willing to create a humorous send-up of itself. The analytical frame of mind that Microsoft most prized did not have much patience with frivolity. It is precisely that difference in outlook that made the early encounters between the personal computer industry and the entertainment industry especially interesting. At the 1993 Big Picture conference, where Microsoft demonstrated interactive television to television and movie people, Nathan Myhrvold was struck by the repartee among the panelists. Though not actors and performers themselves, they were entertaining in ways that computer industry executives never were.

There, for example, was Peter Guber, then head of Sony Pictures, shouting at the top of his voice—even louder than Microsoft's Steve Ballmer—about his philosophy of film-making: If you "grab" people here [points to his head], it's going to be seen by ten people in an art-house theater. If you want a success, you gotta hit 'em here [points at crotch] or here [points at heart]. In the airplane business you'd better get it right every time, Guber explained, but not in his business, where failures were expected. In fact, huge, expensive disasters were just fine, as far as he was concerned, because someone who failed in a big way was destined some day to succeed in a big way. In summarizing his impressions of the conference, Myhrvold wrote Gates, "Interesting recruiting policy, huh? They don't seem to value the same kind of analytical approach that we do." The Hollywood approach to Craig Mundie's résumé perhaps would have been not to inquire about what Mundie had learned, but to discover how much money his previous company had lost.

The analytical faculties of Microsoft's senior managers were put to the test in negotiations with TCI, Time Warner, AT&T, Silicon Graphics, and other partners for an interactive television joint venture. The talks in the middle and latter portions of 1993 were not intended for public discussion, but a *New York Times* story leaked some details and provided the talks with a label, "Cablesoft." As soon as the story appeared, Rep. Edward Markey (D-MA), chairman of the House Subcommittee on Telecommunications and Finance, asked the Federal Communications Commission to investigate the rumored alliance and its power to create a "single, closed standard for television software." Markey's and other critics' immediate assumption—that a standard embraced by a number of parties was ipso facto inimical to consumer interests—was not addressed by public debate because the Cablesoft negotiations never culminated in an agreement.

Though the public may have thought of Microsoft as the 800-pound gorilla, a company like TCI was, in its own domain, a 1600-pound gorilla and was accustomed to demanding—and getting—equity stakes in its partners without having to guarantee that it would carry the partner's programs on its vast cable systems. TCI and

Time Warner insisted on a joint venture form of partnership with Microsoft that would give them half ownership, but their commitments to the project would have remained at their own option, whereas Microsoft's obligation to the project would have been iron-clad. Signing such a deal with such well-known partners was a tempting way to send the message that Microsoft was the odds-on favorite to establish the technical standards for interactive television, but it would have also set a precedent for ceding control and equity that would have caused endless problems when other partners—and there would have to be *many* other partners in this industry—asked for similar concessions. It was too early in the game to give up so much by mortgaging the future. Using the betting metaphor once again, Myhrvold likened the development of interactive television to a game of "500-card stud," and the present historical moment was very early and many cards remained to be dealt. Microsoft decided to pass on Cablesoft.

In 1993, other computer industry rivals announced field trials for interactive television software for 1994, but Microsoft was all too aware of the premature state of the system software that would be needed—Modular Windows would never do. The announcements of imminent field trials were followed as closely as a high-stakes horse race. In early 1994, industry handicappers, observing that the mysterious Cablesoft negotiations had failed, placed Microsoft at the back of the pack. Internally Myhrvold reminded Gates of the technical weaknesses and economic folly of the trials that Microsoft's rivals were announcing. Silicon Graphics, for example, had accepted a deal with Time Warner to prepare a system for trials in Orlando, Florida, that would cost $10,000 a household and whose hasty schedule was no more realistic for widespread adoption than its deployment cost. Externally Myhrvold sought to stem the public perception that Microsoft was already out of the race. He urged a look to the earliest history of personal computers, when there were a "million false starts" before more powerful machines superseded the earliest entrants. The interactive television market had not even begun—there was not a single customer yet. "Suggesting that it's all over is kind of crazy," he said. "By that standard, I guess TV was over in 1945."

The public seemed more interested in reading tote sheets than listening to history lessons, and the company that was making the most noise in claiming to have leaped beyond Microsoft in the interactive television game was Oracle. It posed a potent threat for several reasons. Like Microsoft, Oracle's earliest successes could be said to have come at IBM's expense. Although Oracle based its software for managing large databases on IBM's relational database research, its software was for minicomputers and workstations, brawnier machines than personal computers. Just as Microsoft had become the market leader in many categories of personal computer software, Oracle was the leader in its domain of database software and enjoyed annual revenues that were about half of Microsoft's. Oracle maintained that the problem of how to handle the files that would make up a library of digitized television programming was a database problem, and who knew databases better than they?

Oracle's personality as a company was shaped by its remaining founder, Larry Ellison. Like Gates, Ellison had reaped billions from the appreciation of his holdings of company shares. In fact, Ellison was the only software company billionaire who was not associated with Microsoft. The two men, Gates and Ellison, were often portrayed in the press as "aggressive," but worlds of difference exist within the shared label. There is aggression and then there is *aggression*, and I see the two men as more unalike than alike. An adopted child, Ellison likes to assume the role of a kid who grew up poor in Chicago's toughest neighborhoods but went on to earn advanced degrees from the University of Illinois and the University of Chicago. As drama, it's compelling; as autobiography, it's dubious. His adoptive sister has called attention to Ellison's taking liberties with the family's middle-class background, and university records show that Ellison never received the degrees that he claimed.

Gates's hunger for power, when viewed in isolation, is apparently insatiable. But it seems sedate in juxtaposition with Ellison's drive for growth at any cost, ignoring standard accounting practices or pushing software releases on customers well before the software was fully baked. By 1990, Oracle's sins caught up with it, and the company faced collapse. Its market capitalization fell from $3.7 billion to $700 million in a matter of weeks. Ellison defied calls to step down, brought in outside managers, and restored customer and investor confidence in the company. His timing was exquisite. Oracle was revived just in time to benefit from a then-beginning corporate exodus from mainframes to smaller computers that needed database software, which Ellison's company was in the perfect position to provide. Microsoft had never faced a near-death experience as Oracle had.

The aggressiveness that characterizes the Oracle salesforce in the field is also expressed physically in Ellison's own fitness preoccupations, which stand in contrast, again, to Gates's. Glorying in the adopted persona in which he, in his words, "lives on the edge" in his personal as well as business life, Ellison would need no prompting to recount in loving detail his injuries from his strenuous avocations. When surfing in Hawaii, he suffered a broken shoulder, neck, and three ribs, and punctured a lung, and when he took up bicycling for physical therapy to recuperate, another accident shattered an elbow. Thrice divorced, Ellison made his private life public by boasting of what friends said of him, that "as long as Stanford keeps turning out beautiful 23-year-old women, Larry will keep getting married." In contrast, Gates regards his private life as, indeed, private. Ellison seems to relish using his own private life as a way of making himself, and by default, his own company, more visible. Gates is famously indifferent to the clothes that he wears; Ellison, a fastidious dresser. The longer our list of differences gets, the more we might suspect that Ellison has crafted his persona to set off a contrast with Gates's. But most important of all differences, perhaps, is how the two men, who are the wealthiest pair of college drop-outs in history, regard intelligence. For Gates, smarts are to be sought after and prized without apology, but Ellison's philosophy is "Will is more important than intellect."

If Ellison had not come along, we would have had to invent him, not merely for the contrast in style that he brought to the competition, but also for his wholly different approach to delivering digital television. His approach was based not on personal computers but rather on the computers at the other end of the spectrum, supercomputers. Ellison just happened to own nCube, a new supercomputer company founded in 1990 whose machines were massively parallel systems. These systems were perfectly suited, Ellison insisted, for handling thousands of streams of bits for video-on-demand networks. If Microsoft, in hiring Craig Mundie, sought to create a "virtual" massively parallel supercomputer by harnessing the power of many personal computers, Oracle mocked the very notion that such a network could be an acceptable substitute for the real thing. In the fall of 1993, Ellison told the public that there was no need to wait for the uncertain results of Microsoft's private experiments in interactive television. Oracle's software, running on nCube's supercomputers, was already available for deployment: "It works. It's done." Other competitors were talking about field tests in 1994, but Ellison said his companies were ahead of everyone else and that 1994 would be the year of "serious mass rollout."

Larry Ellison said that many other people shared his vision of interactive digital television, but he admitted that not many shared his own optimistic view about the timing of its delivery to households on a mass scale. One skeptic was Bill Gates. It rankled Gates to hear Ellison go on and on at industry conferences, with journalists dutifully recording every word, calling Microsoft a no-show in the first interactive television trials. Ellison described Microsoft as representing the present, whereas Oracle represented the future.

Gates publicly professed no concern, and in informal chats with journalists, he would ask, what threat could Ellison pose to Microsoft? After all, Ellison had not written a Windows clone. The battle between Microsoft and Oracle was taking place on Ellison's home ground, not Gates's. But Gates did not mention that it was ground that Gates wanted to hold nevertheless, and in the game of "500-card stud" that he, Ellison, and many others had joined, a competitor like Ellison could make perception of a lead self-fulfilling. Myhrvold reported to Gates that an Oracle vice-president had earlier told him that Oracle's strategy was "to lie to some people to get them to write us some big checks and then hope we can deliver later," which might also describe the strategy that Ellison had used to build Oracle's core database business. If you delivered the goods in the end, it worked. Microsoft had to do something dramatic to counter Oracle's publicity offensive. Gates decided to let the press see Microsoft's research in progress.

In May 1994, Microsoft invited reporters to a demonstration of the interactive television technology that carried the code name "Tiger." To emphasize that the information highway was still under construction, the demonstration room was decorated with scaffolding, plastic yellow tape, and hard hats. Mundie proclaimed that an ordinary personal computer would be able to serve up 100 individual video streams and each stream could be manipulated like a VCR with pause, fast forward, rewind, and such. Tiger technology tied the sixteen PCs that were displayed for the demonstration into a "distributed" network permitting video-on-demand that would cost one-tenth that of rival technologies—like Oracle's supercomputer-based system. In a distributed system, all machines share the functionality that formerly had been the responsibility of a host machine. If the hard drive on a particular PC crashed, Tiger automatically switched to redundant drives on the other machines. Microsoft's new technology was a direct repudiation of the model Oracle was offering.

Microsoft hoped for three kinds of press coverage: *favorable* reports of the Tiger demonstration that would show Microsoft's radically different, promising approach to interactive television and quell industry speculation about Microsoft's absence from early trials; *cautioning* reports of a realistic timetable when a full system, of which Tiger was merely one piece, would be ready for release; and *approving* reports of the contribution Microsoft's research group had made to Tiger's development. Some observers went overboard, however, in interpreting the significance of the Tiger demonstration, and stock analysts became excited about the prospects for new revenue in the near future. David Readerman of Lehman Brothers, for example, predicted that Microsoft's interactive television business could bring in "as much as $2 billion over the next few years," a prediction that proved to be overly optimistic, to say the least.

Other reporters were more cautious in their assessment of what they had seen, and some properly noted that a demonstration of a few PCs in a laboratory was not necessarily an accurate indicator of what would happen when the system was actually tried in hundreds of thousands of homes in field tests. Gates himself was skeptical of what could be discovered in a field test of merely a few thousand households— very large numbers of participants would be needed to accurately gauge demand for new interactive services. Though Gates did not emphasize it, small-scale tests in a laboratory also could not duplicate the stresses that would be placed on the network in a real-world setting. In the absence of large-scale field tests, the stand-off between the Microsoft PC-based proposal for interactive television and the Oracle supercomputer-based proposal presented observers with a test of faith. It was impossible to know then which model would prove ultimately to be the most reliable and have the lowest cost.

The Tiger demonstration went smoothly, and Microsoft secured most of the publicity that it had sought. It was now included in the roster of contenders in the interactive television sweepstakes, but it had failed to get reporters to acknowledge the research effort that had made Tiger work. In hindsight, we can see that Gates's and Myhrvold's 1991 decision to establish an internal research group within Microsoft paid sizable dividends in this instance as well as others. Computer scientist Rich Rashid, recruited from Carnegie Mellon, headed the research group, an adjunct to the product development group. Rashid's team investigated cloudy technical questions and modeled in advance the behavior of each of Tiger's constituent components. This work permitted the system design to be tweaked before the machines were physically assembled. When it was time to build the first version, Tiger behaved exactly as the model had predicted.

After the public demonstration, Rashid asked one of the reporters about her impressions and was told that the demonstration was boring because nothing had gone wrong—it seemed suspiciously well rehearsed. The whole point of the design process, Rashid sought unsuccessfully to convince her, was precisely to ensure that nothing went wrong, and in fact the demonstration had not needed much rehearsing. But the reporter had seen only artificial staging in what Rashid viewed as the triumph of thoughtful prior design. Experience here, and elsewhere, taught Rashid that only stories that lent themselves to sports metaphors seemed to reach print. He recalled a story in an industry paper that used football helmets to represent computer companies on a graph showing who was "winning" and who was "losing"—which is just what everyone wanted to know now about interactive television.

The playing field for interactive television was actually quite small. Software for interactive television was going to be sold in a fundamentally different fashion from the way Microsoft peddled Excel or even Encarta. The sales would be to cable companies, not individual consumers, and that meant that the Tiger demonstration was intended to influence a very small set of prospective buyers. Unfavorable speculation in the industry press about Microsoft's prospects in this new area hurt Microsoft only indirectly. When cable company executives visited Redmond, they trotted out the rudest questions that they could pull from industry pundits who had discussed the competition in the interactive television business. In 1994, right after the Tiger demonstration, one columnist pointed out that it was hard to place faith in Larry Ellison's proposed system, given his own vested interests in nCube, the supercomputer company. But then again, he noted, few readers believed that Bill Gates "has your best interests at heart, either." Here, as in so many instances, Gates's negative public image affected Microsoft's attempts to move into newly opening domains of the digital world.

The contention between Gates and Ellison for the central place on the rostrum also revealed another test of the faithful: what consumer appliance would interactive television employ on the household end—a digital television or a personal computer? Originally Gates had thought the answer would be a hybrid box, but as time passed he had revised his thoughts and proposed the idea of a multiplicity of boxes around the house. One box large enough for several people to view simultaneously in a living room, for example, would be considered a programmable television; and another, smaller box sitting on a desktop in a den would be a programmable personal computer that also happened to receive interactive television. Sometimes Gates would declare himself an agnostic about which kind of box the public might most readily accept, and so too did Ellison occasionally.

The two men had too much at stake to maintain agnosticism on the future of computing, however, and their respective companies also put out different perspectives at times. Microsoft's Mundie would say that the future was going to be a PC-centric future, and the digital television set that would go in the living room would be a "subset" of the personal computer sitting in the den. Diametrically opposed to just such a future was Ellison's Oracle, which insisted that as an entertainment medium, personal computers had been a complete failure. An Oracle senior vice president in 1994 declared that "consumers like television and they don't like PCs." The different hardware choices also underlined the confrontation between two dissimilar models for computing. Gates criticized Oracle's "Media Server," the supercomputer specially designed to handle digitized video, as too specialized to be competitive with the cheaper, general-purpose machine, the personal computer. Ellison, in turn, took shots at the supposition that a network of personal computers could match the "graceful scale-ability" that would permit a cable company to expand from a small number of parallel processors to hundreds or thousands.

Gates's predictions that the arrival of interactive television would take a while proved more accurate than Ellison's overexcited whoop of joy that 1994 would be the year of mass rollout. Technical woes and high costs simply would not go away. By 1995, interactive television bliss seemed to be as distant as ever, and at the end of the year, the Time Warner trial in Orlando still had only 3500 customers. Bell Atlantic, which belatedly began its own trials late in 1995 among a few hundred households in New Jersey, estimated that the actual cost per household for full connections to its new network was $17,000. Microsoft kept its own initial trials extremely small in scale, involving only a few hundred employees and Redmond residents and out of the glare of publicity. Oracle, recently so fond of bombastic predictions about rapid rollout, grew uncharacteristically quiet about how its interactive television project was faring. But the most extraordinary aspect of the trials was how quickly public interest had deserted the subject. By the time the trials had begun, the public had become too impatient to wait for an eight-lane superhighway that clearly was a long way from completion. It instead became preoccupied with the rudimentary two-lane, version—online networks reached with modems.

Chapter 10

Toll Road

*B*ARRING UNFORESEEN OBSTACLES, *an on-line interactive computer service, provided commercially by an information utility, may be as commonplace by 2000 A.D. as telephone service is today. By 2000 A.D. man should have a much better comprehension of himself and his system, not because he will be innately any smarter than he is today, but because he will have learned to use imaginatively the most powerful amplifier of intelligence yet devised.*

Martin Greenberger, in *The Atlantic* (1964)

In 1964, when Martin Greenberger, an MIT professor of industrial management, addressed the issue of "The Computers of Tomorrow," he could have focused on technical aspects, just as many similarly titled articles that appear perennially in *Popular Science* and *Scientific American* have done. Greenberger's tack, which makes his essay especially noteworthy in retrospect, was to consider the implications for new business. He foresaw the commercial demand for a ubiquitous information network that used computers—what he called "an information utility." Applications such as medical information for hospitals and clinics, traffic control systems for municipalities, catalog shopping from terminals at home, online libraries accessible from home or office, and computer-assisted classroom instruction revealed the all-purpose nature of such a network.

Anticipating Nathan Myhrvolds's and Bill Gates's vision of a "Wallet PC" in *The Road Ahead* by thirty years, Greenberger

159

described a "money key" that could be inserted into terminals connected to the network that would eliminate the need for currency, checks, cash registers, sales slips, and even the making of change. The "utility" would earn revenue by providing product information, completing sales transactions, and marketing information about the consumers involved in those transactions. (No mention was made of the controversial nature of this latter possibility.)

If Greenberger's prediction about the timing of widely accessible information services ("by 2000 A.D.") seems to have been uncannily on the mark, it is because we have embraced the Internet as the framework for the ubiquitous network. By design, the Internet cannot be brought under any single authority (an aspect vexing to censorious governments everywhere), so Greenberger's idea that a single monolithic "information utility" would collect and dispense information seems highly unlikely. As for how exactly the commercial potential of an "information utility" will be realized, the jury still seems to be out. It is safe to say only that new business models will be required.

In the early 1990s, before the Internet emerged as the most accessible structure, Gates nevertheless clearly saw a change of major proportions looming ahead for the traditional software business, as soon as households were connected to a wide data highway—the fiber-optic–based broadband network capable of sending multi-megabits per second that Microsoft's Advanced Consumer Technology group was assuming for interactive television. The bits would fly over the network to desktop PCs, without needing to be pressed, packaged, and placed on a shelf at a computer store. On this point, Gates and Larry Ellison were in complete agreement. When "everyone is connected," Ellison declared in 1994, "the idea of putting software bits in a cardboard box is nonsense."

Gates was a realist. Though he was certain that the new technology would eventually catch on, he had to be cautious in predicting when it would come to pass. The agonizingly slow diffusion of CD-ROM, as we saw, could leave no lesson other than the importance of a conservative timetable. He also knew that an either/or duality—conventional software distributed via cardboard boxes versus interactive television distributed via broadband networks—was too simple. Before we could reach the Promised Land of broadband, an intermediate stage was necessary: online connections made with modems and ordinary telephone networks. The quantity of bits that could be transferred with such narrowband connections, using even the fastest available modems, was only a fraction of what broadband would be able to provide. But narrowband did have one compelling advantage over broadband: it was already here.

In the fall of 1992, at about the same time that he was hiring Craig Mundie and chartering Microsoft's Advanced Consumer Technology group to begin work on the broadband network project, Gates was giving thought to whether Microsoft should build a business based on a narrowband network. The 1992 musing resulted in the launching of an actual service, Microsoft Network, three years later when Windows 95 was released. During the intervening years, Gates and his lieutenants groped for a viable business model for the service, but the mere knowledge that Microsoft planned to enter the online services market was sufficient to excite competitors and the government. During Microsoft Network's prerelease preparation, outside observers saw in Microsoft a tank that would roll over whatever happened to be in its path. Microsoft managers, however, did not possess any such certainty about outcome; during the network's gestation, no path to a new online service seemed to lead to the prospect of profits.

True to form, Gates's strategy was to assign the project to a young employee on the basis of proven general intelligence, rather than experience in a narrowly defined corner of the computer industry. Gates had sent Rob Glaser and Nathan Myhrvold, for example, off on assignments to learn about new strategic problems—"go figure it out" was the injunction Gates would use—and then report back to him. The person who received this current assignment was Russ Siegelman, a thirty-year-old employee with the rapid-fire speech of someone you'd suspect had grown up in the Bronx, and who had joined Microsoft with a degree in physics from MIT and an MBA from Harvard.

Initially Siegelman had worked in the group that developed network software for offices, and most recently he had been a lead product manager for Windows for Workgroups, the variation of Windows that incorporated some networking capability into the operating system. His project was winding up, and when in November 1992 he spoke to Gates about possible new assignments, Gates offered him a position either as his personal technical assistant or, alternatively, as the person responsible for "figuring out" the online services business. Glaser, Myhrvold, someone in the Office group, and others within Microsoft had written separate memos about pieces of the problem. Gates wanted Siegelman to take a broad view of what Microsoft should do and report directly to him. Gates asked if he would be interested in such a project. The offer did not require lengthy contemplation.

At the onset, Siegelman discovered that Microsoft already had several projects underway that related to online services, but each was going its own way, without central coordination. For example, Siegelman found that the customer technical support group sponsored forums on CompuServe, the Consumer Division was looking into financial services, another division had arrived at a deal with AT&T, Glaser's group was looking into creating portable computing gizmos that could be tied into online services, and Myhrvold's Advanced Technology group was working on a Smart Phone. Not only were these scattered initiatives "opportunistic" and lacking in a common goal, they also lacked research into customer preferences and "usability," the basic hallmarks of what Siegelman called a "product-oriented approach." He anticipated that formulating a strategy to which the disparate Microsoft groups would agree would be difficult because the groups could not even settle on a business model. He urged that the question of "what business to enter" be kept separate from "how to enter."

As he began to look further into what online businesses Microsoft might enter, Siegelman did not initially regard offering an online business for consumers as an automatic given. The consumer market in January 1993 still seemed "risky." (This was just after the holiday season for which the promised Encarta had failed to appear; the hockey-stick effect of CD-ROM sales, fueled by consumer purchases, would not be seen until a year later.) Perhaps, Siegelman thought, Microsoft should enter the online business in a modest way, moving its technical support forums from CompuServe to its own service. In the existing arrangement, Microsoft earned $1 million a year for its share of the fees CompuServe collected, and CompuServe retained what Microsoft estimated to be $4 million for hosting Microsoft's forums. Bringing the forums under Microsoft's own control would mean Microsoft could capture CompuServe's portion of the fees, but the money to be made still seemed pathetically small. Where else could money-making opportunities be found?

Targeting the business user of online services was another possibility. In their favor, business-oriented online services could charge high prices because the data that customers sought produced a tangible pay-off in dollars and cents. But then again, this market was not expected to grow much, and it already had brisk, well-established competition. A general-purpose online service might be viable, but the existing service providers like CompuServe and America Online experienced a high rate of "churn"—almost as many customers dropped the service after an introductory period as signed up. Siegelman's own formative experience in the Microsoft networking group that unsuccessfully had challenged Novell's commanding lead had left him with a deep-seated aversion to challenging entrenched competition head-on. Therefore, calling on another chapter in Microsoft's history, Siegelman suggested that perhaps Microsoft should follow the example of the other online services and simply "gut it out," as Word had against WordPerfect, until Microsoft eventually won. Even in the best of all possible outcomes, it was not clear where a significant new business would appear. In January 1993, Siegelman advised Gates, "There are clearly a couple of multi-million dollar opportunities here, but are there any hundred-million-dollar opportunities?"

After consulting with Siegelman and Myhrvold and meeting with media companies, regional telephone companies, and existing online service providers like AOL, CompuServe, and Dow Jones, Gates recast the central question that had been troubling Siegelman. In a lengthy memo to the company's executive staff in early 1993, Gates removed the uncertainty about new blockbuster markets for online services by saying that Microsoft should be thinking in terms of services of the future when broadband networks were in place, not services of the present. Gates anticipated that pay-per-view or pay-per-song; long-distance calls, faxing, and video telephony that bypassed the local telephone company; software distribution; online shopping; personal and classified ads; travel reservations; ticketing; gambling; multiplayer virtual-reality games; telecourses offered by the best professors; medical information; government services such as license renewal and tax payment—"and everything else besides going to jail or taking your driving test can be done over the system." When millions of homes were connected, the business opportunities would be unlimited. And if Myhrvold's group successfully developed "digital money" stored in a "wallet PC," a PC or television set connected to the network could become a personal automated teller machine (echoes of Martin Greenberger's 1964 vision). Technology, standards, consumer preferences, regulations, and business alliances were all somewhat uncertain. Nevertheless, Gates declared that he had "enough confidence that a large market will develop to make this the priority for new business activity including a willingness to invest hundreds of millions of dollars if necessary."

When viewed from the height at which this enticing future was visible, a narrowband online service thus became one small element of a very big picture. It was a way to immediately "bootstrap," as Microsoft managers liked to say, the company into the service business while the high-speed network needed for broadband communication was being built. Some of the services that Gates had in mind for the future could be implemented without delay, and the underlying design of the services could anticipate the arrival of faster bandwidth. As a result, when it was time to shift to broadband, customers would not have to switch the software that they had become accustomed to using. Microsoft's entry into online services thus would not be a challenge to CompuServe, but an interim move to secure a placeholder and to gain experience that would be valuable when broadband networks and digital convergence would allow Microsoft to compete with the heavyweights who dominated entertainment, communications, and other industries. Where Siegelman, in considering narrowband online services only, had struggled to imagine new hundred-million-dollar businesses, Gates listed multi-billion-dollar businesses for each broad category of future online services. He assigned to the shopping and advertising category alone an estimated $100+ billion dollars of annual revenue. In many of the categories, a comparatively low-speed modem connection could put Microsoft in the information highway business immediately.

Siegelman was persuaded that Microsoft's entry in the online game would not be directly comparable to his earlier nightmarish experience when Microsoft entered the networking game. No single online services provider occupied the immovable position that Novell had held. Yet, as each month passed while Microsoft deliberated about how it should proceed, the subscriber rolls of AOL, CompuServe, and Prodigy kept growing, making the task of competing against them ever more daunting.

Having decided to enter online services, Microsoft faced the classic question of whether to make or buy: Should it start its own service from scratch or purchase one of the Big Three? Concerned that Microsoft was too far behind the others and could not afford the time to build its own service, Siegelman was inclined to purchase an existing provider. Prodigy was based on mainframes, pure anathema. CompuServe was technically more appealing but not for sale. AOL was the remaining possibility, but talks with its head, Steve Case, had failed to persuade him to consider selling. In May 1993, Siegelman told Gates that Microsoft didn't have much choice but to build this thing themselves. Gates agreed and assigned Siegelman to head up the effort within Myhrvold's Advanced Technology group, promoting Siegelman, in effect, from an advisory role to lead manager of a project that would require lots of dollars and developers. Some outside industry analysts did not second the promotion, mocking the notion that Siegelman, young and inexperienced in the online business, was properly qualified. "Microsoft is going to have to stumble and skin its knees," sneered one analyst.

Inexperienced, yes, but also a quick study and not one to be cowed by seniority. When he set up his office within Myhrvold's group and reviewed the work of the ten researchers whom he inherited, he was not afraid to tell them that they would have to start over. Under Myhrvold's direction, the group had been attempting to create an ambitious software protocol that would work without modification on whatever device would be connected to the network, whether conventional personal computer or tiny wallet PC, and regardless of operating system. Siegelman liked "shipping stuff" and, in his opinion, trying to solve some of the most challenging computer science problems on the way to getting online services up and running was not the best way to move quickly. His decision was to "constrain the problem so we can win in the marketplace." Forget the Macintosh, forget wallet PCs, forget anything that was not directly related to having the business ready for the Windows update that would eventually appear as Windows 95 (but was, at that time, due to ship in June 1994). Microsoft Network (MSN) had to be ready, no matter what, when that revision of Windows shipped because, as Siegelman well understood, bundling the software with Windows offered the best chance for the new entrant to make a dent in the share held by the incumbents. And to make sure that it would be ready, Siegelman ordered that the initial services be the basics. What did people use on America Online? Chat forums, bulletin boards, file downloads. These then would be what MSN would start with, too. This would keep things simple and reduce the odds that the system would not be ready when it was time for the new Windows software to ship.

Before Siegelman arrived, the ten-person staff from the research group had not been pressured to deliver concrete products. Now it was a product development team facing a "big-time" deadline. Half of the staff threw up their hands in disgust and left. Siegelman was authorized to hire many people, but as gleeful as he was to have the head count allocation, he faced great difficulty in attracting fellow Microsoft employees to transfer into the new group. Just as Craig Bartholomew had seen in the formation of the Encarta development team, Microsoft employees hesitated to transfer into a new group with uncertain prospects. Before joining the company, at the time of their initial interview, every prospective candidate had answered questions with the earnest consistency of Miss America contestants— each wanted "to change the world." But once they were hired and joined an existing group with established products and predictable updates, they discovered that their role was not to "change the world" but to carry out their assigned piece of the larger whole. It was not as exciting as working on an entirely new product, but it certainly was more secure. When Siegelman was given authority to build his own group for MSN, Microsoft employees had as many negative comments as positive: "This is bogus, bogus, bogus—we can't compete with CompuServe; what does he think he's going to do?"

Nor was it a simple matter to hire many people from the outside in a short time by using the standard Microsoft process of exhaustive interviewing. By December 1994, MSN's head count had jumped to 220, which remained small compared to its rivals'. For example, America Online, at the same time, had 400 employees. In this endeavor, as in preceding ones, Microsoft placed a premium on hiring smarts in wholesale quantities. In late 1993, Siegelman contacted a small, privately funded company, Daily Planet, which happened to be located in another Seattle suburb. Having heard that the company was developing software tools for preparing multimedia content that would be placed online, Siegelman was curious, but Daily Planet's principals initially would not even speak to him. Siegelman had to extend numerous entreaties before they were willing to have lunch, and still more before they were persuaded to show a demo of the company's tools. In the end, Siegelman overcame the initial reticence and talked the company into a friendly acquisition. Just as Microsoft did when it acquired Nathan Myhrvold's company, here, when it absorbed Daily Planet, the program code that came with the deal was discarded—it was the newly acquired brains that were put to work.

Contrary to outside speculation that Microsoft was planning to swiftly obliterate all online competitors with the firepower that would accompany the marketing of the Windows update, Microsoft's internal business plans projected a modest beginning for MSN. In a review with Gates in February 1994, for example, the MSN group forecast that in fiscal year 1995 (ending in June 1995) the service would take in revenue of approximately $10 million and lose $24 million due to start-up costs. The following year would also end in losses. Only in 1997, when expected revenues were put at $340 million, was the first profitable year anticipated.

Even these numbers proved to be too ambitious. The entire MSN timetable depended on the Windows release, which turned out to be late. In January 1994, when the ship date for Windows was still supposed to be June 1994, Siegelman could see that MSN would not be ready by then and asked Gates whether a Plan B should be put into motion. Gates was too optimistic and affirmed his confidence that the Windows group was going to be ready to ship the software as planned. When the release slipped to December 1994, and then slipped again, before finally reaching the street as Windows 95 in late August 1995, MSN had used the gift of additional time to ready the service for simultaneous release. The delays were not wholly a blessing, however. MSN's competitors were busily expanding in the interim. When Siegelman's group was first established, America Online's subscription rolls were about 300,000. By December 1994, they were one million. In 1995, they jumped to two million—then three—then past four. Even allowing for some skepticism about those numbers, as none of the online services permitted the Audit Bureau of Circulations or other outsiders to confirm their validity, the growth in online services clearly was taking off while Microsoft was still preparing its own offering.

The other major untoward development that occurred while MSN was being prepared for release was the rise of the public's awareness of the Internet. In 1993, the media had carried stories about the information highway, ad nauseam. By 1994, journalists had shifted their attention to the Internet. By 1995, they wrote about nothing else. From academic obscurity to media darling, the Internet's arrival on the front covers of news magazines meant that not just MSN and the other commercial online services would be directly affected. Even the domination of Microsoft's Windows itself seemed to be facing its most serious challenge ever.

How best to explain how Microsoft, like everyone else in the personal computer business, was caught unprepared by the Internet phenomenon? It was not that Microsoft refused to believe that at some time, from an unknown direction, the company could very well face a serious threat to its future expansion and health. Complacency that Microsoft's existing businesses would continue to prosper indefinitely was not a Gates failing.

Perhaps a youth factor best explains who would embrace the Internet first. Note the youthfulness of the executives on whom Gates (b. 1955) relied in Microsoft's recent history: for example, Rob Glaser (b. 1962), Nathan Myhrvold (b. 1959), and Russ Siegelman (b. 1962). But, as young as this group was—all still in their thirties—they were not young enough to have spent lots of time connected to the Internet during their college days, as many who were still in their twenties in 1994 had. The oldsters in their thirties thus had neither the personal acquaintance with nor the early visceral understanding of the Internet's potential growth of a Marc Andreessen. As a student at the University of Illinois, Andreessen had been one of the two principal coders of Mosaic, the first piece of software that made the Internet's World Wide Web broadly accessible. He was was all of 23 when in 1994 he co-founded Netscape Communications. Gates may have had the right idea in giving senior responsibility to young managers, but he would have needed still *younger* representatives within his informal advisory council. Their slightly different experiences would permit them to detect technological trends that the thirty-somethings would miss.

Another factor in Microsoft's relative sluggishness in shifting toward the Internet stems from the inability of many Microsoft employees to get out to the Internet and explore on their own. Like other companies, Microsoft's internal corporate network was protected for security reasons by an insulating "firewall" that effectively made it impossible to do much with the outside world other than send and receive e-mail. To make a true outside connection, employees had to scout around the campus for the rare machine that had a real Internet "tap." Two such machines were in the corporate library. They were kept antiseptically separate from the corporate network, lest security be breached and a virus or other mischief be introduced. However, the required sign-up sheets and traipsing to a separate building were hardly conducive to unhurried exploration. None of these security measures was extraordinary compared with those at other companies, but the protection that they were designed to provide worked both ways, isolating Microsoft employees from the Internet as well as vice versa, with baleful strategic consequences.

Not that Gates was wholly unaware of the public fuss that was building around the Internet. But whatever he knew he gleaned as a voracious reader of periodicals, not as a free-ranging Net habitué who lived on the Internet himself. As preparations for MSN proceeded, Gates sent Siegelman clippings about the Internet, persistently asking what Microsoft should do. Siegelman felt that the Internet was overhyped and that the *New York Times* had created a false impression that millions of people were surfing the Net. Siegelman's inquiries outside the company had led him to believe that, except for high-bandwidth leased lines, the present Internet infrastructure could only support several hundred thousand users at a time. Some industry analysts supported Siegelman's position that if the Internet continued to grow as it had been, the infrastructure would collapse under the load. Jeffrey Tarter, the publisher of a software industry newsletter, said in February 1995 that, at that point, it appeared that the Internet would be unable to "scale up without becoming totally impassable."

Even as MSN continued down the path toward becoming a commercial online service with its own proprietary software, Gates continued to press Siegelman about the Internet. In early 1994, Gates viewed the Internet as historically analogous to Microsoft's own DOS operating system in the early 1980s—once the standard achieved momentum, you would not want to get in its way. Siegelman would say that he agreed generally with the comparison, but unlike DOS, the Internet left one nagging question: How do you make money with this thing? It was a reasonable question that had no easy answers, especially because history did not seem to offer any comforting points of reference. The last time that something free and universally used had come along like the Internet Protocol (the openly published standard that all Internet communication was based on and which did not belong to any company) was in the very earliest days of the personal computer industry. Then young Bill Gates had made the case for recognizing, protecting, and commercializing intellectual property rights in order to encourage software developers to improve the state of the art.

In mid-1994, Gates mused that the Internet, because it was nearly free, acted like "gravity," pulling down the prices that commercial online service providers could charge. At that point, fully a year before MSN would actually be released, Gates knew that the company had not yet figured out what it should do for online services. But whatever form the services would take, Microsoft would seek to get more users than anybody else. He asked rhetorically: If you can't get more users than anybody else, why be in the business?

While his online service was still gestating, Siegelman decided to answer the Internet challenge by defining MSN as a superset of private and public online services. It would offer its own subscribers full access to the Internet, which he suggested could be thought of as a "public access channel in a cable TV system." For premium services, subscribers would be invited to visit the commercial offerings on a virtual mall that did not belong to the Internet and which exacted a fee for services used. With an online service thus conceived, Microsoft would benefit from the best of both worlds.

As public momentum behind the Internet gathered speed, the business model for MSN would change again. But even though Microsoft had not originally conceived of MSN as integrally tied to the Internet and had to alter its strategy repeatedly, the episode serves to display one of Microsoft's strengths—the ability to nimbly revise strategy on the fly. Though in late 1993 Gates chose not to exhort the entire company to make all its products "eat, drink, sleep, run, walk, swim, and fly" on the Internet as he would do in 1995, it was not because he was asleep at the helm. Rather, it was because the Internet had not yet become the much-talked-about phenomenon that, we could say in retrospect, became self-fulfilling. The louder the buzz, the more people got connected, the more information was available, the louder the buzz, and so on. Once the positive feedback loop began, the most prominent student—and beneficiary—of the feedback loop phenomenon did not hesitate to redirect his company toward the Internet.

If Gates and Microsoft were caught by surprise by the velocity of the Internet's growth, so too was *everyone*. What about Netscape, the single company most closely associated with the rising popularity of the Internet? When graybeard Silicon Graphics alumnus Jim Clark set up the company in spring 1994, his founding vision was to work on interactive TV technology. And what about Sun Microsystems' Java, the new programming language that became the talk of all Net-savvy software developers in 1995? It was originally developed for "personal digital assistants," the portable gadgets like Apple's stillborn Newton, that at one time—far back in the dim recesses of 1993— were going to be the next big thing.

In those days of yore, Nathan Myhrvold had initially resisted Gates's alarms about a possible industry shift to a Net-centered world because he had not yet seen any indication that the Net would be a congenial home for nontechnical consumers. Indeed, before the proliferation of World Wide Web browsers, the Internet remained a forbidding universe, requiring some familiarity with the arcane commands of UNIX in order to be able to do much of anything. In the early 1990s, Myhrvold believed that customers needed to be offered a wide array of information services to convince them not only to try, but to stick with and pay for, online services. In late 1992, he fastened on an unlikely source of inspiration: France's Minitel system of ubiquitous terminals.

Originally introduced as online telephone directories that replaced printed directories, Minitel had expanded its offerings into credit card sales, banking transactions, and other services. The network to which the terminals connected was slow, the hardware limited, the screens ugly, and yet in 1992 Minitel revenues were the equivalent to about U.S. $1.2 billion—yes, Myhrvold emphasized, *billion* dollars—and 80 percent of that was unrelated to charges for the phone directory. At a time when no revenue was being collected from consumer services in the U.S. portion of the Internet, Myhrvold took France's example of what could be pulled in from a ubiquitous system, even with cumbersome, outmoded technology, as evidence of pent-up consumer demand for information services. By 1994, Myhrvold had come around to the view that the Internet was going to be the network in the United States that, as Minitel had done in France, achieved universal reach into consumers' lives.

Having often urged Microsoft to think about the implications of broad- and narrowband communications becoming an integral component of all personal computing, Myhrvold had already prepared the way by pushing Microsoft to jettison the old model of selling software bits in a box and to embrace a "transaction" model, obtaining a fraction of transaction revenue rather than a one-time license fee when users purchased a box of software. He likened the model that he wanted to try with MSN to that of a shopping mall landlord who charged tenants a small percentage of store sales rather than a flat rent. MSN would invite third parties to offer information and services on the network, and Microsoft would charge the companies a percentage of the revenue they took in. Instead of keeping 70, 80, or 90 percent of the revenues as the incumbent commercial online services did, MSN would only retain 10, 20, or 30 percent, providing a more attractive pricing model for third-party companies that wanted to retail information and services. By the time MSN was launched, however, the primary competition would turn out not to be the other commercial services but rather the Internet. There customers could connect with information providers directly, without a Microsoft serving as intermediary and charging its own cut. When Myhrvold saw this problem looming, he argued that Microsoft had to figure out how to insert its own software into the Internet, independent of MSN. He suggested that licensing Microsoft software for tamperproof, "secure" transactions would bring a transaction fee of 1 or 2 percent just like Visa or Mastercard enjoyed. The charge would not be as large a cut of the action Myhrvold had originally hoped for, but he still hoped that a lucrative business could be built on the basis of sheer volume, the aspect of France's Minitel from which he still derived inspiration.

To the extent that Microsoft could successfully persuade users and information providers to adopt its proprietary software for secure transactions on the Net, a toll road would be possible. If, however, companies such as Netscape continued to gain and protect their market share by giving away or charging only a nominal licensing fee for Internet-related software, Microsoft would have to abandon the toll road and match its competitors with freebies, too.

It was not widely appreciated that in covering the Internet's rise and Microsoft's need to play catch-up, the press had exaggerated the contrast between Microsoft and its competitors. All software companies were in the same predicament and had the same difficulty as Microsoft in answering Russ Siegelman's lingering question: How *do* you make money in this game? The challengers were forced to experiment with business models and various kinds of tolls, too. During 1995, in trying to predict its greatest source of revenues, Netscape oscillated between two possibilities: its Web browser software, used by visitors to Web sites, and its Web server software, used by the hosts. Sun conceded that it expected to receive little revenue from its Java software; its interest in promoting Java was in the indirect benefits to the company. As James Gosling, Java's primary author, reasoned, anything that "contributes to the health of the Internet contributes to Sun's health as well" because Sun workstations were often sold as host machines for Web sites.

If all the players in the Internet software game used common standards, their software packages would be interchangeable commodities and they would not be able to charge much of anything to users. If, however, they each incorporated unique features into their software to differentiate their offerings from competing packages that performed essentially the same function—and hence the software would no longer be interchangeable—the Internet would become balkanized. The World Wide Web had become popular because it consisted of openly published standards. In its early history, any browser could access all the features of any given Web site. Was it realistic, though, to think that the Web would continue to operate in a paradisiacal state, free of commercial motive?

The Web's Internet infrastructure had been built with government subsidy, which was no longer available, and as a labor of love by hackers who were bound by an anticommercial ethos. (Tim Berners-Lee, the British creator of the World Wide Web who was then based at the European Laboratory for Particle Physics in Geneva, had eschewed offers to commercialize his creation and instead placed it in the public domain.) As the network strained under the weight of exponential growth in its use, could it thrive and overcome its present limitations with freeware, without the infusion of developers' investment that commercial software would bring? Denise Caruso, an industry observer, held in late 1995 that the Internet was a noncommercial preserve that should be protected. She chided Netscape for acting to safeguard the proprietary parts of its software: "After working so hard to beat Microsoft to market, it might be nice to wait a while before becoming them." But how could Netscape be expected to give away its software indefinitely? This newest darling of the personal computer world was facing the same wrath that Microsoft had twenty years earlier, when Bill Gates faced the microcomputer hobbyists who were bound by a similar anticommercial ethos.

It is interesting how both camps, then and now, perceived their respective positions as best furthering the interests of the largest number of people. The Software Should Remain Free camp argued, of course, that free software ensured that the benefits of computers would be accessible to one and all. The Software Should Be Commercialized camp claimed that the only way to make software truly useful was to invest heavily in its improvement, and that required charging customers. The ultimate cost to consumers need not be onerous, however, because software development could be amortized across a wide base of users. This is what Nathan Myhrvold had called the million-to-one leverage enjoyed by the consumer who bought a $100 software program that had required $100 million to develop. The Internet merely brought this old standoff to the fore.

Part Four

The Monopoly Game

Chapter 11

The Last War Redux

*T*HE SUCCESSFUL COMPETITOR, *having been urged to compete, must not be turned upon when he wins.*

Judge Learned Hand

Let us initially propose that Judge Hand's declaration may be wrong, that we can imagine instances when it is indeed in society's best interest to "turn upon" or, put more gently, "restrain" a firm that has played the game of free enterprise so well that the game cannot proceed because only one player remains. Hand was correct in pointing to the contradiction that taints governmental restraint of a "winner" who is punished simply for being successful, but historically, how often has the success been attained by means pure and laudable? When we think of the robber barons of the latter nineteenth century, we see a gallery of oily rogues who took advantage of financial systems relatively free of public scrutiny, bribers who manipulated the political system, businessmen whose infrastructure-based empires depended on the transfer of public resources into private hands, or speculators who capitalized on the finite nature of the supply of urban real estate.

The Sherman Antitrust Act of 1890 marked the culmination of public concern about the flouting of the basic operations of a free market by price-fixing cartels, the absence of competition in shipping rates, and above all else, the activities of the Standard Oil Company. The first of the Act's two principal sections outlawed actions that restrained trade whose patently unfair nature would not be regarded as controversial today. The second section vaguely targeted companies that attempted to "monopolize" any part of trade or commerce; it did not spell out where legitimate pursuit of profits shaded into illegitimate attainment of monopoly. It was left vague because Congress was pushed by public outrage to do something about the "trusts," but no one then had a clear idea of what exactly should be done. Nor have the courts since then been able to remove the ambiguity about when to take action and how best to do so.

Enter Microsoft. At first glance, these basic facts of U.S. antitrust history coupled with Microsoft's singular success in the software industry would suggest that it was only to be expected that Microsoft would bring the antitrust issues to the fore. But a different impression emerges if we look at the puzzling way in which the U.S. government has gone about its many investigations of Microsoft. Even if we dissent from Learned Hand's argument and reserve the possibility that even a fair-playing winner may need to be restrained—and ultimately Microsoft may indeed turn out to be precisely such a winner—it is difficult to see where the government to date has come even close to making a compelling case against Microsoft. The way in which the government has blundered along in its pursuit of the company, using technically antiquated and misinformed premises, undermines the very concept of antitrust. History tells us that the nature of Microsoft's domination is fundamentally different from that of Standard Oil, yet the government decided to fight the last war all over again, without recognizing how the circumstances have changed in the digital era.

In his public statements, Bill Gates has taken pains to remove the rawer edges of his and his company's competitiveness; in this, he differs from Oracle's Larry Ellison. To hear Gates tell the story, Microsoft's success is a warm, cuddly "love" story—Microsoft employees simply "love to pursue opportunities." We're not "like an alligator," he defensively told reporters in 1991, after the Federal Trade Commission's investigation into charges that Microsoft had possibly engaged in anticompetitive behavior was made public. In Gates's telling, Microsoft simply produced "these little boxes, these nice little software packages." Where did people come up with the idea that Microsoft was "just sitting up here looking down and thinking, 'Ho, ho, ho, who shall we crush today?'" Well, we can reply that such a caricature of the company could be inferred from the less cautious statements of Gates's own lieutenants, who on occasion have been unabashed in their statements of market-conquering ambition.

When company cheerleader Steve Ballmer addressed the all-company meeting in 1994, he reported in his inimitably best shouting voice that market share in the preceding year had increased for Word, Excel, Powerpoint, and Office. For desktop applications software, "it's MARKET SHARE, MARKET SHARE, MARKET SHARE, MARKET SHARE that counts—because if you have share, you basically leave the competitors [grabs his own throat for emphasis] just gasping for oxygen to live in." Keeping competitors gasping was what "we've got to maintain."

This was not a new sentiment. Three years earlier, Mike Maples had been quite open about the same aim when he told reporters, "My job is to get a fair share of the software applications market, and to me that's one hundred percent." It's a wonderful quotation because anyone who recoils at what Maples said is forced to confront a question that's hard to answer: If "100 percent" is unseemly, what do we want him to strive for? Is 80 percent more reasonable? How about 51 percent? On what basis would we determine what that lesser share should be? And if Microsoft were to accede, should it then restrain its efforts to sell more products if it discovered that it had edged beyond what we had declared to be its "fair" share?

The questions about the propriety of winning by a lopsided margin get especially tricky when we include in the picture the role that we ourselves have actively played as consumers, individual purchase by individual purchase, in making Microsoft successful in operating systems, productivity software, and more recently, home software. This is another instance in which the specter of Standard Oil, which hovers behind the Sherman Act, simply has little to tell us about Microsoft's story. Rockefeller's empire was a kingdom of vertical integration. The expansion of Microsoft's power, on the other hand, has come horizontally with the votes that issue from millions of individual or company pocketbooks. Though Gates oversimplifies when he talks about the process as one of simply putting boxes of software on shelves, he is not all that wide of the mark. We have had plenty of choices as shoppers, and it is our own actions that have served to reduce, or threaten to reduce, the number of choices. *We* are the ones who pursued the less expensive option and accepted Windows as a satisfactory substitute for the Mac, the superior but premium-priced alternative. *We* are the ones who increasingly made bulk purchases of the Office suite, Microsoft's inexpensive productivity software.

Microsoft's success is akin to that of Home Depot, Wal-Mart, Toys 'R Us, Barnes & Noble, or any of the other "category killers" that have come to dominate whichever retail distribution segment they have entered. Though Microsoft is a manufacturer, not a retailer, it too benefits from the public's preference for lowest cost over other considerations, and lowest cost is achieved by having the largest customer base over which to amortize development costs—for both hardware and software. The more customers to be found on a particular operating system platform, the more independent software vendors are drawn to it; the more software that is available, the more purchasers are attracted—and the higher the volume and the lower the prices. The cycle naturally works in favor of the market leader.

We temporarily ignore our predilection to choose the lower priced option when we decry the power of a Wal-Mart or a Microsoft in letters to the editor. But when it comes time to reach for our own wallets, the results speak for themselves. Our wish to impute nefarious motives to the companies that we have made successful is pure hypocrisy. We are also guilty of inconsistency when we complain that the latest version of Windows does not work well with some of our inherited PC hardware. It is precisely because Microsoft chose the path of trying to accommodate as many parts of the raucously competitive, far-flung world of Intel-based hardware that Windows consumers have enjoyed the lower prices that have come from brisk competition among many hardware players.

Apple chose to ignore the din of pleas, from inside and outside, to license its operating system software to other hardware manufacturers. When it finally relented in 1995, it did so tardily and timidly. Until then, it had been able to offer an elegantly integrated package precisely because it knew exactly what hardware the software would work with, a luxury that testers at Microsoft did not enjoy. To the extent that Apple relaxed its monopolistic control of hardware manufacturing, it could hope to increase volume. But if it were to play Microsoft's game, it would soon enough encounter some of the same headaches of hardware/software incompatibilities that the Windows world endures. We might say that the Windows versus Macintosh confrontation is exemplary in that it has presented consumers with a crisply distinct choice between two very dissimilar models. The lop-sided outcome of competition between Windows and the Macintosh, thus, tells us as much about ourselves as anything else.

The vitriol in the complaining voices of Microsoft's foes is remarkable, even after making allowances for the tendency of first-generation business leaders in any new industry to have difficulty sep-arating the personal from the professional. Sun Microsystem's Scott McNealy has referred to Microsoft's dominance in terms that an-nounced the end of "free enterprise" and the arrival of a "controlled economy"—where "everybody winds up driving Trabants." (Wheez-ing East German Trabants? Or just plain Fords?) Keep in mind that McNealy's company sold workstations that might be likened to Ferraris, which he had once hoped would somehow displace per-sonal computers. Tasting gall from the failure of his company's oper-ating system offering, Solaris, his view of Microsoft was not that of a disinterested observer.

What are we to make of Philippe Kahn's statement, made when he was still the head of Borland, that Microsoft's power was like "Nazi Germany's"? Kahn's self-styled role was that of the Allies, supplying the "guts and courage" that kept Germany in check. The outlandish-ness of the comparison stayed with Gates for years. Nathan Myhrvold three years later returned to Kahn's remark as an example of strident criticism that had gone too far: "Say what you want about Windows 95, but it's nonlethal." When Myhrvold spoke at an industry gathering in March 1995, his audience's hostility toward all things Microsoft was so palpable that he began by recalling his speech teacher's advice to think about what the worst thing was that an audience could do to you: rush the podium, tear you limb from limb, and eat your lifeless body? This had always seemed a comfortingly absurd image, Myhrvold said—until that day, when he confessed to the audience, "I'm up here thinking—they just might do it."

The eagerness of Microsoft's competitors to ignore their own strategic blunders is understandable enough. If I were the head of Lotus, who had inherited from founder Mitch Kapor a signed agree-ment with Microsoft to develop a Windows version of 1-2-3 but then had ripped up the contract and bet all the company's chips instead on IBM's OS/2, thus losing the strongest, most profitable franchise in the business at the time, I too would be rather shy about discussing my own company's responsibility for what had transpired. But the government's antitrust investigations into Microsoft's behavior are not so easily understood.

The original Federal Trade Commission inquiry began when the FTC became alarmed by a press release, issued jointly by IBM and Microsoft in November 1989, concerning the companies' plans to bring out a more powerful version of OS/2 and a less powerful version of Windows. The FTC smelled collusion in these plans, discerning a plot between the two companies to intentionally cripple Windows so that the two operating systems would not be competing for the same market segments. The FTC staff spent five months chomping at the bit to go after Microsoft, held back because the Department of Justice initially refused to authorize a full FTC investigation. In the meantime, the staff began to learn the rudiments of the software industry, inviting Microsoft's competitors to provide depositions that served as tutorials. (The sequence is interesting—you would think that the FTC would start its investigation *after* the office gained expertise in the field.)

The FTC staff seems to have been nearly the last group of people to have noticed that the IBM-Microsoft marriage had completely come apart at about the time the joint press release had been issued, and that Microsoft had been working zealously to make Windows 3.0 as strong as it could. By the time that the government staff realized that the hot issue of collusion that had inspired their interest had been doused, they were not about to close up shop. They simply searched for replacement issues and deposed still more of Microsoft's competitors. When the existence of the FTC investigation was made public in March 1991 through an offhand remark by a WordPerfect executive to a Wall Street analyst, whoever in the industry had not already been asked to provide testimony now stepped forward. Gates's public comments about all of this were noteworthy for the appearance of equanimity; he spoke politely of the need to "quickly educate the FTC on our business."

Neither side should have had to "educate" the FTC about the basics of the industry. The unsophisticated state of the FTC's software industry expertise was exposed by the commission's decision to focus on Microsoft's DOS operating system. This decision was greatly influenced by the yelps issuing from Novell, the networking software power that Microsoft had approached on two separate occasions, in late 1989 and in early 1992, to discuss a merger. After the collapse of the second round of talks, Novell's head, Ray Noorda, became Microsoft's most vociferous critic and offered his services to the FTC investigation.

A Microsoft-Novell merger would indeed have raised some interesting antitrust-related questions because Microsoft would have secured a dominant market position in the networking segment of the industry by a means wholly different from the one defended earlier, in which market share is earned one purchase order, one customer, at a time. The FTC, in its wisdom, thought it was most significant that Microsoft had approached Novell the second time for merger talks just days after Novell had announced it intended to acquire Digital Research, the developers of DR-DOS. The government's choice of controversy bordered on the absurd, however. The terms discussed for Microsoft's purchase of Novell were in the neighborhood of $13 billion. DR-DOS's portion of that valuation would have been minuscule; it had a tiny 5 percent sliver of market share in a market that would shrink as post-DOS operating systems took over. Novell's acquisition of Digital Research was only one of many ill-considered purchases that Noorda made in what turned out to be (not coincidentally) his last years at Novell—acquiring the rights to UNIX and the purchase of WordPerfect were also howlers. Novell was not becoming more formidable as it broadened its reach into domains beyond networking. It was becoming unfocused and actually weaker.

Yet the FTC could not shake off its initial assumptions that DOS was crucial to the industry's future health. When, after three years of taking depositions and exhuming hundreds of thousands of pages of internal Microsoft documents, the five-member FTC staff failed to produce a majority in favor of pressing an antitrust action, the Department of Justice itself decided to take on the investigation. It spent another year examining two million pages of documents supporting the investigation into the alleged malfeasance in Microsoft's business practices. More than four years of investigation ended up focusing on the same senescent program—Microsoft's DOS—which by the summer of 1994 was well into its twilight due to natural causes and the progression of the industry. The government was fighting the last war as though time had remained frozen.

The government also revealed scant understanding of the central dynamic that governed the competition for operating system software, that is, the "positive feedback cycle." In this cycle, as we've seen earlier, the more that consumers side with a particular product, the more valuable that product becomes, which increases its attractiveness to still more customers. In the 1980s, two Stanford economists, Brian Arthur and Paul David, showed how the cycle, once started, led to the domination of one technical standard over others by drawing on examples from U.S. history: the triumph of the gasoline automobile engine over the steam engine, AC power over DC power, and the QWERTY typewriter keyboard layout over alternative layouts that facilitated faster typing. David's study of QWERTY suggested that we had become "prisoners of events long forgotten," but he was loathe to suggest government intervention. His only suggestion for remedying such situations when the public had adopted what technically seemed to be the "inferior" choice was to suggest that the government should handicap the leader and favor, in the government's own purchases, the laggards in the race for an installed base or at least whoever was second in market share. If the suggestion, originally made in an essay published in 1987, were acted on today, the government would forbid its agencies from purchasing "Wintel" (Windows software and Intel hardware) and direct all its purchases to Apple.

Brian Arthur also suggested that government should keep more than one technology in a given field alive by artificial respiration through subsidy, if necessary. Without subsidies to ensure "requisite variety," he argued, future Chernobyl-like disasters might reveal that the reigning technology was unsafe and safer alternatives had disappeared. Applied to contemporary operating system competition, would this mean that the government should subsidize IBM's OS/2 operating system (in addition, that is, to the estimated $2 billion that IBM is rumored to have invested in keeping OS/2 alive)? Both Arthur and David were concerned with "tipping," which happens when the competition between two evenly balanced technical competitors first becomes uneven because one side gets more customers than the other, setting in motion the cycle that reinforces the benefits to those who adopt the majority standard. The classic example of "tipping" was when the VHS format for consumer videocassette recorders initially pulled a little bit ahead of the Beta format and then was able to ride the positive feedback cycle to the point of utterly destroying Beta's presence in the consumer market.

How well do these economic principles help explain Microsoft's history? Their application to the story of DOS or Windows is complicated. The government's first three years of investigating DOS seem to have proceeded wholly innocent of the very idea of the positive feedback cycle. Originally Arthur himself thought his writings could be applied to justify Microsoft's market dominance as easily as assail it. He called Myhrvold to offer Microsoft his services in the Department of Justice investigation. Myhrvold referred him to Microsoft Legal, which did not follow up. Miffed because Microsoft never called him back, Arthur hired himself out as a consultant to Microsoft's rivals who were pressing the government to redouble its efforts to sniff out pernicious "tipping."

The confusion about Arthur's theories was compounded because Microsoft did not present a united front in response. When Microsoft's critics hired Arthur to provide some intellectual substance to drape over the skeleton of antitrust conspiracy, Microsoft's chief counsel, Bill Neukom, derided the notion of positive feedback cycles. But the writings and remarks of both Gates and Myhrvold made clear that they, on the contrary, understood the operations of the positive feedback cycle very well. They differed with Arthur only in their interpretation of the relative weight of benefits and harm.

When trying to undermine the concept of positive feedback cycles, counselor Neukom pointed to the examples of once-high-flying software products—the CP/M operating system, WordStar, and Visicalc—all of which had large, seemingly unassailable customer bases and whose publishers would now be shocked to hear that supposedly they had enjoyed a "lock" on their positions. The point that Neukom seemed intent on missing was that though these products were eventually toppled by DOS, WordPerfect, and 1-2-3, respectively, it was undeniably difficult to do. No one appreciated the defensive advantages of an installed base more than Gates. In 1990, for example, when Microsoft's Excel seemed to have no reasonable hope of stealing 1-2-3's market share, Gates acknowledged the difficulty of challenging the entrenched leader: "If everybody at Lotus went on vacation for a year, we'd still have a hard time competing with 1-2-3 because its momentum would still be there." But he had persisted because "once you get to the dominant position, the rewards are incredible." In other words, the potential rewards were commensurate with the challenges of unseating the market leader.

As a society, we seem to be uncomfortable with plain talk about the positive feedback cycle because it exposes our inability to define when a firm's business success becomes harmful to the public interest. One of Gates's earliest recorded comments about the software business was in 1981 when he said, "I really shouldn't say this, but in some ways [the way the software business works] leads, in an individual product category, to a natural monopoly." With its "I really shouldn't say this" and mention of "natural monopoly" in a single breath, this statement would seem to be the perfect smoking gun, the self-incriminating blurting of a contemporary robber baron. In fact, lawyers representing Microsoft's competitors these many years later continue to use this quotation, stripped of its original context, to great dramatic effect. But if you consider what Gates originally said preceding and following that sentence, you will find that the "monopoly" is one of momentum, earned not by foul means but by building "user loyalty, reputation, and salesforce"; by "properly" documenting, promoting, and pricing software; by training users; and by navigating the strategic challenges in an industry characterized by high fixed and low marginal costs.

On other occasions, Gates pointed to the operation of what he called the "herd" effect—"90 percent of the people in this industry are the herd." The herd effect hindered Microsoft's attempts to gain market share for its spreadsheet on the DOS side where Lotus had the attention of the "herd," but it worked in the company's favor on the Macintosh side where in the mid-1980s Microsoft's Excel far outsold Lotus's Jazz. The reason Microsoft sold twenty copies of its Mac product for every one of Lotus's was not because it was significantly better technically—Gates himself said it was only marginally better—but because, Gates observed, once the market anoints a leader the entire universe of third-party support—"all the books, all the templates, all the training, all the [stores'] stocking,"—heads in the direction of the leader, too.

This was precisely the phenomenon of "tipping" that so concerned Brian Arthur. Arthur's list of five sources that contributed to what he called "increasing returns to adoption" of a particular technology are at work in the software industry and have greatly contributed to lowering the costs of personal computing:

1. *Learning by Using*—the more a given technology is used, the more is learned about it, and hence the more likely that it will be improved further.

2. *Network Externalities*—the more members that join a network, the more valuable joining the network becomes. (Telephones are the best illustration.) Arthur emphasizes that the attractions of one network serve to weaken consumers' willingness to hold out for a technically superior alternative that does not have as many members.

3. *Scale Economies in Production*—These are unquestionably as important in the personal computer industry as anywhere else.

4. *Informational Increasing Returns*—This refers to how the risk-averse tend to adopt the leading technology because it will be better understood and thus adoption is less likely to contain unknown risks.

5. *Technological Interrelatedness*—Adoption of a given technology spawns various subtechnologies and technical infrastructure that make it increasingly difficult to displace the technology. Or put another way, the existing infrastructure serves to keep costs low.

Arthur's original illustration of the "increasing returns to adoption" was of gasoline engine technology, and the refineries, filling stations, and auto parts industries that depended on it. Applied to personal computers, this particular source of increasing returns seems to apply more to hardware than it does to software, and within software, it applies more to operating systems than to the software applications that ride on top. In any case, here as in the other sources that tend to reinforce "increasing returns to adoption," it should not be forgotten that the "increasing returns" refer to the "returns" reaped by consumers.

Nathan Myhrvold cheerfully embraced Arthur's writings to show that the concern about the monopolies of the past was misapplied to today's high-tech industries such as personal computers, which are dominated by the positive feedback cycle. The VCR market "tipped" in VHS's favor not due to accident or market manipulation, but for two other reasons. First, VHS tapes originally could record two hours of video, whereas Beta tapes could only accommodate one hour, too short for a movie or ball game. Second, VHS was licensed widely to many manufacturers who brought out a variety of VCRs, whereas Sony, who controlled Beta, chose not to license the technology broadly. The parallel between this pairing of VHS and Beta, on the one hand, and Microsoft's DOS and Apple's Macintosh operation system, on the other, is easily drawn.

In a 1993 draft of an article entitled "Telling It Like It Is" that was originally intended for publication in a mainstream business publication, Myhrvold applied the theory of the positive feedback cycle to the history of DOS. The widespread adoption of DOS did not lead to higher prices, as predicted by the classical theory of monopoly. Just as VHS and audio CD standards were licensed inexpensively, so too was DOS licensed to computer manufacturers cheaply, for about 1 percent of the price of the system, making it the least expensive major constituent "component." In all of these cases, the nature of the positive feedback cycle, which operates only by increasing the installed base of customers, served to reward open licensing policies and encourage third-party support.

Perhaps the most controversial portion of Myhrvold's defense of the theory was when he observed that, in the history of computers, the market share leader in operating systems gets about 90 percent of the market, the runner-up has about 90 percent of the remainder, and so on. In applications software that runs on top of the operating system, the positive feedback phenomenon is at work, too, but it does not bring customers as many benefits, so the distribution is not quite as dramaticaly skewed. Nevertheless, a pattern is found in application software categories too: the leader gets 60 to 70 percent of the market and the runner-up gets 60 to 70 percent of the remainder. Two years after Myhrvold made these observations, another software category—the suite of productivity applications—had become important. When a well-integrated suite like Microsoft's Office became widely adopted, it brought out every one of Arthur's five sources of tipping, enhancing the effects of the positive feedback cycle. By 1995, Microsoft's Office had a 90 percent share of the suite segment of the market, exactly what Myhrvold's earlier remarks had predicted.

The consistency of the positive feedback cycle phenomenon suggests that people see considerable benefits in choosing technology that others have also chosen. Microsoft understood the phenomenon early, but the pattern would appear with or without Microsoft. Novell's seemingly secure dominance in the network software market, for example, suggested that the same cycle was at work. What distinguishes these latter-day examples of near-monopoly in operating system or networking software from near-monopolies in other industries of the previous century is the extent to which the modern examples expressed consumer evaluation of the technical, financial, and ancillary benefits of sticking with the same software others had chosen.

The issue of consumer choice was also on the minds of the staff of the Department of Justice. Because its investigation into Microsoft's alleged anticompetitive practices failed to show substance, the Department of Justice retreated to the simplest notion of consumer choice: the government wanted all consumers to explicitly choose their operating system software when ordering a new personal computer. Microsoft had enticed most PC manufacturers into blanket licensing agreements for particular models. In the agreements, they paid Microsoft a very low fee for the right to load DOS and Windows on every machine that left their factory, rather than paying a higher fee for each copy of DOS/Windows that was actually placed on a machine.

This arrangement of paying Microsoft "per processor" purchased from chip suppliers, not on the basis of actual copies loaded onto assembled machines that left the factory, pleased Microsoft because it eliminated the need to closely scrutinize every manufacturer's operations. It also went a long way toward eliminating piracy in operating system software. Before per-processor licensing, manufacturers were tempted to avoid paying for system software licenses by shipping machines "naked." In such cases, consumers were likely to install copies of a friend's operating system—"borrowed" or "stolen," depending on whether the vantage point was that of the customer or of Microsoft— rather than purchase a retail copy. But per-processor licensing outraged Novell, IBM, Sun, and NeXT, the other publishers of operating system software for Intel-based machines, who argued that neither personal computer manufacturers nor consumers were willing to later pay an additional charge to have alterative operating system software installed. They maintained that this constituted "unfair competition," denying consumers "choice."

The Department of Justice, unable to come up with anything more damaging in the way of charges against Microsoft, eventually concurred and placed this issue at the center of the consent decree that Microsoft was persuaded to accept in July 1994, in which the company agreed to end per-processor licensing. The government claimed a victory in the name of consumers. Microsoft, which had not had to confess to any wrongdoing, declared a victory, too, for having been implicitly cleared of serious charges. The company expressed relief—prematurely, it turned out—that the distraction of lengthy government investigation was now behind it.

Commentators failed to question, however, the government's presumption that the consent decree represented a victory for consumer interests. Per-processor licensing was the ultimate expression of a bulk rate. The consent agreement meant higher charges, and in the end who would absorb these charges, the manufacturers or the consumers? We can also ask why manufacturers would preload PCs with operating system software that was not what the market wanted to see. Let us also not forget that machines that came bundled with DOS/Windows were no different from machines that came bundled with a CD-ROM encyclopedia or other kinds of software. Consumers were perfectly free to purchase an alternative, so where was the absence of choice? If the publishers of the other operating systems had become so discouraged that they withdrew from the market entirely and only Windows remained, the issue raised by the Department of Justice would be more interesting, but this was not the case in 1994. Even in the extreme hypothetical case of Windows becoming the sole surviving operating system, we would need to see a rise in prices—classical "monopoly rents"—before we could assume we were being harmed by our own collective decision to settle on this one operating system. As Microsoft's lead in market share grew, in other software categories such as word processing, spreadsheets, and databases, Microsoft's prices, happily, had declined. The trend could be reversed, but until it is, the historical evidence from this particular industry would suggest that the market still seems to function well even when Microsoft dominates, counterintuitive though this may be.

The government's consent decree should be praised perhaps more for what it excluded than what it included. Microsoft's competitors frequently complained that its operating systems developers gave Microsoft's applications developers privileged information that was not made available to others, which gave Microsoft's applications an unfair advantage. The proposed remedy was to break Microsoft up into two separate companies, a possibility that the Department of Justice chose not to pursue in the decree.

Microsoft's defense of the interactions of its systems and applications groups was not helped by its own record of wildly inconsistent claims over time. Back in 1983, Steve Ballmer averred a "clean separation" between the systems and the application software developers, a separation so inviolable that Ballmer likened it to the separation of "church and state." The separation did not appear to be as clean as Ballmer claimed. For example, at an industry show in the fall of 1989, Microsoft demonstrated a forthcoming version of Excel that took advantage of some operating system features on which spreadsheet competitors had not yet been briefed. When challenged, Ballmer retreated to reasoning that it would not be in Microsoft's interest to jeopardize the acceptance of its operating system business, which then accounted for the bulk of the company's revenues, by favoring its own application developers and angering outside application software developers, whose support was critical for the operating system. But this claim, even on its face, became meaningless when revenues of Microsoft's application business surpassed those from the operating system. So Microsoft's official stance changed. By 1991, Mike Maples declared that there was no "Chinese Wall" separating the systems and applications groups and as far as he knew there never had been. Gates added subsequently that he himself had never used the term "Chinese Wall."

The Chinese Wall issue should not be dismissed peremptorily. If Microsoft's applications secured their leads by virtue of insider or advance knowledge of undocumented system calls, the implications for competitors would indeed be grave and the formal separation of Microsoft's systems and applications groups might deserve serious consideration. Yet Microsoft's competitors have not presented any convincing evidence that their lagging competitive position can be attributed to special advantages Microsoft's internal applications group enjoyed. The Gang That Couldn't Shoot Straight is the term that independent industry observers often revert to when looking at the history of how Microsoft's competitors in applications resisted the company's call to switch to Windows. The stories of how Lotus, WordPerfect, Ashton-Tate, Borland, and the other former leaders in various application categories were inventive only in devising ways to shoot themselves in the foot are painfully visible and should not conjure sinister thoughts of an internal Microsoft cabal.

We can also challenge the implicit suggestion that Microsoft's applications enjoy commercial success out of proportion to their technical merits, as judged by independent reviewers in industry and consumer magazines. Gates would truculently, but correctly, invite critics to "name a Microsoft product that's successful and isn't a top-rated product—we don't have one." And how are we to explain Microsoft's ability to dominate the word processing and spreadsheet applications categories for the Macintosh to an extent greater than it enjoys even for Windows, despite its seemingly disadvantageous position as an outsider, lacking privileged access to Apple's operating system developers?

The most persuasive argument in favor of leaving Microsoft intact came not from self-interested Gates and fellow Microsoft officers but from an unlikely quarter: Gordon Eubanks, the chief executive officer of Symantec. Symantec was a software company about one-twentieth the size of Microsoft whose software products, primarily utilities, were especially susceptible to Microsoft's encroachment because each operating system revision incorporated functions that had formerly been available only through separate software packages like Symantec's. Despite his company's vulnerability, Eubanks was consistent in defending Microsoft as a fair-playing competitor and urging other independent software vendors to spend less time griping and more time improving their products. Addressing his peers at an industry conference, Eubanks could not resist tweaking the audience with the Yiddish expression, "The person who can't dance often says the band can't play." He reminded his counterparts that those "thinking of revolution" should realize that their unhappiness with a Microsoft-dominated industry should not be mistaken for consumer unhappiness: "The peasants are not pissed." If Eubanks, of all people, could regard the competitive landscape as one that remained essentially fair, the claim indeed deserved to be regarded seriously.

The 1994 consent decree that the Department of Justice and Microsoft agreed on still had to be ratified by a federal judge, and it was placed in the jurisdiction of Judge Stanley Sporkin, where the investigation, which had begun with so little sophistication on the government's part, then became outright farce. Having read James Wallace and Jim Erickson's unflattering 1992 book about Microsoft entitled *Hard Drive,* Sporkin decided that the Department of Justice had not gone far enough in demanding changes in Microsoft's business practices. The content of his grumbling showed a lack of familiarity with the industry. For example, he wanted the government to outlaw "vaporware," the announcement of products before their release. This utterly impractical proposal would mean that customers would be denied any idea of when to expect updates or new software releases. But most disturbing was Sporkin's automatic disdain of evidence that originated anywhere but in the single book that he regarded as so insightful. When one of Sporkin's friends suggested a second book that he might consult, Sporkin declined, asking rhetorically, "Who knows what I might find?" The remark, unlikely to be entered in the annals of the finer moments of American jurisprudence, drew laughter in the courtroom, but the judge was not joking at all.

Microsoft's lawyers were understandably upset—and so too were their supposed antagonists, the Department of Justice's lawyers—about the weight that Sporkin accorded this one book. Sporkin refused to examine the government's reasoning in its argument that it had arrived at the most stringent settlement that the evidence gathered in four years of investigation warranted. When Sporkin rejected the consent agreement, both the government and Microsoft appealed. A three-judge panel disqualified Sporkin on the basis of his reliance on *Hard Drive* and his acceptance of briefs hostile to Microsoft that were submitted by lawyers for three anonymous clients. A new judge was assigned on a random basis to review the original consent decree and gave his approval in August 1995, bringing to an end one extended chapter in the government's scrutiny of Microsoft. But even before this chapter had concluded, another chapter of a strikingly different character had begun and had already been concluded with a conspicuously different outcome.

Chapter 12

The Home Front

O NCE THE UNITED STATES *had an antitrust movement without antitrust prosecutions; in our time there have been antitrust prosecutions without an antitrust movement.*

Richard Hofstadter, "What Happened to the Antitrust Movement" (1964)

When speaking on the record for reporters, Bill Gates modulates what he has to say about the competition depending on the formality of the occasion. The more formal the occasion, the more bland the comment, which in most cases has been bleached of the sardonic tone that shows off Gates's mind at its sharpest. Throughout the lengthy antitrust investigations into his company, Gates was asked incessantly about the government's curiosity. Sometimes, instead of hewing to the line that it was only proper that the government look into this new, strategically important industry and satisfy itself that competition was indeed alive and well, Gates would betray a wave of irritation. In 1991, when the Federal Trade Commission had just begun its investigation, Gates sarcastically ascribed the case to Microsoft's neglect of politely saying "thank you" to its competitors. The next year, when asked what the ultimate outcome of the investigation might mean to Microsoft, Gates answered that the very "worst case" he could think of would be if he happened to trip on the steps of the FTC building.

As for the complaints from a competitor such as WordPerfect that Microsoft's Word owed its success to insider knowledge about the Windows operating system, Gates suggested a simpler explanation of WordPerfect's lagging market share. WordPerfect started its Windows development three years late and spread its developers across six or seven different operating systems instead of the two on which Microsoft focused. "Isn't that a more logical explanation than flying saucers for why we have better Windows applications?" he asked. The discussion in preceding chapters supports Gates's position. The dominating position first of DOS, then of Windows, was the outcome of a perfectly natural pattern of positive feedback loops, and the commanding hold of Microsoft's various applications was a result of smart execution, continual improvements, tenacity—and of consumers voting with their pocketbooks.

For evidence of the still healthy state of competition in the personal computer software industry, Gates in the summer of 1994 pointed to the continuing efforts of companies like Apple, IBM, Sun, and Taligent to write competitive operating systems. "It's not like anybody's given up," he could say then. As for specific categories of software programs, home banking was an area in which Microsoft "went in and at least so far, we haven't captured a very high market share." The months that followed Gates's 1994 statement would bear out his claims, but in complex ways.

The operating system competitors did begin to "give up," at least in maintaining direct competition against Microsoft, so the landscape for operating systems that Gates had described accurately in 1994 was less competitive a year later. But the industrywide shift in attention to the Internet served to render the operating system battles of the past less relevant. Consequently Microsoft would face more, not less, competitive pressure as the battlefront shifted. Gates's mention in 1994 of home banking and the tacit reference to Intuit as the unnamed competitor that had thwarted Microsoft's attempts to gain market share fall into a different category altogether. As convenient as it was for Gates to be able to present Intuit as Exhibit A when arguing that Microsoft had not obliterated all its competition, he was at that very moment privately exploring with Intuit the possibility that Microsoft would abandon the competitive fray—by acquiring Intuit lock, stock, and barrel. That the two companies ultimately would remain competitors was not Gates's own preference.

Intuit's continuing success in the personal finance software category was especially galling to Microsoft because it was based so clearly on the same philosophy of outsmarting its marketplace foes, letting brains get the better of brawn, on which Microsoft had prided itself in its own climb to the top. Moreover, Intuit darted into the very same store aisles and tweaked Microsoft's nose with its cleverness, such as in the marketing ploy that had enabled Quicken to take advantage of the launch of Windows 3.1. Intuit also daringly won over PC hardware manufacturers, the very group with which Microsoft had enjoyed the longest, coziest relationships of any software company.

Even as they were readying the launch of the first Windows version of Quicken, Intuit's executives were thinking about how best to equalize the tremendous 100-to-1 disparity between Microsoft's salesforce and its own. They realized that Intuit needed to secure bundling deals that would get Quicken into the hands of as many customers as possible, which meant striking deals in which the company forwent anything but a token payment from the PC manufacturers. The trick was to create a special version of Quicken for such bundles that would not have all the features of the regular retail version (to give customers a reason to upgrade in the future) but *would* have the most popular features (to avoid being perceived as a "crippled" version that customers would not bother using). Striking the right balance was delicate, but Intuit swiftly succeeded. The company hired several veterans with experience in creating such bundles, designed a special version of Quicken with ample features that a new user would not exhaust for months, and jumped quickly ahead of Microsoft in this important form of distribution. Microsoft could only admire Intuit's nimbleness and try to catch up.

For those with an antiquarian interest in Microsoft's very early history, it's amusing to recall that Bill Gates, in an interview in 1982, had shown himself amenable to literally giving away software through hardware bundles in order to secure market share. The occasion was the release of MS-DOS 2.0, and he said at the time that the software was being made available freely to computer manufacturers so that it would be widely distributed. "Frankly, an operating system is more of a strategic move than an economic product," he had said, explaining "you wouldn't expect to find a huge percentage of a software company's income ever coming from an operating system." Subsequent events, of course, revealed business possibilities he had not then imagined. Manufacturers, and indirectly their customers, turned out to be willing after all to pay a small price for operating systems, and, by virtue of volume, Microsoft did very, very well in this segment of the business. But down the road, the latter-day Microsoft was timid about deploying Money in bundles, just as the company had initially spared Encarta from inclusion in demeaning give-away bundles.

In 1993, Microsoft's Money group was intensely focused, not on distribution, but on the development of its next upgrade. The new version was to finally provide the electronic banking features that had been planned for version 1 but had been left on the cutting-room floor at the last minute and then had to be excised again from version 2 because Microsoft lacked a payments processing partner when Intuit contractually blocked it from working with Checkfree. For version 3 of Money, Microsoft had found an untested partner smaller than Checkfree, a new outfit called National Payments Clearinghouse, Inc., and had persuaded four banks to work with it to provide electronic banking services to future Money customers. Late in the drive to have the new version of Money ready for the fall of 1993, however, Microsoft's developers discovered that though the partner banks were on schedule to complete their portion of the code, Microsoft's own code once again would not be ready. So the company had to decide whether to go ahead with the new release without electronic banking or to postpone the release until that feature could be included. Not wanting to repeat the dismal history of the first two releases, Microsoft chose postponement. The peak selling season arrived for 1993, and Intuit had a field day offering its new upgrade while Microsoft was still stuck with its old, weak version.

Finally, in January 1994, Microsoft was able to bring out version 3 of Money with electronic banking features, beating Intuit to market with a major innovation. The highly fragmented nature of the banking industry—over 12,000 separate banks in the United States alone—made it difficult to entice prospective Money customers with just the four banks that were initially linked to the software. But the mere possibility of customers using electronic banking transformed the category into a strategically important one in the eyes of Gates and his senior managers. Revenue from the personal finance category of software was too small for Microsoft to be much concerned about Quicken's commanding lead over Money. But as the point of entry for a future market in electronic banking, personal finance software would be critical. The same thought had occurred to U.S. banks, and most saw a sinister motive behind Microsoft's interest in developing this new corner of the software business. The banks wondered, what would prevent Microsoft, after enticing them to build up electronic banking, from dispensing with its role as intermediary between customers and banks and becoming a bank itself? Consequently most banks did not welcome the arrival of Microsoft's banking-enabled Money.

When the Money team faced a product review meeting with Gates in February 1994, the only cheery news came from Europe. Money was the market leader in both France and Germany, thanks to Intuit's slowness in launching an international effort, and netted Microsoft $42 a unit, all in retail sales. This was a princely sum that could not be matched in the United States, where Microsoft received just a third of that for each retail package. The bulk of revenue for Money, such as it was, came from bundling deals in which Microsoft received the less-than-princely sum of $1.50 a pop, which in most cases turned out to be the last money Microsoft would receive for those copies. Most customers who received the Microsoft personal finance package preloaded on their newly purchased computers never purchased the regular retail version of the software. The budget for the fiscal year that would end the following June called for Money to deliver a modest $5.2 million in revenues. Given that the holiday season had passed and the product had only reached about half of its assigned revenue quota, the outlook for meeting its sales goals was not bright. In terms of raw numbers of units, thanks to bundling efforts, Money could claim about 15 percent of the personal finance market. Measured in terms of actual revenue, it had less than 10 percent of the market.

A bleakly clearsighted Jabe Blumenthal led the presentation to Gates: Intuit "owned" the category; it made few missteps; it was broadening its financial services offerings and expanding into new markets and computer platforms. Microsoft's own Money, on the other hand, had yet to capture significant market share or even market awareness of its existence. Unlike Quicken, Money did not have companion programs like Intuit's small business accounting and personal income tax packages. And, to make matters worse, the large tax preparation firm H&R Block was entering the fray with its recent purchase of MECA, the company that held the third place in personal finance software. Microsoft could see no way to extricate itself from its marginal position in this category.

A *Newsweek* reporter was permitted to observe this 1994 product review meeting. The story that would later appear described Blumenthal in unflattering terms ("lean, hawk-eyed, predatory in manner") and characterized Gates as a money-mad cartoon character, carried away by fantastical visions of world domination. *Newsweek* reported that the mere thought of capturing a slice of revenue on all electronic banking transactions was sufficient for Gates to forget his disappointment with Money's performance. It said he pounded triumphantly on the conference table and exclaimed, "Get me into that, and, goddamn, we'll make so much money!"

One sentence in particular, in which Gates was reported to have declared that banks were "dinosaurs" and Microsoft could simply bypass them, would endure long after the rest of the story had been forgotten because it seemed to confirm the very fear that banks had of Microsoft. Those who were present later recalled that Gates had said that bank *computer systems* were dinosaurs, not the banks themselves, which after all Microsoft had been assiduously courting. Gates would spend the next two years attempting to correct *Newsweek*'s version, but once in circulation, the banks-are-dinosaurs phrase attributed to him simply would not die.

One way of considering Money's position in early 1994 would be to think of Microsoft as David, not Goliath. In terms of the key index in the software business, head count, Intuit had more than 1000 people focused on nothing but personal finance and related software. Microsoft had only about 60. If Microsoft wanted to catch up with Intuit, it could match Intuit's investment in hiring an equivalent number of people to focus exclusively on the same corner of the industry. Debt-free Microsoft certainly had the cash to do so. At this time, its cash reserves were so large that even the company's in-house reporter was amazed to learn from Mike Brown, the company's vice-president for finance, that the kitty held $3.2 billion. The reporter was dumbfounded that the money was "just sitting there in the bank." Yes, Brown said, it was kept in short-term investments, awaiting Gates and Myhrvold's decision about what to do with it.

In the past, whenever it lagged behind the market leader, Microsoft would choose to take the arduous path of redoubled internal effort. It would marshal an overwhelming number of smart employees to improve Microsoft's product until it was, at last, truly competitive and able to win over buyers, one wallet at a time. But this time, in the spring of 1994, Gates decided to dip into the cash kitty for a quick fix and simply acquire Intuit. Unlike the half-hearted inquiries that had been made earlier, in 1989 and 1990, this time Microsoft would negotiate in earnest, offering whatever it would take to accomplish a friendly acquisition.

This move represented such a departure from the company's past that it deserves a moment's consideration. By that point, Microsoft had increased its revenues to $4 billion a year without deviating too often from its long-established pattern of growth through internal effort, not by acquisitions. Past departures from this pattern had been the occasional licensing of outside products (Flight Simulator); the acquisition of smart people by purchasing an outside company, retaining the people, and discarding the code base (like Nathan Myhrvold's little company, Dynamical Systems); or the acquisition of an established company with special technical expertise that would help jump-start Microsoft's own homegrown skills in new technical areas (Fox for databases, Softimage for computer animation, and Vermeer for Web page creation). Much earlier in its history, in 1983 and 1984, Gates had sought a merger with Lotus, which at the time was much bigger than Microsoft and turned the offer down. Gates was glad afterward—on its own, Microsoft grew to a market valuation of $50 billion by the time Lotus was acquired by IBM in 1995 for $3.5 billion. And, in a few cases, Microsoft had investigated acquisitions that would have meant an instant leading position in market share—the proposed merger with Novell comes to mind. But preliminary talks, like those between Microsoft and Novell or the earlier ones between Microsoft and Lotus, can be found at some point in the past between virtually any two players in the personal computer industry. The combinatorial possibilities are myriad, and the talks have usually aborted before advancing far. In the end, Microsoft's growth had been built by attracting its own customers, not by buying them wholesale through a major merger.

During the previous antitrust battles with the Federal Trade Commission and the Department of Justice, Microsoft and its external defenders had argued that Microsoft's less skilled competitors—the Lotuses, the WordPerfects, the Borlands—had no basis for complaining because Intuit's success with Quicken showed that company size did not necessarily determine whose product would win when pitted against Microsoft. The quality of the product, the effectiveness of the marketing, and the success in building brand loyalty were what Microsoft had emphasized in gaining the lead in other categories of software—and Intuit had, too, in personal finance. Microsoft managers always told their employees that Microsoft's market share lead in spreadsheets, word processing, and the like permitted no complacency and had to be defended each day with continual product improvements. If Microsoft were to abandon the competition with Intuit and simply "buy" its way out of its problems with Money, the sermon it had been preaching would have been undercut. If Microsoft managers really believed that a strong product can always topple a market leader, why did Microsoft dodge the hard fight for market share when it found itself staring uphill?

The proposed acquisition of Intuit presented a tricky public relations problem. It also automatically gave the government an opportunity to scrutinize the transaction, which could result in a legal challenge. Growth that is achieved by dint of internal effort is the product of thousands of small corporate decisions, no one of which is visible in the way that the acquisition and absorption of an outside company would be. That is one reason the Federal Trade Commission, and later the Department of Justice, brought in such a meager haul at the end of their multiyear fishing expedition investigating Microsoft's dominance in operating system software. But if those agencies earlier had seemed pathetically desperate to come up with something, anything, that would permit the government to rein in Microsoft, they now would have no need to concoct a case. To find a good example of two competitors raising troubling questions about the likelihood of greatly diminished competition in the wake of their proposed merger, you would not have to look beyond the proposed marriage of Microsoft and Intuit. And the adverb "greatly" did not even precede "diminished competition" in the guidelines for reviewing horizontal mergers that the Department of Justice and the Federal

Trade Commission had issued jointly in 1992 for precisely this kind of case. The government's alarms would be tripped by the mere likelihood that the acquiring company would be able, in the wake of diminished competition, to impose at least a "small but significant and nontransitory increase in price."

Microsoft executives turned to their attorneys for an estimate of the odds that the courts would challenge and then block the merger. The legal staff, true to form, hated just such a request. It sought to instead lay out the legal precedents that defined a range of possibilities, without attaching numerical probabilities to a particular outcome. The attorneys did encourage the executive committee to push forward with the proposed merger, proposing the "Fix It First" defense. The government's guidelines focused on the increase in market share that the acquiring company would gain as a result of a merger. Well, then, the reasoning went, if Microsoft's net increase in market share in personal finance software would be *zero* as a result of divestment of its own product, Money, the government's objection to the merger would have no basis. With this optimistic reading from the legal department, Microsoft executives felt that the chances that the Department of Justice would block the merger were small. They were no doubt also emboldened by an unfortunate syllogism based on the previous experience with the government's antitrust staff, which suggested that the government's lack of a good case against the company in the past meant, ergo, the government would *never* have a good case.

From May until September 1994, high-level Microsoft executives engaged in secret talks with Intuit about a possible deal. During this time, the Money team was kept in the dark, in case negotiations did not reach the desired end, and also because, even if the deal were to succeed, its only chance to pass government muster would be if Money were sent elsewhere. The more work that was done in the meantime to ready the next release, the easier it would be to unload the software on a willing buyer.

Microsoft proceeded as if it could handily meet anticipated government objections. On the eve of the announcement, Money's managers were at last told of the negotiations, and one was sent to Utah to sell Money to Novell, conditional on completion of the Intuit merger. When the details with Novell were finalized, the Microsoft bid for Intuit was announced in October. It came as a surprise to the employees of both Microsoft and Intuit, who so long had regarded the prospective merger partner as The Enemy. Now, suddenly, they were to embrace. For Intuit, the adjustment of course was easier. For the Quicken group, Microsoft's willingness to buy the company was sweet vindication—little Intuit had forced the Giant to cry for mercy. And all of Intuit's shareholders had concrete reason to rejoice: Microsoft's bid for the company included a premium of more than 50 percent of its current market valuation. The company, which had earnings of only $25 million in the previous year, was now valued at $1.5 billion. Scott Cook's holdings of Intuit stock would be worth $360 million.

For Microsoft employees who had no direct connection to the Money group, the news of the merger was astounding. It marked a dramatic break with Microsoft's past. For some who stood in the hallways to talk about the deal, it conjured unsettling images—J. D. Rockefeller was mentioned by name, with a shiver. For Money's developers and marketing personnel, the news that Quicken would displace their own baby was humiliating. These employees did not face exile to Utah and would remain with the company, but for the time being they found themselves in a curious purgatory. They would not yet be permitted to transfer to their next positions within Microsoft. They had to stay at their stations and continue work on the next version of Money in order to honor the terms of the agreement with Novell, which did not want to be handed code that had sat moldering for a year. Given these circumstances, we might guess that the developers' morale would be low and the resulting work uninspired and careless. But, in fact, the work resumed and proceeded well, better in many ways than normally, unimpeded by the usual requests for changes from the marketing team or the whims of upper managers. These developers were left on their own—and their professional conscientiousness would turn out to be of great benefit to Microsoft in ways no one at the time foresaw.

Unfortunately for Microsoft, however, Novell, the ostensible beneficiary of the transfer, lost the middling interest it had had when it agreed to provide a new home for Money. The ebbing of enthusiasm was not due to onerous terms: Microsoft could not have made it easier without literally giving the product away to a future competitor.

What Microsoft ended up offering Novell was a deal that maintained a facade of a "sale," but which was unlikely to cost Novell much of anything. No initial payment was demanded; an inconsequential royalty of 10 percent was to be paid on net sales of Money in its first post-transfer year; and to sweeten the deal, Microsoft guaranteed Novell millions of dollars if Money did not fare well. Still, Novell developed cold feet, not only about accepting a new personal finance package, but also about continuing its poorly performing experiments with other application software, like WordPerfect, which diverted the company from shoring up its embattled core business in networking software. Novell had belatedly asked itself why it thought it was going to be more successful with Money than Microsoft had been. And if it could do no better—even to do as well would be difficult—why would it want to be in that business at all? By March 1995, Novell's CEO, Bob Frankenberg, was actually urging the Department of Justice to block the pending Microsoft-Intuit merger that supposedly was going to yield a gift to his own company.

During the six months between the announcement of the proposed merger and the filing of the Department of Justice suit seeking to block it, and even as their ally Novell abandoned them, Microsoft and Intuit still maintained a cheery optimism. The executives at both companies told their respective employees not to worry about fallback positions in case the merger was not consummated—the deal would go through, so they should plan accordingly. Confident of the desired outcome, Gates talked matter-of-factly in public about Microsoft's impending shift to a new business model centered on capturing a slice of revenue on transactions, the shift that the *Newsweek* reporter had portrayed darkly as behind-closed-doors plotting just half a year earlier. When the Department of Justice announced its suit, Gates reflexively responded as if this latest challenge was based on as weak a case as the earlier government challenges to Microsoft, vowing to fight on in the courtroom in order to make the merger happen.

The brief that the Department of Justice filed in U.S. District Court opposing the merger makes interesting reading. The transfer of the number two product in the category, Money, to a third party did not much impress the Department of Justice reviewers. They reasoned cogently that Novell's willingness to fund losses after exhausting the Microsoft subsidy was doubtful, given that the product was strategically much less important to Novell than it had been to Microsoft, which was eager to expand into electronic banking and other transaction-intensive services. And prospective new competitors likely would be frightened away by the prospect of facing Quicken once it was in Microsoft's hands, where Intuit's strengths would be wedded to Microsoft's considerable power, which had enabled it to secure the number two position in market share in this category before the merger.

The brief also made a fuss about a subpoenaed memo in which a Microsoft executive vice-president reported his initial negotiations with Intuit's Scott Cook. Cook had been told that Microsoft had not invested in the head count to the degree that this strategically important area deserved, and "I tried to tell him how much we could do with $1 billion; I tried to be nonthreatening, but let him know we would do something aggressively." Making a much more damaging argument, the brief used the remark as evidence that Microsoft, if it remained separate, would continue to invest heavily in improving its product, egging Intuit into additional improvements—a textbook case of competition that would benefit consumers. The government wanted to know what evidence there was of a comparable commitment to Money on the part of Novell if the product were to be transferred into its hands.

A subtle but important inconsistency on Microsoft's part suggested that the transfer of Money to Novell would be less significant than the company claimed. In the terms of the deal, Microsoft had promised to turn over to Novell all the code, associated intellectual property rights, customer lists, and documentation for Money, and to provide some technical assistance from a few of its own developers during a short transition period. Yet, when it spoke elsewhere of its merger with Intuit, Microsoft said that the most important asset it would acquire in the deal would not be Quicken's code, but rather Intuit's employees and the skills that Scott Cook and company would bring to Microsoft's organization. Indeed, the prizing of people over code was a hallmark of Microsoft's previous acquisitions. Why, then, was Novell supposed to be in a good position when the Money code was delivered to its doorstep without permanent transfer of the code's parents?

Microsoft's lawyers had three principal responses to the government's objections. The weakest one was its proposed Fix It First defense. The company grudgingly conceded that Novell did not possess strengths identical to those of Microsoft. But the law did not require that the recipient of a divestment perfectly match the original owner. (The government could have counterresponded that Novell did not know the first thing about the consumer software business; it was ready to bolt even without having taken a risk-free try.) As for the tacit criticism that the merger would remove one of the few categories of software applications in which a personal computer software company other than Microsoft held a dominating lead, Microsoft's lawyers were ready to argue that the successes Microsoft had in other fields were not legally relevant. If the government wanted to make an issue of it, it would have to change its own merger guidelines. (Possible counterresponses might have been: the acquiring company's lead in other categories *is* germane; and since you mentioned it, fine, we'll amend the guidelines.)

Microsoft's strongest defense was that the area of electronic banking was still in a nascent state. It was far too early for any company, or even combination of companies, to establish a durable lead. The financial assets of a combined Microsoft-Intuit would eventually be dwarfed by those of large banks that would surely get into the action themselves. If merged, Gates and Cook said, the resulting, larger company could speed the process of automating financial transactions, bringing the more progressively minded banks into the electronic age more quickly and helping put computers to work for customers earlier rather than later. The very month that the government filed its complaint opposing the merger, the argument that Microsoft-Intuit would not be all that large received some indirect support when BankAmerica and NationsBank, the nation's second and fourth largest banks, respectively, announced that they jointly were purchasing MECA, the publisher of the third-place personal finance package. But it was a very distant third place, and this was an inexpensive way for the banks to dabble. It was a $35 million deal, not a multi-billion-dollar commitment.

The arguments in defense of the merger offered, at best, long-term benefits to consumers at the price of immediately eliminating the two-horse race between the market-leading Intuit and the lagging-but-eager-to-win Microsoft. After the government's objections to the merger were spelled out and Microsoft's attorneys laid out the likelihood of another year's delay before a trial and even more time before an appeal would finally settle the matter, Gates reconsidered his vow to pursue the deal in the courtroom. Employing his trademark practicality, he wisely decided to back out. Microsoft formally withdrew its offer.

As is customary in such cases, Microsoft extended to Intuit a $46 million payment as salve for the distraction that the uncompleted transaction had been to the target company. However, Microsoft need not have been concerned; Intuit had reaped priceless positive publicity in the course of this adventure. By the time the merger was called off, the price Microsoft was prepared to pay for Intuit had passed $2 billion (thanks to the appreciation in the interim of the Microsoft stock to which it was tied). No other software company had made headlines as Intuit had for being so valuable that Microsoft would offer to pay a then-record sum to acquire it. Microsoft's bid also validated the importance of the category of personal finance software. Actually the aborted merger was the second time that Microsoft had helped Intuit validate the business—the first time was when Microsoft entered the category itself with Money, which arguably helped Intuit far more than hurt it in bringing attention to this largely ignored corner of the market.

After the announcement that the merger had been called off, Intuit's stock price could have collapsed, but it not only remained aloft, it levitated still higher. By the end of 1995, its market value was $3.6 billion, or more than twice as much as Microsoft had originally bid (even though some observers had criticized Microsoft's offer for providing too rich a premium above the prevailing market price). This high market valuation reflected the credibility Intuit had gained by being Microsoft's desired quarry. The favorable publicity extended worldwide, and even Intuit's recruiting efforts benefited. In belatedly launching stronger marketing for Quicken outside the United States, Intuit found itself deluged with applications from strong candidates who had refused to return the phone calls of Intuit recruiters the previous year. The episode also conferred credibility on Intuit in the eyes of banks. Before the merger announcement, Intuit had not succeeded in signing up a single bank for electronic banking; after the merger collapsed in 1995, Intuit was able to line up several banks, which were glad to have a credible alternative to the demonized Bill "Banks Are Dinosaurs" Gates.

The end to its quest to acquire Intuit left Microsoft in worse shape in some ways than when it had started. Its business relationship with Mastercard was in tatters, and Money's reputation was damaged by the company's fumbled attempt to abandon it in favor of Quicken. Fortunately for the company, Microsoft developers had not just been going through the motions while the merger deal was still on. They had made great progress in readying the next version of Money, which would serve as one of the early applications written for Windows 95.

Internally, at least, the Money group received sympathy for their travails in the preceding months. No, Gates did not immediately raise the group's budget by a billion dollars for new head count, as Microsoft had threatened Intuit it would in the controversial memo ("I tried to tell him how much we could do with $1 billion") seized on by the Department of Justice. But after having averted the expenditure of $2 billion on the proposed merger, almost any request from the Money group for head count would seem puny. (The same effect worked for Encarta whenever Microsoft had considered, then dismissed, the purchase of existing printed encyclopedia businesses.) The Windows 95 marketing group took special pains to back the promotion of the new version of Money, a mild form of favoritism that probably would not have happened had it not been for the ordeal that the Money group had endured. A November 1995 reorganization formally recognized within Microsoft the strategic importance of the personal finance category by establishing a Desktop Finance *Division*. Initially the division's only product was Money, but its elevation to the same organizational plane as the entire Consumer Division signaled the importance that Gates placed on its future role in the company.

Having discarded the proposed merger, Microsoft and Intuit resumed the tough competitive battle that had engaged them earlier, each spurring the other to adopt improvements that directly benefited consumers. By December 1995, Money was no longer the technically hapless product it had been in its earlier incarnations. Walt Mossberg, the personal computer columnist for the *Wall Street Journal*, expressed surprise to see that "Microsoft has finally turned

Money into a very respectable competitor." Mossberg's review only examined the two companies, not so subtly emphasizing that, in personal finance, it was a simple two-contestant race. But, noting the improvements that both companies had built into their products, Mossberg concluded, "It's enough to make you glad that merger fell through."

The appearance that Microsoft and Intuit had simply resumed their rivalry where they had left off was deceiving. While both companies jockeyed for the best positions for their personal finance products in the proprietary pipelines from homes to banks (Checkfree and NPCI) or from homes to merchants (Microsoft racing to tie its products to MSN; Intuit, to America Online), the underlying assumptions were quietly crumbling as the growth of the Internet shook up existing models.

The Internet was especially relevant to personal finance software, whose potential benefits could be realized not with a stand-alone program but rather with the program tied to financial information outside the home. Software companies and banks alike were uncertain of the outcome of the change. Would the Internet allow companies like Microsoft—and Intuit—to provide their customers with bank-like services, as banks feared? Or would banks be able to reach their own customers without having to pay a tithe to software company intermediaries? Caught up in the new mania of ubiquitous networking, everyone was shouting out conflicting self-interested visions. Thus, to the Internet we now turn.

Chapter 13

Preemptive Attack

O NCE UNDERSTOOD, *the implications of IBM's monopolistic hold on the basic equipment of the information revolution are frightening. It is as if in the past, a single company had held a worldwide monopoly over the steam engine; or over the making of steel; or, later still, over automobile production.*

Richard Thomas DeLarmarter, in *Big Blue*

If I saw this quotation and was told that DeLarmarter was an economist with eight years of experience on the staff of the Antitrust Division of the Department of Justice, I would have difficulty guessing the publication date of his book. The federal government filed antitrust suits against IBM at different times—in 1932, 1952, and 1969. The last one, the famous thirteen-year government siege from 1969 to 1982, ended with the government's withdrawal for ideological reasons (what might be called the Reagan Administration's *anti*-antitrust philosophy). The suit became the model, retrospectively, of the irrelevance of antitrust prosecution in ill-chosen cases. As we now know, IBM would be caught unawares by the popularity of its own personal computer introduced in 1981, by the capacity for third parties to improve it, and by the new industry that grew around it. We cannot assume that the generalization to be drawn here applies in all industries, but in this particular one, the operations of the market served to rein in the power of a company that had seemed omnipotent without the assistance of the Antitrust Division.

DeLarmarter's book depicting IBM as the monstrous monopolist, unstoppable without government intervention, appeared not in 1956, not in 1976, but in *1986*. It was the fruit of four years of research, following his unhappy departure from federal employ when the government withdrew its case against DeLarmarter's nemesis. Oblivious to the changes in the computer industry in the interim, DeLarmarter untiringly beat the drum against his old bête noire. The same obliviousness to the passage of time and changing circumstances was also to be found in good measure among DeLarmarter's colleagues at the Department of Justice. They had their sights set on Microsoft for so long that they could not bring themselves to move on, even after Microsoft withdrew its bid for Intuit and even after Microsoft acquiesced to the consent decree that settled the minor issues of operating system licensing. Just as DeLarmarter could not let go of IBM as the personal computer industry blossomed, so too the next generation at the Department of Justice could not let go of Microsoft as the Internet's popularity ramified throughout the industry.

The target for the Antitrust Division's ongoing investigations of Microsoft in 1995 was the yet-unborn Microsoft Network (MSN). No threat is as fearsome as the one that has yet to actually appear, and such was the case with MSN in the minds of the Department of Justice staff. The government regarded MSN's affront to competition as so grave, and the Department of Justice's solicitation of testimony from Microsoft's competitors to bolster its own oppositional stance was so transparently one sided, that many industry observers began to speculate that the government would not permit Microsoft to release Windows 95 if the company insisted on keeping easy MSN sign-up part of the new operating system. The government normally maintains a strict public silence about all ongoing antitrust investigations until it decides whether to take formal legal action. In this case, however, with the plans of most players in the personal computer industry tied in one fashion or another to the release of Windows 95, a cloud of uncertainty now fell on the entire industry, not just on Microsoft. In early August, the government issued a brief press release confirming that it was investigating MSN and "other issues associated with possible anticompetitive practices relating to Windows 95," but that it did not expect to complete its investigation prior to August 24, which was the appointed day of the rollout of Windows 95. This served to dispel the concern that the new Windows would be held up, but it left a large question mark over the future of MSN.

The central argument that the other commercial online services were only too glad to explain to the sympathetic ears at the Department of Justice was that MSN would enjoy an unfair free ride into homes along with the new operating system, an advantage that would be denied to them, MSN's soon-to-be competitors. Microsoft's response was reasonable. Everyone in the commercial online services industry gave out introductory discs that provided free trials. These were the same discs that contributed to the high churn rates in the industry, with many people trying the online services and many fewer staying and paying. The prevailing "industry standard" at that time was to provide initially free sign-up to as many people as possible. Yes, it was convenient for Microsoft to be able to use another product, Windows, to convey MSN to new users, but other online services— magazine publishing giant Ziff-Davis's, for example—also had tie-ins with other products or media. MSN was no different from the others—its online services had to be compelling enough for users to stay after the free trial expired. So where in MSN's plans was the dire threat to freedom, justice, and the American Way?

When Windows 95 finally appeared on August 24 and MSN formally debuted, nothing occurred as earthshaking as Microsoft had hoped and MSN's competitors had dreaded. Consumer acceptance of Windows 95, especially among those who were considering upgrading the system software on older personal computers, was guarded. Sales of the new operating system in the remainder of 1995 were only about two-thirds of what Microsoft had hoped. The unfair "advantage" of MSN's ability to ride the Windows 95 magic carpet now was revealed as a disadvantage, too, because MSN worked only with Windows 95. Thus, if the new operating system was slow to take off, so too would be MSN.

Technical problems also contributed to a less than auspicious start for MSN. Even though MSN software had been placed in the hands of 200,000 beta testers prior to release, perhaps the company's widest beta test for a product other than an operating system, MSN was formally released into the market in August as flawed and limited as any other first version. *P.C. Letter*, an industry newsletter, commented that MSN was in such a sorry state that Steve Case, the head of America Online, had wasted his time beseeching the Department of Justice to unbundle MSN from Windows 95. Instead, Case and his colleagues would have done much more damage to MSN "by just mailing out MSN disks far and wide" and letting consumers see for themselves what a "loser" MSN was. An analyst at Dataquest was no kinder, describing MSN as the "Yugo" of online services.

Before MSN was released, its rivals had claimed that it would have as many as 9 million subscribers by the end of 1995, or more than the Big Three online services combined. In fact, MSN struggled to provide satisfactory performance on its glitch-ridden network to 500,000 subscribers, a milestone it reached only in November. During the same period, America Online added 700,000 subscribers, and its acceleration in growth seemed only to increase after MSN's release. AOL gained another 500,000 customers in merely one month and by late December had 4.5 million customers, a threefold increase since the beginning of 1995. At the very same time that the Justice Department was sharpening its knives to go after MSN, Microsoft's own rivals were growing handily on their own, and consumers were the principal beneficiaries because MSN's lower prices had spurred its rivals to cut their prices, too.

If the script for this story were to follow that of other inauspicious product introductions, Microsoft now would remove MSN's technical shortcomings one by one, and with relentless improvements the company would fight its way uphill against the entrenched competition. But Microsoft's original plan to combat the powers of AOL and CompuServe had been rendered less and less relevant as the months had passed during MSN's development. By the fall of 1995, the battle against America Online resembled fighting units stranded on a remote atoll, far from the central theater defined by the Internet.

In early 1995, MSN had put out the word to prospective third parties that it would welcome as many kinds of information services as could possibly find paying customers. Microsoft intended then to make its money not so much from monthly subscription fees as from a portion of whatever revenues the third-party providers of information collected on the network. The call for content-providers had been successful—too successful. Microsoft was deluged with 15,000 applications from content-providers and forum managers, far too many for a small staff to screen. Russ Siegelman proposed that to keep the task of making these arrangements manageable, MSN should initially focus on a handful of areas (termed "beachheads" by MSN managers). Families with children would be one rubric for information services; small/home offices and PC enthusiasts were others. But when Siegelman presented the plan to Gates in early 1995, Gates rejected it. He felt that MSN must have at least as many services as AOL did and directed Siegelman to sign up more content-providers.

At that point, Siegelman still conceived MSN as entering an existing business, commercial online services. But by early summer 1995—even as the Department of Justice was busy investigating MSN's impending monopolization of online services—Gates realized that commercial online services in toto could not continue to carry on as if the Internet was not changing the rules. He revoked his earlier injunction to match AOL, convinced that lots of content would appear on the Internet soon enough without the intercession of traditional online services. Microsoft's only possibility of a viable business for MSN, then, would be to develop unique content on its own or with select content-providers with whom Microsoft would work to provide special content and services, accessible via any other company's Web browser. By the time MSN actually rolled out, the goal Microsoft had in mind was not to vanquish AOL, CompuServe, and Prodigy, but to simply attain profitability somehow in the coming Internet era of freely available information.

In the original business model, it was easy to see who had to be bested—AOL—and what would be necessary in order to do so. But in the revised model, it was not clear at all how money could be made. Paul Allen's company, Starwave, located down the road and staffed with a number of former Microsoft employees, showed that a profitable niche for a particular kind of online service could be created in conjunction with the Internet. For sports enthusiasts, Starwave offered a free Web site that aggregated scores and sports stories—information that was available elsewhere but repackaged attractively. Advertising from sponsors brought in revenue from this basic level of service that attracted as many "eyeballs" as possible. For access to unique sports information, visitors were invited to subscribe to Starwave's fee-only online sports service for $5 a month. Still, because of its limited scope, Starwave's experiment fell short of providing heartening evidence that the general public would be willing to pay for a broad array of information on the Web.

Within Microsoft, there was no consensus about how to price its own online services in the future. Gates was fond of talking of how consumers would be glad to pay a small amount, say, a nickel, each time they visited a Web site of interest, and by virtue of volume, seemingly tiny usage fees could add up to a considerable revenue stream. But contrary voices within MSN expressed doubt that the public would accept such fine granularity in fees. Would people really buy *Time* magazine articles one at a time? Or to put it another way, after becoming accustomed to flat-rate charges for local telephone calls, would consumers happily embrace a new price regime for local calls that, similar to their long-distance service, was based on the duration of each individual call? Merely asking such questions, which involved social psychology as much as business strategy, reflected the widely held conviction that the Internet's popularity threw all comfortable assumptions of the past into doubt.

Uncertainty led to intellectual efflorescence, though the participants were in no position to savor the moment. The future of the personal computer itself was now in doubt—many in the industry began rethinking the ideal size and cost of the computer that would tap into the Internet. When the first CD-ROM specifications were developed, Gates had searched the horizon for incipient signs of a threat to PCs from below, such as CD-I players or game machines hooked up to a television. Again in early 1995, the threat from the low end reappeared as competitors and industry observers began to prognosticate that a new kind of machine would soon supplant the personal computer as the consumer electronics device for the masses.

"Telecomputer" was the term proposed by Gordon Bell, a patriarch from the minicomputer era. It would be a machine that would be used expressly for connecting online to the Internet, combining the price of the telephone and the functionality of the PC. To keep its cost minimal, it would have to be "dumb," bereft of its own microprocessor and hard drive storage, but it could tap into machine intelligence and mass storage residing elsewhere on the network. Nicholas Negroponte of MIT's Media Lab was pleased by such talk. He pointed out that Nintendo had just released a game machine whose technical specifications—32-bit RISC microprocessor, extraordinary 3-D graphics, digital stereo sound, and so on—resembled those of a Silicon Graphics workstation, yet its suggested retail price would be $199. That the standard price for personal computers remained stuck at $1500 was proof, Negroponte argued, that their prices were held artificially high and that American technology companies were averse to entering a commodity business. They would prefer selling one million machines at $1500 to selling 10 million at $150. These musings, along with those contributed by others, were sent via e-mail to Nathan Myhrvold, the point man defending the PC battlement.

Could history be repeating itself, and a small box designed just to access the Internet—a "Web crawler," "Internet terminal," or "Network Computer," as others called it—be about to do unto PCs as PCs had done unto larger machines? (A computer scientist needled Myhrvold: "Mainframes are forever, right?") Comfortable with historical analogies, Myhrvold did not contest the method, but he did reject what lessons were to be drawn. Everyone was familiar with Moore's Law, but some other laws derived from past experience would be decisive here, too. Myhrvold argued that users' expectations and desires grew faster than the ability of either software or hardware to satisfy them. And consequently software developers would use up new computing resources at a rate slightly faster than they would become available. Given the unlimited nature of human ambition, there would never be an end to the desire for more features in software.

The reason that Moore's Law had not led to steadily diminishing prices for personal computers was that consumers' hunger for absolute power and new capabilities increased at least as fast as software developers could deliver ever more sophisticated hardware. A $200 game machine might seem much cheaper than a $2000 personal computer, but keep in mind, Myhrvold said, that if you amortize the cost of the PC across the many different uses to which it is put, the price difference is not all that great. The programmability of a general-purpose computer like the PC continued to be a key advantage over less expensive and less capable variations. Home users were increasingly voting in favor of the PC, Myhrvold pointed out, outselling Sega or Nintendo in the previous year.

Rob Glaser, who had left Microsoft and had founded Progressive Networks, which provided audio software for computers connected to the Internet, was interested in Gordon Bell's proposal of a telecomputer. He wondered aloud about the practicality of setting a single, unchanging standard for the telecomputer and letting the normal progress of Moore's Law push the price of the machine down and down, eventually making it affordable to everyone. Glaser had derived his own lesson from history through painful experience. When Microsoft and Tandy introduced the first multimedia PC, they had based it on Intel's anemic 286 chip in order to make the machine as affordable as possible and consumers had steered clear of it, perceiving it as a "bad PC."

The microprocessor was at the heart of the PC revolution, and no equivalent new development was visible that would upset the existing dominance of the personal computer. The long-term impact of the Internet, Myhrvold speculated, would be to *increase* the price of a personal computer. The more that online computing proved it could do to change consumers' lives, the more consumers would demand improved hardware and software to realize the potential. Twenty years ago, the typical home budget did not even have a category earmarked for computing. Now, 30 percent of households had a personal computer; over 10 percent had two or more. Myhrvold thought the percentage of household income that would be devoted to computing had nowhere to go but "UP UP UP." He drew another historical analogy: just as the advent of the affordable automobile had led families to increase the percentage of their income that they devoted to transportation, so too computing would come to rival transportation or any other major expense category in the household budget.

Transportation could be used to draw another kind of historical comparison, likening MSN and the other commercial online services to toll roads running in parallel to the toll-free Internet. Would the quality of the toll road and its roadside attractions be sufficiently compelling to entice users to forsake the freeway? One reason the Internet excited such interest in the personal computer industry was because it was *not* part of Microsoft's dominion and seemed to offer a fresh opportunity to change the rules. Larry Ellison, whose plans for rapid rollout of interactive television had fizzled, wasted no time in seizing the Internet in its stead as the opportunity to smash Microsoft's hegemony. In October 1995, Ellison announced Oracle's plans to introduce a low-cost "Network Computer" in 1996 that would cost about $500 and would resemble the "Web crawler" that Bell, Myhrvold, and others had considered, though it would incorporate a low-cost microprocessor. With the bravado of a challenger and without analyzing the if's and but's, Ellison waved away the PC. Too expensive, he declared: "PCs are old hat."

To defend the idea that fully capable personal computers would prevail, Myhrvold turned to, of all places, the classified ads for additional support. Isn't it curious, he asked, that there are so few used computers for sale? The answer to the mystery, he hypothesized, was that potential buyers simply were not much interested in machines, regardless of low price, that could not compete technically with the newest offerings. Why should we expect that a crippled Web crawler would be in great demand either? But his conviction did not interfere with his appreciation of smarts in others. He put Gordon Bell, the originator of the e-mail thread proposing a telecomputer, on Microsoft's payroll, adding still another name to Microsoft's lengthening list of distinguished computer science figures from academe and industry.

This early debate about Internet terminals may have turned out to be a passing moment of extreme polarization of positions. All parties reconsidered their definition of a personal computer. Microsoft revived projects that included a scaled-down version of Windows for handheld gizmos and another one that would link a stripped-down PC to a television set, saving the consumer the expense of a monitor. And as design work on Oracle's Network Computer proceeded, the company revealed that Ellison's declaration that PCs were "old hat" was premature. The Oracle-designed box would have a microprocessor in it after all—not made by Intel and not able to run Windows, but a microprocessor nevertheless. So the revolutionists seemed to be unable, at least initially, to make a clean break from the "PC" model after all. Both the revolutionaries and the ancien régime were moving toward the middle.

Gates's decision to reorient every Microsoft business—and in MSN's case, every business-to-be—to unconditionally embrace the Internet was manifested in steps over the course of 1994 and 1995. Between October 1994, when Gates dispatched a memo to senior managers titled "Sea Change Brings Opportunity," and May 1995, when he followed up with "The Internet Tidal Wave," his thinking underwent significant change. In 1994, his primary focus was on the impact of network communications on office documents; by mid-1995, however, the Internet had assumed "the highest level of importance." What's particularly striking is that Gates understood the potential impact of the Internet's rapid rise on all aspects of Microsoft's business by applying the model of positive feedback loops that had served the company so well in the past. The Internet, Gates wrote, had benefited from the self-propelling loop in which "the more users it gets, the more content it gets, and the more content it gets, the more users it gets." Gates urged all members of his executive staff and their subordinates to use the Internet and see for themselves.

Internet-based profits were not within view, but then again, the company could not wait. The only certainty in such a situation was that profits would *not* be earned if Microsoft remained rooted in its pre-Internet position. To undertake a major shift when the company had continued to earn record revenues and profits required a leap of faith, moving as one Microsoft manager put it "where the puck's going" instead of where the puck actually was. And the shift was influenced by history more than by anything else. In 1995, Gates thought that the best analogy for explaining the significance of the Internet—both the opportunities and the dangers it presented to Microsoft—was not the beginning of the Windows phenomenon, but even further back, at the arrival of the IBM personal computer and the dawn of a distinct PC industry. Now, as then, existing businesses that stood still, heedless of the change, would be extinguished by the process of competition. Gates's 1995 alarm echoed Myhrvold's 1993 "Road Kill" manifesto, which had named Microsoft as among those companies whose existing businesses were endangered by the arrival of the information highway, and which covered the entirety of modern Western history to provide historical analogies.

Gates had to proselytize his Internet message within Microsoft because of internal sneering at the limitations of the Internet as it was then constituted. Currently the Internet was well short of providing the fiber-based broadband network linking all households on which the information highway projects had been premised. Forget video-on-demand; even as a conduit of static graphics from a single Web page, the Internet was creaky and slow. The influx of users and the resulting congestion were causing long delays that produced more frustration than euphoria. But if an engineer had graded the IBM PC in 1981, Gates reminded everyone at Microsoft, that report card would have been dismal, too. It was precisely because hundreds of companies were formed to solve the original PCs' technical problems, and because the number of software developers who accepted a single software standard for the machine reached a critical mass, that the IBM PC became the seminal computing event for the 1980s. So too, Gates predicted, hundreds of companies would address the technical limitations of the Internet and, in so doing, flourish. No one could have predicted that a Compaq or a printer division at Hewlett-Packard would appear and become multi-billion-dollar operations; no one would be able to tell who the specific winners in the Internet era would be either. But Gates was certain that the same pattern of what he called "nonobvious" winners would repeat.

The pattern that Gates anticipated did not take long at all to appear, and for a "nonobvious" winner, we could hardly do better than nominate Netscape and its dramatic rise from nowhere. The company's initial public stock offering and the sensational increase in its stock value during the remainder of 1995 made it deservedly the darling of Wall Street. When Netscape went public in summer 1995, the yet-to-show-a-profit company had an instant market cap of $2 billion. By October it was $3.5 billion, and by December its market cap had reached $5 billion. Due to the announcement of its first quarterly profit of $1.4 million, Netscape's price-to-earnings ratio was briefly a stratospheric 2187 when Microsoft's ratio, until then regarded as a bit overpriced, was 36. Netscape's rise to prominence in the industry happened with breathtaking speed. The company was founded in April 1994, its first product entered beta testing that December, and it went from zero to a multi-billion-dollar valuation in little more than a year.

In this amazing tale, the press nearly overlooked several important points. The Netscape story, regardless of whether its stock subsequently remained aloft or not, had already served to thoroughly and unalterably negate a key assumption of the Department of Justice and of Microsoft's other competitors: that Microsoft had an unbreakable choke hold over the industry. As we have seen, Richard Thomas DeLarmarter argued in 1986 that IBM's hold on the computer industry was absolute. And in 1994, Gary Reback, an attorney that

Microsoft rivals retained as a "friend of the court," revived the notion of a stranglehold and applied it to Microsoft. But here, as before, the software market showed how tenuous a "stranglehold" actually was. The Department of Justice seemed perfectly oblivious to the implications that the Netscape Cinderella story had for its continued obsession with Microsoft.

Perhaps most important of all, the rush of investors to Netscape and other companies most directly associated with the Internet phenomenon reflected not an accidental development that happened to reinvigorate competition in the software market, but rather the manifestation of mundane forces at work. Even if Microsoft seemed, amid all the attention paid to the newcomers, to be in an unenviable position of playing catch-up, all of the fuss about the Internet confirmed precisely what Gates had been arguing all along: that, in the software business, the barriers to entry were low—the software company's principal assets were smarts, not capital-intensive assembly plants like those required in the automotive industry. Smarts in the form of twenty-something college graduates could be had cheaply.

The positive feedback cycle and consumer preference for buying the market-leading products reinforced the leader's position. But such protection could evaporate the moment the next change arrived, and the same forces that helped a leader build a dominating market share would operate with the same speed to unseat an incumbent when market support shifted to a newcomer. There was no enduring protection that would save any company from the stringently cold winds of competition. Even as Netscape's Andreessen worked to undermine Microsoft, he was serving, inadvertently to be sure, as the perfect poster boy for Microsoft's campaign to explain the realities of competition to the government.

When Gates explained to his own employees how Microsoft would address the threat Netscape posed in the struggle to control the software standards for the Internet, history again served as a guide. When Excel had been introduced at a time when Lotus's 1-2-3 held overwhelming market share, Microsoft had not attempted to demand that prospective customers make a clean break. Excel embraced 1-2-3's macro language, which was used to store commonly used keystrokes and formulas, and simply built on top of it. Microsoft would apply the same principle of "embrace and extend" in the competition to control Internet-related software standards.

The challenge that Microsoft faced in attempting to repeat its own history was reflected at a computer industry conference in the fall of 1995. The ambient sentiment that the Internet was going to pose the most significant challenge to Microsoft's power in the industry was crystallized in a speech, "Why Microsoft and Intel Don't Matter Anymore," given by Roger McNamee, a venture capitalist. McNamee argued that the coming New World Order in the personal computer industry would center on communication, not desktop-centered productivity software. He also predicted that the importance of the Internet would be in the triumph of openly published software protocols available to one and all, replacing the proprietary standards held closely by Microsoft.

Dear to Gates's heart as the idea of controlling standards was, even if Microsoft failed to maintain control, its future was not necessarily as dim as Microsoft's critics assumed. As *Windows Watcher* editor Jesse Berst pointed out, Microsoft did not have any control over the Macintosh's standards, yet its Macintosh programs were top sellers. Nor was Microsoft's relatively late start in adopting a top-to-bottom Internet strategy necessarily going to be an insurmountable handicap. Compared to its rivals, Microsoft had been ten years late in introducing a database program for the desktop. The delay, however, did not prevent Access, the database program that Microsoft eventually released, from taking the top spot in its own category.

MSN's late start was in some important ways a blessing because it did not have to worry about easing any existing business—with a massive infrastructure, business assumptions, and revenue streams—into an Internet-centered future as America Online and CompuServe did. America Online already had hedged its bet on commercial online services by investing modestly in a separate Internet access service called Global Network Navigator, but that was not a fundamental shift in strategy. Microsoft was a bit bolder. In 1995, Gates predicted that the Internet's future place in computing would be as all-pervasive as electricity. Therefore, just as no company has a separate "Electricity Division," neither would Microsoft establish an "Internet Division." When Gates reorganized the company in early 1996 and established what he had a few months earlier declared was not needed, the new Internet group did represent a tactical about-face, but it did not represent the sudden arrival of the Internet religion on the Microsoft campus—Gates had without question caught the religion by May of 1995, the time of his "Internet Tidal Wave" memo. In the wake of the reorganization, he did not revoke his charge to all Microsoft divisions to reorient for the Internet. He simply added a group that would focus exclusively on software tools for the Net.

At MSN, as elsewhere, from Gates's office on down, historical analogies provided points of reference in the rethinking of strategy. Bill Miller, MSN's director of marketing, in 1995 likened Microsoft's position when facing the Internet to that of his previous employer, Digital Equipment Corporation, when it first faced the personal computer. DEC had smart people and they could see that the threat was real. But DEC's business, based on VAX minicomputers, assumed that each piece of hardware would sell for $100,000+ per box, each piece of software would sell for $50,000–$60,000, and 100,000 employees were needed to run this business. A PC box that sold for $2000 and related software that sold for $100–$300 a unit had grave implications for DEC's existing business. But even if the company could see where the business was headed, how could it get from here to there? By dismissing 90 percent of its employees? Not easily done. For the same reasons, Miller sympathized with the Encyclopaedia Britannica managers when they had confronted Microsoft's Encarta and been as paralyzed as DEC had been.

Gates was anything but paralyzed. In fact, by all the evidence, he positively relished the jolt out of complacency that Netscape had given his company. He told the assembled employees at the 1995 company meeting that he welcomed the attention Netscape was receiving and even the taunts that had been hurled Microsoft's way from observers who said, "Hey, Microsoft, aren't those guys going to knock you off?" It was precisely the "dynamic" of facing a crew of similarly smart competitors (for a refreshing change, he implicitly suggested, comparing Netscape to the fumble-prone Lotuses and Novells who had been Microsoft's most potent competitors) that "really gets us going, gets us thinking." He was correct in his assessment that challenge brought out the best in the company. Furthermore, the basic strengths that had served the company well to date would bolster Microsoft's response to the Netscape challenge.

Following MSN's debut and the internal reorganization to re-orient all Microsoft groups toward the Internet lodestar, MSN was unshackled from Windows 95. The MSN developers who had been working on the below-surface plumbing were moved to the operating systems group. This freed Microsoft to better compete with new-comers like Netscape and entrenched veterans like AOL, all of whom were ecumenical in accommodating many operating systems in their desktop software. The portion of MSN responsible for content has-tened its plans of becoming a World Wide Web site, abandoning its own proprietary software interface. The shift left MSN's smaller con-tent providers, who had invested in developing software to work with MSN's non-Web format, understandably upset, but the future of non-Web online services was now uncertain, and it was not within Microsoft's power to stem the Internet tsunami. (Content providers for CompuServe soon enough received the same bad news: the ser-vice was shifting to a Web format, too.)

Microsoft's embracing of the Web brought immediate benefits. Instead of having to fight Netscape and AOL on separate fronts, Microsoft was now free to arrange business alliances that would have been impossible before. The most breathtaking change was its suc-cess in securing the support of AOL—so recently MSN's number one archrival—in fighting back the challenge of Netscape in the market-place war between competing Web browsers. In March 1996, AOL agreed to exclusively distribute Microsoft's browser, Explorer, in the millions of packages it distributes to customers in exchange for Microsoft's willingness to provide easy one-click access to AOL as a standard option in Windows 95.

Microsoft's ability to quickly adapt to an Internet-centered soft-ware universe and pick up new allies was also demonstrated when Steve Jobs, one of the more vociferous critics of Microsoft, sang the praises of Microsoft's software and the company's receptivity to forg-ing deals with other software companies like his own NeXT Software. "This is really weird," Jobs said when he clambered on stage at a Microsoft-sponsored conference in early 1996. "Netscape is treating us just the way you would expect Microsoft to treat us."

The MSN managers still wondered where the compelling content would come from that would validate their newly created concept of a for-profit Internet online service. They took some inspiration from their neighbors in the Consumer Division's Encarta group, which had persevered through the discouraging years before their flagship product reached the light of day and had been so helpful in showing both the industry and consumers the capabilities of CD-ROM technology. Current Web offerings were no further developed than what had been available on CD-ROM in the late 1980s. Until Web sites offered something more interesting than electronic brochures, an Internet online service would not progress very far. Encarta showed that content would eventually catch up with the delivery technology.

Encarta also showed that being a relative latecomer was not an insuperable handicap. In the competition with the print encyclopedias, Microsoft had been able to deploy assets that the older encyclopedia companies lacked: large investments, software knowledge, and "being quick on your feet through a period of trial and error," in the words of Myhrvold, who held up Encarta's shining example in a 1995 memo about the Internet. Myhrvold reasoned that "you can almost always buy the old skills and assets, but the new ones are not available anywhere."

Actually, Encarta provided MSN with more than just inspiration; it also provided the online service with some of its initial content. A year prior to MSN's debut, the Consumer Division had been asked to prepare to make Encarta and the reference works collection Bookshelf available to the future MSN subscribers. Encarta's managers resisted, arguing that online usage would cannibalize sales of the CD-ROM and that the payment that MSN would send over to the Consumer Division on a per-capita basis would fall short of the revenue lost from retail sales. Gates instructed Consumer Division head Patty Stonesifer, and Stonesifer passed the word down the chain of command: product groups were not individual fiefdoms—if MSN needed the help of other groups within Microsoft, it was to receive it. Subsequently Encarta and Bookshelf were among the offerings made available to MSN's beta testers, and they proved popular.

After MSN was formally introduced, the arrangement turned out well for the Encarta group after all. It had taken a leaf from Intuit's playbook, which had altered Quicken for bundles placed on new PCs in such a way that the product remained useful but still fell short of all the features that the regular retail version possessed. Microsoft's Encarta group created a slightly different version of its encyclopedia, called Encarta Intro, which lacked an atlas, timeline, video clips, and other ancillary features that the regular CD-ROM version had. Every time it was consulted, Encarta Intro served as an advertisement for the retail Encarta.

It perhaps was not surprising to see newly born MSN scramble to find a viable business model after the Internet shock had dashed its original one. More surprising was the Consumer Division's ability to undertake major strategic changes even though, by the fall of 1995, it had grown to 800 employees with annual revenues of about $800 million, nearly double the 1994 level. When price competition threatened to erode market share—when Encarta's nominal retail price was $99 and the street price was $85, but the prices for the other CD-ROM encyclopedias dropped to the $55 range—Microsoft decided to chop its own prices. Microsoft and other software companies had learned that surveying consumers for their reactions to proposed prices produced notoriously unreliable data. (The earliest Encarta survey research had indicated, after all, that consumers were supposedly happy with a $395 price for the CD-ROM.) So the company decided to test some alternative prices in the field. To avoid ill will if anyone should discover that some consumers were paying a higher experimental price than others, Microsoft sought out a territory far from the curious eyes of the computer industry press, and in Nebraska it tried out $79, $59, and $49 prices for Encarta. Sales surged at the $49 point, so in October 1995 the new suggested retail price became $49. The other Consumer Division titles were repriced proportionately downward as well, even as sales were strong.

The Consumer Division also proved adroit in other respects. It discarded its earlier strategy of producing many titles using similar templates and instead focused its resources on categories (like encyclopedias) that would require heavy investment, deterring the entry of me-too competitors, and that would have the depth in content and features to produce sales year after year. And it gave up its "Consumer Division" name, when a February 1996 reorganization sent its software products like Works and Publisher to rejoin their kin like Word and Excel, while Encarta, Bookshelf, and some other groupings were joined with MSN in a newly created "Interactive Media Division."

The capacity of the organization to learn as it proceeded was evidenced also in the much savvier management of manufacturing arrangements and retail distribution issues. When Encarta had entered its first holiday sales season in 1993, only one manufacturing plant was available to press its discs and only one small box company had the esoteric equipment necessary for the unique, heavy cardboard casing and it could only produce a few thousand boxes a week. When demand exceeded forecasts, this manufacturing capacity fell far short of what was needed. In 1994, a less costly and more easily manufactured box was adopted, and for the 1995 holiday season, five plants stood at the ready for orders for Encarta.

By hiring more managers with retailing experience, the entire Consumer Division had become more adroit in managing the distribution channel. Like Intuit, Microsoft looked to companies outside the computer industry and brought in more professionals from Procter & Gamble, Nestlé's, Nabisco, Coca-Cola, and Nike. Details of Microsoft's holiday promotions with its retailers were finalized and made available in the preceding summer, when retailers needed the information. To ensure that inventory on store shelves was adequate and displayed well, Microsoft contracted with jobbers to visit 4500 store fronts every month. For its largest 600 retail accounts, Microsoft's own managers personally visited each account *weekly*. These were the basic operational details of "blocking and tackling" that were standard practices in other consumer product fields.

The unglamorous work at the retail end of the business helped to make software ubiquitous. This ubiquity in the consciousness of consumers was the little-noticed precondition for the Internet, which not much earlier had been almost exclusively an academic network, unknown to newsmagazines. As a generic product category, software first had to become omnipresent enough to be demystified in the popular mind. Diffused within the consumer economy to the point that it no longer stood out, sold not at special software-only emporia but everywhere, and priced like an ordinary household item, it influenced public consciousness just by sitting on shelves at the local Wal-Mart or on palettes at Price/Costco. For Windows 95, Microsoft took pains to place the software in some 20,000 outlets, many of which did not even customarily sell software. But even outside of that campaign, by 1995 Microsoft software was carried regularly by 12,000–15,000 separate outlets, a distribution network that rivaled any other kind of consumer article outside of foodstuffs. This reach was not accomplished overnight, as we saw when looking at Encarta's gestation; nor was it accomplished singlehandedly, as we glimpsed when tracing the outlines of Intuit's history. But historically speaking, the arrival of software in the midst of a broad mass market happened in a blink.

Legacies

*H*AVE NOT GREAT MERCHANTS, *great manufacturers, great inventors done more for the world than preachers and philanthropists? Can there be any doubt that cheapening the cost of necessities and conveniences of life is the most powerful agent of civilization and progress?*

Charles Elliott Perkins,
President of the Chicago, Burlington & Quincy Railroad (1888)

*W*E'RE BENEFICIARIES *in what's been the largest single legal creation of wealth we've ever seen on the planet in a decade.*

John Doerr, Silicon Valley venture capitalist (1994)

*B*EWARE OF TOO MUCH GOOD *staying in your hand. It will fast corrupt.*

Ralph Waldo Emerson, in "Compensation" (1841)

An updated version of Charles Elliott Perkins's argument resides at the core of what Microsoft, as well as all the other software and hardware companies in the personal computer industry, promise us—that with ever more powerful personal computers and a communication web to link them ultimately will come a brighter future for us all. We can hope that such will be the case, yet somehow we should be suspi-

228

cious, perhaps outright dismissive, when we hear Bill Gates articulate our secret hope. When Gates asks us to listen to what may or may not be credible claims about the social benefits that personal computers can bring, as he did in *The Road Ahead*, it is difficult for us to pay close attention; we are transfixed by his wealth. To be asked to disregard Billionaire Bill's wealth is no more possible than to obey a directive *not* to think of an elephant. I have endeavored to keep Gates's wealth out of the narrative thus far, but the omission was flagrantly artificial. Let's now look at the issue.

Since Perkins's time (1840–1907), the public has been keeping close track of who among us are the richest. In 1840, the publisher of the *New York Sun* published a pamphlet of *Wealth and Biography of the Wealthy Citizens of New York*, listing "persons estimated to be worth $100,000 and upwards" and appending to each name an estimate of net worth, just as *Forbes* provides today. The guide proved so popular that new editions were produced regularly, with, as the publisher claimed fifteen years after the pamphlet's inauguration, "not a single copy of any one edition being left unsold." Over the years, various publications would carry out an unofficial census, with its attendant tasks such as canvassing individuals for estimates of the privately held wealth of others. Although the defining threshold of noteworthy wealth has climbed, the public's insistence on counting, assaying, and scrutinizing has hardened into customary habit—there can be no such thing as an unknown billionaire in this country.

We, the nonrich, assiduously collect and savor the delectable stories of greed unbound, of John D. Rockefeller, for example, as a young man often confiding to his then business partner, "I'm bound to be rich. Bound to be rich! BOUND TO BE RICH!"

Gates's Nominal Net Worth	
1986	$315 million
1987	$1.25 billion
1988	$1.1 billion
1989	$1.25 billion
1990	$2.5 billion
1991	$4.8 billion
1992	$6.3 billion
1993	$6.2 billion
1994	$9.35 billion
1995	$14.8 billion
1996	$16.5 billion

Oh, what sweet pleasure indeed to have been there, too, and observed Rockefeller in such richly revelatory moments, sprouting horns and displaying the unseemly avarice that serves as our solace for Fate's bestowing the millions on him and not on us.

Bill Gates has been unwilling to allow us to view him through the defining prism of wealth. From the moment Microsoft stock was offered to the public in March 1986, he has adamantly—and to no avail—maintained that the fuss was misplaced. He has insisted that his wealth was tied to Microsoft stock, paper assets that were volatile, not necessarily easily converted to cash, and deserving to be distinguished from "real wealth." In 1986, when Gates was merely a very wealthy thirty-year-old centimillionaire, this tack stretched credulity. When he became a billionaire the next year, it became harder to accept. In the early 1990s, as sales of Windows software expanded and the value of Microsoft stock brought the value of his holdings up so swiftly that by 1992, at the age of thirty-six, *Forbes* anointed him as the wealthiest American, his continued avowal of being merely a billionaire *on paper* was private metaphysics, a perspective to which the public did not subscribe.

What the public much preferred was playing the parlor game of "Bill Could Buy . . ." These mental exercises ranged from the quasi-silly to the quasi-serious. When his net worth reached $8.2 billion in mid-1994, for example, a Seattle reporter used the occasion to figure out that this wasn't the loose change that most people have in a cookie jar. In Gates's case, the jar, if filled with quarters, would weigh more than 1000 Boeing 747s. A bit more substantive, however, was the calculation that if Gates were to spend $1000 a minute, 24 hours a day, his wealth would not be exhausted for nearly 16 years. Two years earlier, a rather arresting observation was made about Gates's personal net worth and the size of his business competitors. If he were to sell his Microsoft holdings, then worth $7.3 billion, and use the proceeds to buy and promptly discard the entire year's production of his closest 99 competitors, Gates still would have been worth more than Rupert Murdoch or Ted Turner.

How does Gates's wealth compare to the fortunes of his richest-in-their-time predecessors—the Astors', Carnegie's, Rockefeller's? It's not an easy question to address. The first inclination is to do the math to adjust for inflation. Then the comparison that can be made—Rockefeller's fortune in today's dollars would be worth well over $10 billion—seems straightforward enough. But the apparent comparability is misleading. In some respects, the dollar's purchasing power went much further in an earlier age. John Jacob Astor's contemporary, essayist and poet Ralph Waldo Emerson (1803–1882), could support his wife and four children, his mother, and the household's five servants, in a spacious house set on a six-acre estate in Concord, Massachusetts, on a mere $3000 a year. Adjusting for inflation, we arrive at a supposedly comparable $45,000 a year—obviously well short of what would be needed today. But, to complicate matters further, the purchasing power of today's dollar goes much, much further in other domains. Not just Emerson, with his modest income as an author, but even John Jacob Astor, fur trader and real estate investor nonpareil, with all of his millions could not purchase anything equivalent to a household personal computer and the software that are within the means of today's middle-class households.

In the late nineteenth century, the public wanted to know, just as it does now, what incantations would summon the genies who award business fortune—though, in the earlier tradition, proper "character" was considered the salient basis of wealth. In both the nineteenth century and the present, we also see public fascination with the daily routines of the wealthiest. A hundred years ago, the question *What is it like to be so rich?* often lurked behind polite inquiries and caused the rich to react defensively. A suspicious person such as Leland Stanford, Southern Pacific titan and one-time governor of California, was observed bridling at a friend's greeting of "How do you feel this morning, Governor?" with a wary, "Wouldn't you like to know?" Today, our journalistic proxies drill down with unapologetic directness and repeatedly ask: How *does* it feel?

The most interesting lessons to be learned from questioning the rich, I venture, are not found in the replies, per se, but in what such encounters tell us about ourselves and our own expectations about our wealthy quarry. As a general rule, we can say that the American public has a cinematic taste for the drama inherent in the self-made fortune built from modest origins—the more modest, the better. We are attracted to the implicit promise that similar opportunity is within our own grasp. Much less interesting, of course, are the instances of large fortunes that grew from inherited smaller fortunes.

What is to be done, however, with Gates's family history? On the one hand, it is one of upper-middle-class privilege, exemplified by the attendance at private Lakeside School, which offered the precocious Gates early access to time-shared computers before the dawn of truly personal computers. On the other hand, the intangible advantages of Gates's background are harder to catalog, such as the quality of the education or the sense of feeling intimate with the corridors of power from early experiences as a page, first at the state capitol, then in Washington, D.C. Yet Gates did not need the most familiar and tangible possible advantage: seed capital. One of the peculiar, transitory characteristics of new ventures that ride the advent of epoch-defining technology is that little capital may be needed, and such was the case of Microsoft. Barriers to entry were so low, gross margins were so large, and the industry grew so fast that Gates did not need to seek anything but token venture capital nor did he have to sell most of his original holdings to finance the company's growth. The same had held true for others who would become computer industry billionaires: Bill Hewlett, David Packard, and Ross Perot. Historical circumstances meant, in the end, that Gates's family did not play any significant role in the founding of Microsoft. Thus the story, with its muddle of privilege helping indirectly but not directly, is a disappointment to those hungry for sizzle.

We can always hope for the possible glimpse of a pagan dance to lucre, as in John D. Rockefeller's case, and so Gates is asked, with all manner of imaginative variation, how he feels about being the richest or second richest person in the country. The question often serves as a set-up so that our sensitive instruments can best detect the hidden truth (... *Late at night, he descends to the counting room, where in the darkness he caresses his bars of gold bullion* ...). But the question also flies in the face of consistent evidence that Gates happens to be someone who simply does *not* spend much time whatsoever thinking about the money. What's fun to observe, when reviewing some fifteen years of journalistic tennis in this court—serve, parry, lob, parry, smash, parry—is the particular way that Gates chose early on to handle this question and the Gates-watchers' response, in turn.

Before Microsoft's initial public offering, Gates's net worth was unknowable. When Gates was asked to estimate what it would be, he expressed impatience—Who knows? Any numbers that anyone might conjure would be "just silly"; what would be the point in speculating? After Microsoft went public, Gates's net worth henceforth became a matter of public record, but Gates remained impatient with the continuing questions about how he *felt* about it, what did it *mean* to him—the curiosity of a therapeutic culture applied to business. He developed a standard answer: *Billionaire?* That's only a product of abstract multiplication. I don't have X billion dollars, I merely own stock.

As intelligent and canny as Bill Gates is, he has nevertheless been rather myopic in thinking that this kind of reply would make the billions vanish so his interlocutor would cheerfully move on to other topics. What happens, of course, is that the interviewer delights in the obviousness of this attempted legerdemain and digs in. In 1990, for example, a reporter took evident relish in exposing Gates's linguistic sophistry when he asked about Gates's net worth:

Q: What does all the money you have mean to you?

Gates: I don't have any money; I have stock. I own about 35 percent of the shares of Microsoft, and I take a salary of $175,000 a year.

Q: Yes, but you sold about $30 million worth of Microsoft stock, didn't you?

Gates: About a year ago.

Q: Most people still consider that "money." Don't you?

Gates: Yes, that's money . . . that's money.

Q: Now that we've established that you do have money, what does it mean to you?

In more private contexts, Gates suspended the campaign to educate the public about the distinction between paper wealth and cash. At a semi-public conference in 1994, Gates briefly mentioned that, the day before, Microsoft had been assessed a large judgment in a patent infringement suit, and his lawyers had informed him that he'd just lost $120 million. He concluded, "So I kind of had a bad day yesterday." The remark drew a long, appreciative gust of laughter—we've all had similar experiences, right?

The self-deprecating humor of which Gates is capable is not often glimpsed publicly because of his resistance to being publicly defined by his wealth. He responded with a little joke in 1994 when an interviewer for *Playboy* asked him about his parents' reaction to his accumulation of wealth. I hide it from them, Gates began; yes, it's buried in the lawn, and bulging a bit. But then, as if this thread in the interviewer's interest seemed to hint that perhaps the entire Gates clan secretly practiced a pagan Money Dance in the back yard, Gates abruptly cut off the joking: "My money is meaningless to them. Meaningless." And to make sure there was no misunderstanding, he emphatically added, "We never talk about money."

Microsoft Share Prices
Averaged over six months, adjusted for splits

1986 First half	$2
1986 Second half	2
1987 First half	5
1987 Second half	6
1988 First half	7
1988 Second half	6
1989 First half	6
1989 Second half	8
1990 First half	13
1990 Second half	15
1991 First half	22
1991 Second half	29
1992 First half	40
1992 Second half	41
1993 First half	44
1993 Second half	40
1994 First half	45
1994 Second half	58
1995 First half	73
1995 Second half	93
1996 First Half	105

Gates was consistent in what he said. Not only did he spend little time thinking about it, but so too, he always urged, should we. The value of the stock would be volatile, he warned often—and presciently, the week before the October 1987 market crash, when his paper losses would extend to more than $350 million. Immediately after the crash, he and other Microsoft executives remained as unconcerned about the drop as they had been about its preceding rise. They kept repeating that theirs was a long-term perspective, unfazed by momentary fluctuations. In July 1995, Gates had a couple of *really* bad days, suffering a $2 *billion* drop in the value of his Microsoft holdings. When reporters pressed him for a comment, he answered with the same uninflected reply and shrug as before: "Investing in tech stocks is a high risk." The lack of visible emotion displayed by Gates exasperated reporters. Laugh, cry, tear your hair—we will forgive you your billions, but please, for God's sake, show some emotion!

How do we wish he would comport himself as Microsoft stock climbs—and climbs—and climbs? It would seem that we want a swagger in his step and high-volume braggadocio, like that displayed by Donald Trump (Before the Fall, in the 1980s). Gates refused to oblige. Year after year, Gates urged Wall Street analysts to listen to the company's conservative projections for the upcoming fiscal year. And year after year, when Microsoft surpassed those projections, the analysts became less willing to heed the company's constant lament that its increase in size dictated slowing growth. Erring by under-estimating growth earns no credit in our society's judgment. Neither does Microsoft's compensation system, which has rewarded Gates on the basis of equity holdings, not salary, an arrangement that requires a longer term perspective. It is strange how unremarked this aspect of Gates's wealth remains.

Gates's spending habits have been the subject of extensive commentary, which in some respects has merely been a continuation of the public's longstanding critique of the comportment of the wealthy. But, in another respect, the commentary has taken a new, distinctively modern twist. Scrutinizing Gates can be frustrating: vilification would be much easier if Gates were a consistent spendthrift, instead of merely an occasional one. Knowing that Gates flew coach on domestic flights and frequented McDonald's, an interviewer in 1990 summarized his impression that "for a man of your wealth, you're not a great spender." Gates had said, yes, spending had "just never grabbed me." This did not work in his favor. Instead of softening the public's judgment, Gates's parsimony only helped to embellish the press's characterization of Gates as a freakish figure. The public was not consistent, however. Compare how the modest living style of older, paternal figures like Sam Walton or Gates's friend Warren Buffett was received in such a strikingly different way, forming the very different image of the Endearing Billionaires of Simple Tastes.

Every time Gates reached for his wallet in public, the entire world received a report of the transaction. Or if he allegedly did *not* reach for his wallet, as when a trade paper's gossip column claimed Gates had been sighted at a hotel bar walking out without paying his tab, with angry waiter giving chase. Or if he did not carry his wallet on his person, as in a Chicago reporter's gleeful description of Gates rushing from a convention center into a chauffeured car as his facto-tum shouted to another aide, "Do you have his wallet?" The assistant jumped forward and handed the wallet over, and the reporter concluded that here was the ultimate level of success, being so rich "you have someone who carries your wallet." Gates laughed the next day when told of how the newspaper had depicted the scene. He had merely heeded the public relations staff's order to never give a presentation with anything in your pants pockets that jangled or bulged. Learning of the news story, Gates predicted that years later people would say he had a "personal money carrier," a prediction now fully realized with this mention.

If Gates's failure to be "grabbed" by the spending impulse was a disappointment and prompted attacks suggesting that he was somehow deficient, his start on constructing a massive home on the shore of Lake Washington in 1990 should have been more in keeping with what we expect. But, of course, it served only to open him up to other varieties of attack—for extravagance. The underground garage, which would take up almost 6000 square feet, could accommodate 26 cars, and would alone cost an estimated $1.1 million, meant in one commentator's words that "Bill's cars will live in a larger, more expensive home than 99.9 percent of the earth's population."

The domiciles of nineteenth-century millionaires were also the focus of attention in their day. There were the mansions along Fifth Avenue in New York, along Lake Shore Drive in Chicago, on Nob Hill in San Francisco, in Newport, the Hamptons, and wherever the rich collected. Unlike the ostentatious nineteenth-century faux-castles of the New World (or real castles transplanted stone by stone from Europe) that helped to inspire Thorstein Veblen's treatises on the conspicuous consumption of the "leisure class," the design that Gates chose in an architectural competition for his house was "subdued." The winning architect attempted to make the house blend in with the landscape, to make the consumption as *in*conspicuous as possible.

The nineteenth-century estates were widely viewed as a devastating commentary on what one contemporary called "the injustice of concentrated wealth." The offensiveness of the mansions was mitigated by the consoling thought that, whether intended or not, their labor-intensive construction served to redistribute wealth. William H. P. Faunce, John D. Rockefeller's one-time pastor, declared in 1893 that once a wealthy benefactor—even a "misanthrope"—loosens the purse and "begins to spend his money in the most selfish and ostentatious luxury, he is an involuntary benefactor of that city." In contemporary times, this line of defense does not seem a very compelling form of redistribution. Doug Kelbaugh, the chair of the University of Washington's department of architecture, sounded the same note as critics had a century earlier, that a luxurious home like the one Gates was building served to call attention to the wide gaps between rich and poor. He suggested, only half-jokingly, that Gates's architect "do penance" by designing low-income housing.

When Gates spoke of his plans as the house was being built, he allowed that, yes, he "guessed" it was "indulgent." But he forwarded a partial justification that was never heard in the previous century: that, as a showcase for new multimedia applications of personal computers, the house would serve Microsoft's interests and so could be seen as paying for itself indirectly. It was this theme that Gates used in *The Road Ahead*, too, where he completely abandoned his attempts to deflect the public's curiosity about his house and instead sought to show that the experimental aspects of the technology that would be incorporated in the house would be all that it had in common with William Randolph Hearst's San Simeon. Unlike Hearst's estate, Gates's would not be a "monument to excess," he avowed.

That Gates felt compelled to attempt to justify his house is itself an interesting confirmation of the omnipresence of the tribunal of public opinion. And if he had not embarked on this large "indulgence," he would not necessarily have avoided criticism, either. Just as Rockefeller had been assailed by Ida Tarbell in 1905 for the *unpretentiousness* of his homes ("They show him to have no pleasure in noble architecture, to appreciate nothing of the beauty of fine lines and decorations ... "), so too Gates's failure to spend on a home a sum proportionate to his net worth assuredly would have been interpreted as evidence of an Otherness that the public wanted to inscribe upon him. Even with the costly San Simeon North taking shape, Gates was still being pressed by the public, his unbidden auditors, to shake loose more of his coins, to take fuller advantage of his means.

For the most part, I regard the public discussion of Gates's house as benignly amusing. Building an extremely large, architecturally innovative house on a publicly visible shoreline is not an inherently private activity. The occasional references to larger social issues posed by the spectacle, even if not supported by much substantive discussion, fit the longstanding historical tradition of similar architectural critiques. But the particular way in which public discourse operates today forbids the object of the media's attention from preserving much privacy. *Everything* is now fair game.

When ABC's *20/20* profiled Gates in 1991, the subject of the new house came up, naturally enough, but the interviewer was not interested in architecture. The questioner zeroed in on the large number of bedrooms included in the architectural design. Were those for children that then still-unengaged Gates planned to have? Gates said, well, yes, they could serve as children's bedrooms. That reply wasn't explicit enough, so the follow-up question got to the heart of the matter: Would you like to have children? (Is this a common question to ask of a childless adult who was not a close personal friend?) As soon as Gates answered yes, the interviewer was then emboldened to explore the most intimate nether region of all, the nexus of money and sex: Aren't you worried that the women you are dating are gold-diggers? "Well," he replied, "I like to go out with smart women and so they're smart enough to know they're not going to get my money."

Ah, television reporter heaven! The coup was not in what Gates had said literally, but in his forgetting the last protective barrier that prevented public access to the sanctum sanctorum. Like houseguests that do not wait for an invitation, the public now made itself quite at home in Gates's bedroom—ostensibly on the seemingly innocuous pretext of curiosity about Gates's money. The *Wall Street Journal* asked Gates if he would require a future spouse to sign a prenuptial agreement. Gates again failed to see that by answering—he said he would never ask for a prenuptial agreement—he would be helping to completely erase whatever line had separated public from private. Answer a question like that, and why not have the public come right in and take seats by the bedside?

I don't regard the public's curiosity about prenuptial agreements among the wealthy to be improper; I'm as curious as anyone else. And one of the most amusing moments at the 1993 Microsoft all-company meeting—after Gates announced his engagement to Melinda French, a Microsoft manager, but before the wedding—was when comedian Dana Carvey, the emcee hired for the day, had Gates on stage in a mock *Tonight Show* interview and put a variety of personal "questions" to Gates. Gates laughed gamely throughout the routine, which at times resembled a one-person roast. Finally, Carvey asked, with a sly smile, "What the people want to know, I think, is—it's just kind of awkward to ask you—have you talked . . . prenuptial?" When the roar in the arena had subsided, Gates asked laughingly, "That whole list of things I told you not to bring up—we're going through that, one by one, right?" Carvey smiled mischievously and held up the stage prop that had been prepared for the prenuptial joke. It was an enormous, catalog-like document with hundreds of pages, so large it would have been visible at the rear of the Kingdome.

It was a fine moment, I thought, because it provided a way of publicly—or actually *semi*-publicly because it was a meeting for Microsoft employees, not the general public—yet innocuously, broaching a private matter without actually intruding the way that demanding an actual answer from Gates did. The joke did not transform the private into public disclosure. The joke was as much on us, for our curiosity, as it was on anything else, and it did not inflate the curiosity into a hard-news item. This incident was wholly different from the occasions when the press badgered Gates about prenuptial agreements, even after the wedding. The press was aware that whatever Gates could be cajoled into disclosing—or even what he did *not* say—would then be compared to earlier statements, very publicly dissected, and then supplemented with a story of a proxy doing Gates's dirty work in securing French's signature—all in the most public of forums.

My concern is not primarily for Gates's equanimity. It's fine with me if we, the public, want to criticize him and the power he wields—if we decide, after seriously discussing the issues, he deserves the criticism. And I'll lose no sleep if Gates is the butt of barbed jokes, even if they are *entirely* at his expense and not even partially at our own. What I wonder about is how the fascination with "celebrity lifestyles" has warped public discussion. Is it any wonder that we rarely examine the larger, nontrivial issues posed by the aggregation of wealth in the hands of a single person? It's not Gates, ultimately, who loses the most by the trivialization of discourse. It is the rest of us who are robbed of the opportunity to discuss a serious subject—the disposition of great wealth in a democratic society—free of the tawdry.

The ascension of the personal computer industry should raise larger social questions. Venture capitalist John Doerr's "largest single legal creation of wealth we've ever seen on the planet in a decade" was the market capitalization of companies in the industry. By his estimate, between 1982 and 1992, the companies that had been established since the advent of personal computers—including companies like Microsoft and Apple, but excluding older companies like IBM and Hewlett-Packard—witnessed an increase in market valuation of $100 billion. The same companies also had generated $100 billion of revenue in that decade. By all appearances, the pace of wealth created by the industry has not slackened a whit since 1992. Understandably its leaders take pride when calling for historians to recognize, without delay, the place of personal computers in history. The rapidity of the industry's growth could be seen as the manifestation of the operations of the microprocessor that lies at the heart of the personal computer. If today's 166-megahertz Pentium chips run at 166 million computational cycles a *second*, it is poetically (but not logically) appropriate that PC companies' growth has collectively proceeded at astonishing speed, too.

Remarkable though this record of accomplishment has been, it is difficult to reconcile the incomprehensibly fast metronome by which the personal computer industry measures the passage of time—in which a calendar year, like a dog's year, represents the eventfulness of seven years in more established industries—with the slower metronomic beat to which historians are accustomed. Microsoft, which Gates has proudly identified from its formal incorporation in 1975 as the very first company founded to write software for personal computers, has the longest history among its software counterparts. Yet even its two decades would constitute an all but invisible dot on a timeline used by France's Annales school of historical writing, the postwar historians who showed the usefulness of looking at historical change from a long-term perspective, such as a millennium.

Doerr's giddiness in contemplating the paradox of brevity and hypergrowth that defines the personal computer industry's history to date is shared by other industry leaders. They all seem to assume that the positive impact of 130+ million PCs is so obvious as to be utterly unnecessary to substantiate. Bill Gates does not go so far as to ask us explicitly to accept a variation of the "What's good for General Motors is good for us" dictum, but to reassure us of the social contributions of the personal computer industry, he does return perennially to the vague claim that the machines are "empowering." It's not just Doerr and Gates—the entire world of personal computers is saturated with the comforting notion that the machines can, by their nature, unleash individual potential and transform society. Thus the humdrum of business in personal computers is itself a form of peaceful revolution.

I am not convinced that this is so. It seems to me that the brief history of the personal computer industry reveals a paradox of progress and no progress. On an individual basis, the personal computer has unquestionably served to increase the individual's mental productivity, and as the use of networks has expanded, a single machine's usefulness has been exponentially increased, as well. Thanks to Moore's Law, as we've seen, the machines themselves have become ever more powerful and capable while their price has remained steady. Who would want to deny what a boon this ongoing technical progress has meant for individual consumers? But the paradox is that the stories of individuals, who will gladly state that they would never consider returning to life as it was before the personal computer, do not add up to a society that has been made over in visible, fundamental ways.

Zeno's Paradox presented the puzzle of the arrow that seemingly could never arrive at the target because it must first traverse half the distance, and after it does, it must then cover half the distance that remains, and so on, an infinite number of times. Here is Zeno's Paradox in real life. We make apparently great progress: the original IBM PCs in the Intel branch of the family history giving way to XTs, to ATs, to 386s, 486s, Pentiums, Pentium Pros, and so on. An ever larger percentage of the nation's households acquire the machines and get wired into humming cyber communities. Yet we also do not seem to have improved any of the usual measures of social well-being, as measured by real income in all but the upper two quintiles of income distribution, degree of job security, investment in education, amity among racial and ethnic groups, accessibility of health care, freedom from crime, quality of environment, and all the other items that bear more directly on the quality of life than the problems that personal computers have been able to address so far.

Is it unfair to hold personal computers responsible for failing to help somehow to ameliorate the larger social problems of the contemporary moment? My response is that the personal computer industry cannot have it both ways. It cannot demand that historians bestow the ribbon that affirms its significance, yet also insist that the industry be judged only by its own preoccupations—like John Doerr's celebration of the decade of $100 billion generated in "wealth," without giving thought to how widely other Americans have reason to celebrate.

At Microsoft, Gates and his lieutenants were aware that personal computers had failed to effect revolutionary social change. One example was Myhrvold's skepticism of how radical a revolution could be if, as in the advent of spreadsheet software, its implicit rallying cry was "Death To Columnar Pads!" As he sketched out his thoughts in 1993 about the information highway and the possibilities for change that would be enabled by new technology, he had no shortage of ideas that would affect the political system in ways that fully deserve the adjective *radical*. The geographical entities on which our representative democracy had been based, he argued, presumed a commonality of interests among neighbors that no longer holds true. Myhrvold suggested that he had more in common with a computer industry counterpart who lived in Massachusetts than he did with the retired couple who lived next door in Washington State. Why not shift to virtual communities as the organizing basis for politics, and why not use cumulative voting to give more political power to those in the political minority? Give every American 535 votes to apportion in any way he or she wanted among a national slate of candidates, and "there would be a very different set of people in the House, and a very different set of political dynamics."

In the oral history that Gates recorded in 1993, he conceded that social change in the wake of personal computers had been small, but he anticipated that major change was ahead in the way that "markets are organized," in the way "people educate themselves, or socialize, or express their political opinions." Two years later, in *The Road Ahead*, he was unable to do much better in providing concrete specifics of significant social improvements to be found in the here and now, rather than in the feathery clouds of the future. Even for the future, most of the illustrations he provided were solutions to the rather trivial vexations encountered when shopping, commuting, and going on vacation. Gates told us that the information highway will help us find out about new restaurants, or easily change reservations for restaurants, or learn about Eddie Bauer boots before embarking on a vacation to the Everglades, or mount a citizens' campaign to have the timing of a traffic light changed. These and the many similar examples offered in the book serve unwittingly to underscore the gap between Gates's lifestyle, spare though it may be within the Billionaires Club, and those who are not club members and face more pressing problems.

Let's consider, for example, such problems as the dismantling of federally funded welfare programs, the long-term decline in real wages for blue-collar workers, the disappearance in many cities of jobs that formerly had permitted African-American men to support families, and the absence of a ladder that permits workers who hold minimum wage jobs to advance. How will the information highway serve to ameliorate these and similar problems? Gates is silent.

As for the prospect of technologically based unemployment, as employers learn how to deploy personal computer technology to operate more efficiently, achieving "friction-free" technology, Gates acknowledges that, yes, there will be job displacement. But he offers as sop a simplistic economic lesson: "Each time a job is made unnecessary, the person who was filling that job is freed to do something else." He goes on in the same sanguine voice to reassure his readers that there will be "plenty" for everyone to do, blithely ignoring the concept of "structural unemployment." Whether society could put the labor that has been "freed up" to work on socially useful tasks is not the issue, as a glance at our public schools, health clinics, home-care services, parks, and other community resources shows all too painfully. The question is: who exactly is eager to hire and thus *pay* for that newly freed up labor to be redeployed, in a time of continued downsizing in both private and public sectors? Perhaps Gates's view of life on the outside has been distorted by the anomalous position in the contemporary landscape of Microsoft and its brethren in the personal computer industry, with their unrelenting growth in head count.

Distorting, too, is the wisdom received from economic history, of the kind that many economists, historians, and popular writers like Alvin Toffler are fond of citing, arguing that just as there was dislocation in the transition from agriculture to manufacturing, so too will there be dislocation today as we collectively roar down the highway. But we are supposed to take comfort in the reassurance that ultimately all who are willing to work will become gainfully employed. The fatal problem in this analogy is that, in the past, we never had anything quite like the personal computer revolution. Its labor-saving effects can be applied *simultaneously* in the very places that would have been the most likely places we would have expected to absorb those displaced, the newest sectors as well as the older ones. For example, the computer software that has decimated the ranks of human operators who handle long-distance phone calls does not create offsetting demand at software companies for customer service representatives who handle requests over the phone. Software is being utilized to automate customer service, too. Thus there is no haven where its efficiency-producing effects—or put more bluntly, its job-destroying impact—will not be felt. For Gates to cheerily assert the hope that the number of new jobs created by companies such as his own will nicely match the number of jobs that are eliminated by the dramatically enhanced productivity that is derived from more intensive use of PCs and networks is an act of faith, not based on science or history.

It is here, when Gates puts on the robes of the clairvoyant, that his pretense that his financial situation is not publicly relevant causes problems. How objective can we expect him to be when he reports to us that he has given considerable thought to the "difficulties" posed by the technological changes that he describes and celebrates and has found that "on balance, I'm confident and optimistic." His declaration that "I think this is a wonderful time to be alive" invites the snide response from those standing on the other side of a class-defined gulf, who might suggest that anyone who was the richest person in the richest country in the world of course would be ebullient.

Gates makes imminent problems, such as growing disparity in access to computer skills and information resources between the affluent and the poor, simply disappear with a sunny declaration that it will be otherwise. I do not doubt that the economic, educational, and political reforms that he says are enabled by, or impelled by, technological advances will indeed come to pass. What I am skeptical of is whether their overall impact will significantly ease the most pressing problems that shape the quality of contemporary life. Improvement should not be assumed, especially given the operation of Zeno's Paradox that we have witnessed in the twenty years of personal computer "revolution" so far.

If Microsoft and its allies and competitors succeed in their business aims but the most acute social problems are aggravated, or at best, left untouched, we might ask whether Gates's future philanthropic activities are likely to be of much help. When asked about his plans, Gates has never sought refuge in a Libertarian sanctuary, claiming that society has no right to ask. Consistent with his offhand manner when talking about his lack of interest in spending his wealth, he has publicly evinced no interest in holding on to his wealth, either. He has declared on a number of occasions that his children will not be heirs to a family-run "dynasty" and that he planned to give away "95 percent" of his wealth, sparing his children from a "debilitating" inheritance.

As of 1995, Gates's philanthropic gifts had totaled about $22 million, obviously small compared to the value of his Microsoft holdings. The public record included a few notable gifts to his alma mater, Lakeside School, to the University of Washington, and to the United Way. Some, such as a 1992 gift of $6 million to Stanford as the lead gift on a new building that was named the Gates Information Sciences Building in honor of the lead benefactor, and the channeling in 1995 of royalties from *The Road Ahead* into experiments in deploying PC and network technology in schools, were not wholly separate from Microsoft's own interests. Gates's record of philanthropy has left him open to public criticism. In 1991, when it appeared that the Mariners would leave Seattle, the team's fans displayed banners pleading "Bill Gates—Save Us." (Though Gates did not "save" the team, the group of investors that did step forward included some Microsoft millionaires, including Rob Glaser and Carl Stork.) Gates is assailed when he does give as well as when he does not. In the same year, when Gates presented the University of Washington with a $12 million gift, of which $11 million funded a new program in molecular biology and the remaining million went to the university's computer science department, the campus newspaper complained that the humanities had been ignored.

Acting through his company, Gates did not shirk social responsibilities. He campaigned regularly for employees to join him in participating in United Way pledge drives, and since 1992, Microsoft has matched all charitable contributions up to $12,000 a year for every Microsoft employee. Gates has said consistently that he has not given the bulk of his wealth away to date because overseeing Microsoft requires too much of his attention. Later in life, he said, he will be able to give philanthropy due attention. In the meantime, "to the degree Microsoft can do well," he reasoned, "it's just that much more to give later."

If we return to Henry Ford's example, we should not be too impatient to reap the largesse of Gates's bounty. In his late fifties, Ford was still nattering about how he detested "professional charity" and "coddling" by social services. The Ford Foundation, established in 1936 when Ford was seventy-two, was a transparent maneuver to shield Ford's stock from estate and income taxes. The thought that his money would help fund Roosevelt's New Deal was anathema, driving the old man to embrace the "professional charity" that he had always scorned. Even then, he sought to prevent the foundation from diversifying its portfolio and offering shares in the Ford Motor Company to the public. "I'll take my factory down brick by brick," he promised, "before I'll let any of those Jew speculators get stock in the company." So, measured against Henry Ford, almost any wealthy figure who follows is likely to look positively saintly. Observers who are upset with Gates's failure to make philanthropy a central personal occupation perhaps are a bit too impatient.

Or perhaps I am overly patient because I do not expect a Bill Gates Foundation to have a transformative impact on society. Yes, compared to the individual net worth of the rest of us, a $16 billion kitty to carry out good works is a sum that might momentarily appear sizable enough to make most anything possible. But compared to the size of contemporary urban problems in the United States alone, it's a pittance. As an exercise, let's imagine that Gates would be able to somehow cash out his position in Microsoft stock without affecting its share price. A kitty of $16 billion would last how long if exclusively applied, say, to funding federal government commitments to education and training? (About three and a half months.) Or how about if the entirety was devoted to easing the federal government's burden in investing in health care and related research—separate from Medicare? (About a month and a half.)

Defenders of our major philanthropies will respond to this line of objection by arguing that their funds, and presumably Gates's in the future, are best used not for routine needs but to demonstrate new solutions to old problems, for "highly leveraged" situations, as they say in business, in which the foundation's investment is superseded ultimately by "other sources"—code words for the government. In an era of expanding government services, as in the post–World War II decades, this model of philanthropy worked fine, but it does not work well today. Existing philanthropies have been forced to face the dismal fact that government funding of promising pilot projects has all but disappeared. So the philanthropies must either continue to fund short-term projects that lead nowhere or burn up their assets quickly if they attempt to expand their funding of short-term, narrow projects to long-term, expansive ones. Neither course is promising, and that is why I am not waiting for a Gates Foundation to begin disbursing the founder's wealth.

If private philanthropy, wielding even the largest of personal fortunes, has so little hope of making a difference, and the political prospects for a more activist government are also bleak, where can we turn? We should turn back to a most unlikely source, that loathsome national hero, Henry Ford. Not for the example of the Ford Foundation, but rather for something Ford did much earlier, which turned out to have had far more positive social impact than the Ford Foundation—or all of the major foundations combined—would ever have. On January 5, 1914, Ford and his co-executive James Couzens raised the pay of their workers in dramatic fashion, doubling overnight the prevailing minimum wage to what was then an unheard of five dollars a day. The news caused an immediate sensation worldwide. Forty years later, on the anniversary of the event, *The Economist* would remember it as "the most dramatic event in the history of wages," and the French praised Ford for contributing in 1914 "more to the emancipation of workers than the October Revolution of 1917." Today, however, it seems to have been all but forgotten. Now it is particularly timely to exhume this chapter from the nether region of national memory.

The Ford Motor Company in the early teens was in a position that might be compared to that of Microsoft. It was a profit machine that was making money in unseemly fashion. Prior to 1914, the company's executives were becoming ever richer, its customers were offered ever cheaper automobiles, and yet company coffers continued to swell. Even though pay increases in October 1913 had brought the wages of Ford workers up to or above those of competitors, it was becoming embarrassing for the company to sit on $28 million in cash while paying its workers $2 or $2.50 a day.

Historians do not agree which of the two, Ford or Couzens, should be credited with the idea of doubling wages, but the documentary evidence seems to point to Couzens as the one who first suggested to Ford that a "five-dollar day" would be "the greatest advertisement any automobile concern ever had." Ford immediately grasped the public relations dividends that would be reaped and readily agreed. The two men called reporters in to provide details of what they referred to as neither "charity nor wages" but "profit-sharing." Rather than paying a bonus at the end of the year, workers would receive the bonus in their regular paychecks. Workers who were twenty-two or older would receive the increase immediately; those younger had to demonstrate that they were "sober, saving, steady, industrious" and would not fritter away the increase in "riotous living." Ford and Couzens estimated that the boost in wages would cost the company $10 million in the first year.

The point that should be underlined here is that the wage increase was not prompted by the need to retain veteran workers in a tight labor market. In fact, a worldwide depression had created pools of unemployed and increasingly desperate workers. If Ford had acted "rationally" to minimize labor costs, he could have lowered wages instead of raising them. Nor was the pay increase necessary to reduce high turnover rates that had accompanied the introduction of monotonous assembly line work. By late 1913, the turnover rates had already been reduced to acceptably low levels by other, more modest reforms. It was precisely because the Five-Dollar Day was introduced at a time of depressed business conditions when it was *not* needed to retain the loyalty of Ford workers that it had such an electrifying impact on the world, an impact that took even Ford and Couzens by surprise.

To the *Cleveland Plain Dealer*, the Five-Dollar Day "shot like a blinding rocket through the dark clouds of the present industrial depression." In seven days, the press of New York City alone devoted over fifty columns, much of it front-page news, to Ford Motor and its profit-sharing plan. The *New York World* called Ford "an inspired millionaire"; another newspaper ran the headline, "God Bless Henry Ford of the Ford Motor Company." Cartoonists had fun depicting workers riding in chauffeur-driven limousines. In one such cartoon, a wealthy gentleman tells his chauffeur, "Hawkins, will you step over to the pay window and get my wages? I quite overlooked the matter last week."

Ford Motor and other automobile companies were enjoying a period of expansion when other industries were in a depressed state, so it is not surprising that unemployed workers seized on the news of the Five-Dollar Day as their salvation. Ten thousand men gathered outside the Ford employment office in the wee hours of the morning, hoping to be hired. "No Hiring" signs dispersed the crowds temporarily, but thousands of men from other cities descended on Detroit on the same quest and refused to budge, despite snow and a bitter wind. After days of standing in the cold, their desperation culminated in a rush on the factory gates. The police turned on water hoses, drenching the crowd in the subfreezing weather. Finally the unemployed abandoned their hope of being hired.

Ultimately, however, millions of workers who did not work for Ford benefited by the Five-Dollar Day. The fulminations of other employers against Ford's innovation tells as much about its broad impact as testimonials from the workers themselves. Also telling were the editorials that worried most about the raised expectations that Ford was nourishing among plebeians who worked for other employers. The *New York Times* dismissed the Five-Dollar Day as "Utopian"; the *Wall Street Journal* called Ford a traitor to his class and predicted that the wage boosts—"economic blunders, if not crimes"—would return to plague him, the industry, and "organized society."

The dark predictions that Ford's wage plan would bring ruin to him and others proved wrong, of course. At Ford's factories, even though total wage costs in 1914 more than doubled over those of the previous year, labor costs for each car produced increased only modestly, due to increased productivity of workers, machines, and mass-production methods. The actual cost for the bonus turned out to be almost half of the $10 million expected, and even that could be viewed as a bargain in advertising because it created priceless good-will for the company among prospective customers. The durability of that good-will can be seen in a public poll taken more than two decades later, in 1937, at the time of Henry Ford's violent suppression of union organizers at his giant Rouge plant. Almost 60 percent of Americans polled still believed that the Ford Motor Company treated its own labor force better than any other company.

It is difficult to trace precisely what the impact of Ford's Five-Dollar Day was on other employers because of the advent of war in

Europe, the rapid growth of the U.S. armaments industry, and then the entry of the United States in the World War in 1917. These events introduced a variety of other factors that influenced the operations of the national labor market. The Ford Motor Company would find that it had to establish a Six-Dollar Day and then a Ten-Dollar Day to keep up with inflation. None of the subsequent raises drew anywhere near as much attention from the press as had the Five-Dollar Day in 1914.

In a general sense, we could argue that what Ford did, without being fully aware of the implications, was establish the principle that workers should be paid high wages because mass production requires mass consumption—the two cannot be separated. As Henry Ford's obsessive resistance to unions would subsequently make clear, the paternalistic nature of a unilateral decision like the Five-Dollar Day was more dear to him than sharing the company's profits with his workers. But as hard-fought as the union struggles at Ford and elsewhere were, still, it was Henry Ford's action in 1914 and the happy results for the company and its workers that may have instilled somewhere in the national consciousness the thought that a high-wage, high-consumption economic model that defied conventional economic wisdom worked out well for capital and labor alike.

From the 1950s through the 1970s, employers, unwittingly for the most part, followed the spirit of Henry Ford's Five-Dollar Day, paying white- and blue-collar workers more than they may have had to. To make this observation does not imply a naive hope that employers can simply return by force of will to the less competitive—and globally speaking, extremely insular—world of America in the 1950s. But the reason I dwell on Ford and the Five-Dollar Day is because it does show us the possibility of great change when a business leader captures the world's attention with a singular innovation. The significance of the Five-Dollar Day stems from its influence, acknowledged or not, on other employers. If Ford had remained the only employer to pay dramatically higher wages, the most important outcome historically would not have followed: the mass production/mass consumption model requires broad participation. Ford could not prosper by relying on the bulging pocketbooks of its own workers alone to provide the demand for its automobiles. For all to prosper, other employers also had to let go of the notion of paying their own workers the bare minimum. Another way of talking about all this is to call attention to the important role of subjective factors and the psychological receptivity of the public to Henry Ford's announcement.

Perhaps Bill Gates stands in a position that is not unlike that of Henry Ford on the eve of January 1914, in which an epoch-defining reform that he adopts could win instant worldwide attention and help persuade others to adopt a course that would improve the lives of others in ways that could never be achieved by even the wisest disposal of his own personal wealth. What the contents of the reform or program might be, I do not know. (Though, as I have hinted in passing remarks about *The Road Ahead*, I feel strongly about what does *not* fit the bill—the increased proliferation of personal computers and travel on the Internet will not necessarily ameliorate any urgent social problems.) It would not be a literal successor to the Five-Dollar Day, updated for the 1990s. As we saw, Microsoft already bestows generous stock options on its software developers and some options to the other employees. What else should it do? Reverse the outsourcing trends that never occurred to a Henry Ford in the 1910s? Change the status of the cafeteria workers and shuttle-bus drivers on the Microsoft campus from outside contractors to regular employees? The world's reaction would be a yawn.

Should we look to Gates to do something bold and clever that would shake us all out of the comfortable assumptions that the system that we presently have, of crumbling social infrastructure amid pockets of flourishing growth such as at Microsoft, is the best we can do? Maybe the very beauty of Microsoft's physical campus, which I credit for contributing to the company's success, makes it all the more difficult for Gates to feel the urgency of the problems that sit beyond view. But even if Bill Gates felt the urgency—like Bill Clinton, *felt our pain*—why should we look to a business figure as a source of authority on matters not directly related to his business?

I like to think that Gates has intellectual resources that Ford, the ultimate anti-intellectual, never possessed. Ford, after the fact, would claim that the Five-Dollar Day was inspired by Biblical passages and by Emerson's essay on "Compensation," but his biographers give no credence to his attempt to conjure forethought where so plainly there had been none. But even if Ford blundered onto the action that would have the most positive influence, cannot Gates come up with an equivalent boon for society by deliberation—sitting and thinking?

We should not forget that Henry Ford provides a cautionary example as well as an inspirational one. If the Five-Dollar Day turned out to dramatically increase the public's regard for Henry Ford, it also served to dramatically increase Ford's high regard for his own brilliance. As the mail and requests from the press for interviews poured in and his reputation flourished, Ford began to believe that his wisdom extended far beyond automobile production and labor relations. The gold standard, capital punishment, the causes of war, the theory of evolution, foreign trade, alcohol, railroads—he had single-sentence solutions for them all. After the Five-Dollar Day, Ford launched one crusade after another that had nothing to do with the automobile industry, such as promoting "peace" in Europe by chartering a ship and sailing across the Atlantic, or insisting that "wheat is the divine food," or funding newspapers that wrote of nothing but the dastardly deeds of the "international Jew."

The modern-day example of Ross Perot's ready answers to all contemporary problems certainly gives me pause, too. And the Forbes family provides the full nightmarish gamut of possible roles that the very wealthy can elect to assume, roles that Gates has thankfully shown no interest in to date. They range from Malcolm's full-time preoccupation with flouting his wealth to Steve's bid for the presidency based on a flat-tax platform of the rich, by the rich, and for the rich. Gates has not shown any inclination to run for elective office himself, and if he does, he can be reminded of what he said in 1991 when a British interviewer surprised him by asking if Gates had been asked to run for Congress. Gates, clearly taken aback, replied, "No, people don't do it like that over here, you don't get asked to run. I'm a software person, not a politician."

I could be persuaded that just as a Henry Ford, convinced of his own omniscience, was a dangerous figure, so too perhaps it is best for us all that Gates has not been lured to tackle problems that fall outside his expertise. Gates tends to be a bit vague or unrealistically positive about solutions to gritty social problems. For example, having pondered how the exodus of the affluent from the cities, helped by the convenience of telecommuting, could worsen the already weak tax bases, Gates preposterously proposed that the urban infrastructures in such cases would be "less heavily loaded" because of the high-income exodus, hence not worse off, on balance. Perhaps it's best that he does *not* claim special expertise on all manner of problems. And we should take care not to send the message, as Ford's public did, that we presume that Gates's opinions on all manner of topics are equally wise.

Henry Ford's example instructs us in an important lesson about not only the potential power of a business figure, but also in the public's power in shaping the person's outlook. Until now, Gates has not been nearly as attentive as Ford to how the public views him. His concern has been how the public's view of himself affects Microsoft. In the future, he will likely become more concerned with the public's opinion of his contributions to society, not just to his own company. We then may collectively have an increasingly important role to play in Gates's future biography than we realize.

In the meantime, Microsoft has much to teach us if we can put aside a caricature of Bill Gates as the Devil and overcome our instinctive antipathy toward smarts. We must resist the temptation to unload on a scapegoat our uneasiness about a future beset with serious problems, only some of which will be the product of technological advances. We do not need to continue to view Gates as an outsized iconic face—removing the horns from his head only to substitute an equally large smiley face to depict Saint Bill would be silly, too.

We should instead see Gates and his employees in their actual size, and therein resides their utility to the rest of us. We can see in their experience the attention they devote to thinking as thoroughly as possible but not paralyzingly slowly either. They act with provisional answers, knowing that experience will feed back to provide new input into an unending process of reevaluation and revision. In Microsoft's example, we can find a celebration of cerebration, which can serve as a tonic antidote to the inheritance of anti-intellectualism. If the future is daunting because most of all it necessarily remains opaque, we must redouble our conviction to learn whatever we have to in order to think our own way through to our destination.

Acknowledgments

When Elizabeth Kaplan first suggested that I take on this project, I pronounced myself not interested: the shelf of books on Microsoft is already a long one, I sniffed. She knew better than I did that once I began, I would discover a plenitude of unexplored topics and in the end have lots to say. I am thankful that she persuaded me to have a look.

For interviews, I wish to thank the following current or former employees at Microsoft: Steve Arnold, Craig Bartholomew, Carl Bates, Ed Belleba, Susan Boeschen, Richard Bray, Ryan Carey, Tom Corddry, Peter de Vries, Libby Duzan, Bill Gates, Rob Glaser, Sonja Gustafson, Charlotte Guyman, Karen Hargrove, Alan Hartman, Dave Heiner, Tom Ikeda, Edward Jung, Martin Leahy, Tom Lopez, Bill Miller, Peter Mollman, Craig Mundie, Mike Murray, Nathan Myhrvold, Peter Neupert, Jessica Ostrow, Sanjay Parthasarathy, Rick Rashid, Greg Riker, Russell Siegelman, Charles Simonyi, Linda Stone, Nils von Veh, Min Yee, and Natalie Yount. For help in the company's library and its archives, I would like to thank Jeff Abbott, Kris Kaeding, Chris Shannon, and Kyle Wagner. For interview arrangements, responses to queries, and logistical help, Josh Baran, Jon Lazarus, Andrea Cook, Sharleen Grove, Mich Mathews, and John Pinette provided all that I requested, and cheerfully too.

I am also indebted to others unconnected to Microsoft for their assistance: Mari Baker and Eric Dunn of Intuit; Terri Childs, Christopher Hopkins, Ken Wasch, and Sara White of the Software Publishers Association; Mark Eppley of Traveling Software; Howard High of Intel; Christine Milazzo and Jon Leibowitz of Reed Exhibitions; Mike Kwatinetz of Paine Webber; Deborah Sanders of Multiple Zones International; and Ken Williams of Sierra On-Line.

San Jose State University's College of Business provided indispensable help in many forms, including the technical assistance of Luciano Canziani, whose patience is apparently bottomless.

At the University of Washington, Nancy Britanyak of the Department of Computer Science helped me track down a videotape that turned out to be most valuable.

Gail Hershatter applied an astringent skepticism to a preliminary draft, as she has done many times in the past; the revised draft was much improved thanks to her close reading.

For advice and insights, I wish to thank Lee Gomes, Joe Nocera, and Greg Stross.

In guiding the book into print, John Bell of Addison-Wesley greatly helped me tighten my presentation and discard as many academic mannerisms as I could be persuaded to relinquish. Margaret Hill deftly wielded a copyeditor's scalpel, and Pat Jalbert kept the project on track with calm efficiency.

The last person I should thank remains unknown: I never found out who exactly at Microsoft acceded to my request that I not be accompanied by representatives of the company's public relations firm when I was on the campus. Sometimes the absence of professional "helpers" can be the greatest help of all.

—July 1996

Introduction
Camping with Henry and Bill

1 *Wired* article: "On Hating Microsoft," *Wired*, April 1996, 155.

2 No right to review the results: See Stephen Manes and Paul Andrews's discussion of the centrality of this same condition in their biography, *Gates: How Microsoft's Mogul Reinvented an Industry—And Made Himself the Richest Man in America* (New York: Doubleday, 1993), 458–460. The concern for maintaining a strictly independent vantage point has earlier precedents. For example, when Ford Motor Company agreed to help write the history of the company after Henry Ford I's death, the historian who led the study, Allan Nevins, also took pains to explain the authors' absolute independence and disinterestedness. See Allan Nevins, *Ford: The Times, The Man, The Company* (New York: Charles Scribner's Sons, 1954), vii.

4 If not Henry Ford: The place of Gates's company in the public consciousness is ahead of Ford's namesake company at a similar point in its history because Microsoft has received a disproportionate amount of publicity. Let us compare Microsoft's prominence in the news with Ford's larger competitor, General Motors, the nation's largest industrial corporation (ranking first on the *Fortune 500*, defined by revenue, compared to Microsoft's 250th position). In 1995, the *Wall Street Journal* ran 1033 articles that mentioned Microsoft Corporation, or almost three articles every weekday, for a year. During the same year, Gates himself was mentioned in 168 articles in the *New York Times*. By contrast, GM's chief executive appeared in only 21 articles. See "Bill Who?" *New York Times*, 31 December 1995.

5 Ford on history as "bunk": *Chicago Tribune*, 25 May 1916. Ford's biographers have noted the contradiction between Ford's professed attitude and his establishment in the late 1920s of an industrial museum and his re-creation of an early American village.

5 Gates on "waste of time": "Bill Gates & Paul Allen Talk," *Fortune*, 2 October 1995, 86.

5 Gates on "future is what matters": Bill Gates, "PC Empowerment," syndicated column, issued 10 October 1995.

5 Gates on Microsoft maintaining its place: Bill Gates, with Nathan Myhrvold and Peter Rinearson, *The Road Ahead* (New York: Viking, 1995), 275–276.

5 Ford as cautionary example: In 1994, Gates said of Henry Ford: "Ford is not that admirable—he did great things but he was very very narrow-minded and was willing to use brute-force power too much. His relationship with his family is tragic. His model of the world was plain wrong in a lot of ways. He decided he knew everything he needed to fairly early in life." See John Seabrook, "E-Mail from Bill," *The New Yorker*, 10 January 1994, 61.

5 Gates willing to delegate: G. Pascal Zachary, "The Once and Future Microsoft," *Upside*, April 1995, 28.

5 *Fortune 500* rankings: "The Fortune 500," *Fortune*, 29 April 1996.

6 Intel and Microsoft earnings: for rankings, see "The *Business Week* 1000," *Business Week*, 25 March 1996, 154, 158. Data for calendar year 1995 were used instead of the companies' varying fiscal-year calendars.

6 Lewis's study: David L. Lewis, *The Public Image of Henry Ford: An American Folk Hero and His Company* (Detroit: Wayne State University Press, 1976). Lewis states that the book was the product of nineteen years of research, a claim that is wholly credible in view of the scholarship that informs the work.

6 Ford captured reporters' attention: Original article from *Boston Post*, 18 August 1928. Cited in Lewis, *The Public Image of Henry Ford*, 222.

7 Gates's friendship with Buffett: When Gates reviewed Roger Lowenstein's biography of Warren Buffett for the *Harvard Business Review*, he spoke about his friendship with Buffett at length, but emphasized the intellectual ties between the two. He said nothing at all about their recent China trip together (which also included a former president of the University of Washington and a teacher expert in the

nuances of contract bridge as travel companions). See Gates's review in either the January/February 1996 issue of *HBR*, or the reprint, "Gates on Buffett," in *Fortune*, 5 February 1996, 102–104.

7 Bernays's lunch with Ford and Edison: Edward L. Bernays, *Biography of an Idea: Memoirs of Public Relations Counsel* (New York: Simon and Schuster, 1965), 451.

7 *Times* review of Ford's *My Life and Work*: "Finding the Winning Card in Business," *New York Times*, 15 October 1922.

7 Ford's autobiography: Henry Ford, in collaboration with Samuel Crowther, *My Life and Work* (Garden City, NY: Doubleday, Page & Company, 1922).

7 Suppression of other books: Lewis, *The Public Image of Henry Ford*, 215 and footnote 14 on 521.

9 Microsoft persuaded IBM: Manes and Andrews, *Gates*, 154–163.

10 Multiplan versus 1-2-3: "Manzi vs. Gates: Software's Blood Feud," *Business Week*, 4 June 1990.

10 Gates on "world's best plumbing": "How Bill Gates Keeps the Magic Going," *Fortune*, 18 June 1990.

14 Sven Birkerts, *The Gutenberg Elegies: The Fate of Reading in an Electronic Age* (Boston: Faber and Faber, 1994). The subtlety of Birkerts's arguments about the nature of reading a printed book, and how the electronic world displaces the act of "deep" reading, sets his collection of essays well apart from the work of other Cassandras, such as Clifford Stoll's *Silicon Snake Oil: Second Thoughts on the Information Highway* (New York: Doubleday, 1995).

Chapter One
Sitting and Thinking

16 Thoreau quotation: Henry D. Thoreau, *Walden*, J. Lyndon Shanley, ed. (Princeton, NJ: Princeton University Press, 1971), 111.

16 Gates's "sit and think": "This Week With David Brinkley," 3 January 1993. During the interview, Gates was asked about what George Will (self-introduced as "one of your grateful stockholders") characterized as the U.S. government's attempted encircling of Microsoft. Did this betray, Will asked, the government's lack of understanding of a historically new industry? Gates replied that he was not at all surprised that the government was looking into the workings of the computer industry, given its importance, and he mildly expressed a hope that the gov-

ernment was "enlightening" itself as it delved into an unfamiliar realm. Then he suggested that one of the difficulties that the government faced in coming to a better understanding was grasping the nature of the work itself.

18 Coupland's description of the campus: Douglas Coupland, "Microserfs," *Wired*, January 1994, 88, 146. Also in Coupland's book, which incorporated the original story: Douglas Coupland, *Microserfs* (New York: Regan Books/HarperCollins, 1995), 2, 38.

18 Gates on "private thinking and private discussion": "Bill Gates Reveals Secrets of Success—His and His Employees," *Wall Street Journal*, 8 November 1994.

19 Gates's reserved parking space: The decision was also apparently prompted by a rash of incidents in which strangers seeking a job or a donation accosted him in the parking lot. See "William H. Gates," *USA Today*, 16 January 1991.

21 Letter-writer urging telecommuting: Phil Zack, "Microsoft's Split Personality," *MicroNews*, 19 August 1994.

21 Company line on telecommuting: Mike Murray, "Wouldn't It Be Oil Smarter To Telecommute?," *MicroNews*, 18 March 1994.

22 Fell on deaf ears: "Microsoft Unplugged," Microsoft Annual Company Meeting, 1994.

22 Nonmandated benefits: "The Company Meeting (Part 2)," *MicroNews*, 12 August 1994.

22 Food and beverage subsidies: "The Company Meeting Q&A," *MicroNews*, 22 October 1993.

22 "Anything with caffeine": "Culture Club," *Newsweek*, 11 July 1994. The same article stated erroneously that "the cafeterias are open until midnight."

22 Having an outside life: "Microsoft Unplugged," Microsoft Annual Company Meeting, 1994.

23 On-site childcare: Jon Shirley, at 1988 Annual Company Meeting, and Mike Murray, at 1994 Annual Company Meeting. Shirley's remarks in 1988 alluded to the fact that the request had been presented at earlier annual meetings as well.

23 Other benefits: "The Company Meeting Q&A," *MicroNews*, 22 October 1993. Mothers received eight weeks of short-term disability leave, which, combined with the four weeks of infant-care leave, yielded a three-month maternity leave.

23 Shirley's injunction against bare feet: 1988 Microsoft Annual Company Meeting.

23 Percentage of invitees: "Microsoft Whiz Keeps Tabs on Technology," *Seattle Times*, 7 March 1994.

23 Letter from Ben Goetter: Ben Goetter, "Work Standards Are a Joke!" *MicroNews*, 27 January 1995.

24 Reaction to this manifesto: "A Joke, Indeed," *MicroNews*, 3 February 1995.

24 Picture of Goetter: *MicroNews*, 10 February 1995.

24 Gates on "ownership": Videotape of Gates's interview with local Seattle media, 4 August 1993.

24 Employees who own stock: The percentage of employees who own at least one share of Microsoft stock is publicly unknown. What *is* known is the percentage of shares owned by employees versus nonemployees. In 1993, Gates owned 28 percent; Paul Allen, 11.2 percent, and Steve Ballmer, 5.3 percent, other officers and directors, about 2 percent; and of the remaining, employees held "about 20 percent." "Company Meeting Q&A Summary," *MicroNews*, 20 October 1993.

25 Gates's "shows our culture": "Microsoft Unplugged," 1994 Microsoft Annual Company Meeting.

25 Estimates of their net worth: A skit performed at the company meeting in 1994 reveals how the outside viewed Microsoft:

New Employee: Is it true that 92 percent of all Microsoft employees are millionaires?

Mike Murray: Wait a minute. Did you say *million*aires, or *billion*aires?

Employee: Millionaires.

Murray: That whole comment is stupider than Jupiter. I don't get where it comes from. Roger, 92 percent!? What do you think it really is?

Roger Heinen: I don't think it's anything like that. I think it's 86 percent.

"Microsoft Unplugged," Microsoft Annual Company Meeting, 1994.

27 Wall Street firm: Michael K. Kwatinetz, "Microsoft's Mixed Blessing: A Wealth of Rich Employees," *Bernstein Research Weekly Notes*, 14 February 1992. Kwatinetz's methodology for estimating the value of

the holdings of developers hired in 1989 is presented in detail; if his methodology had flaws, Microsoft did not explain them when the company complained that his estimate of the number of millionaires was too high.

More recently, another source estimated in 1995 that about 3000 of Microsoft's employees were millionaires. See Michael A. Cusamano and Richard W. Selby, *Microsoft Secrets: How the World's Most Powerful Software Company Creates Technology, Shapes Markets, and Manages People* (New York: Free Press, 1995), 116–117.

28 Wall Street report: Kwatinetz, "Microsoft's Mixed Blessing."

28 Lower turnover: Until 1994, Microsoft experienced an annual turnover-rate of 7 to 8 percent, and only a small portion involved software developers. In 1994, the turnover rate increased to 10 percent, not only in Microsoft's U.S. operations but also in its foreign operations. Concerned that the increase might indicate that retention would become difficult in the future, Microsoft closely monitored the turnover rate.

28 Employee asked at the annual company meeting: Microsoft videotape, General Session of the National Sales Meeting, Day 4, 1993.

29 Gates on "those guys" in Silicon Valley: "The Met Grill," *Metropolitan Home*, July 1985, 23.

29 Campaign to eliminate frills: "Shrimp and Weenies at Microsoft," *MicroNews*, 11 June 1993. The phrase "Shrimp and Weenies" is credited to Nathan Myhrvold.

29 "Every penny counts": Excerpt from Mike Murray memo. See "Shrimp and Weenies at Microsoft," *MicroNews*, 11 June 1993.

29 No limos: In 1991, Gates and Ballmer offered a limousine ride to a rival's CEO, Jerry Kaplan of GO Corporation, at an industry trade show. It is interesting to see Ballmer's need to offer an embarrassed explanation of the unusual extravagance, which seemed to violate the company's well-known stricture against the use of limos. Ballmer told Kaplan that the hotel Microsoft employees were staying in for the show provided it without charge because the company rented so many rooms. For what other company would the limo have been a source of embarrassment? See Jerry Kaplan, *Startup: A Silicon Valley Adventure* (Boston: Houghton Mifflin, 1995), 214.

29 Murray's "a day at a time": "Is Your Job Safe?," *MicroNews*, 11 June 1993.

30 Request for more volleyball courts and more parties: "How About More Volleyball Courts?," *MicroNews*, 21 May 1993.

30 "Time is money": "The Real Debate Is Weenies vs. Beans," *MicroNews*, 25 June 1993.

30 Turning computers off at night: "Is This Man Making Too Much Money?" *MicroNews*, 3 March 1995.

30 Cash kitty: "Brown Has Fun While Meeting Microsoft's New Financial Challenges," *MicroNews*, 22 April 1994.

30 "We should appreciate": "How About No More Whining," *MicroNews*, 28 May 1993. For another letter in a similar vein, see "Of Shrimp, Weenies and Beans If You Don't Like It Here," *MicroNews*, 2 July 1993.

30 "Do a slow burn": "Microsoft Doesn't Owe You Club Med," *MicroNews*, 25 June 1993.

Chapter Two
Smarts

32 Thayer quotation: William M. Thayer, *Tact, Push, and Principle* (Boston: James H. Earle, Publisher, 1882), 65.

32 "Cromwell built the finest army": Anonymous, "Why I Never Hire Brilliant Men," *American Magazine*, February 1924, 118, 122.

33 Whyte's "Fight Against Genius": William H. Whyte, Jr., *The Organization Man* (New York: Touchstone Books, 1956), 205–217.

33 Hofstadter on business's antipathy toward the brilliant: Richard Hofstadter, *Anti-Intellectualism in American Life* (New York: Alfred A. Knopf, 1966), 236.

34 Breathed described Gates: "Tycoon," NBC Special With Tom Brokaw, 28 May 1995.

34 Unflattering physical descriptions: For an interesting example of unflattering characterization, see Jessica Maxwell, "Macro Meets Micro," *Washington*, September/October 1988, passim. Maxwell's piece concerns The Brain, Gates, meeting The Brawn, the Seattle Mariner's Brian Bosworth, who had signed what was at the time the largest rookie contract in NFL history. The two men were compared in terms of physique—Bosworth could bench-press 450 pounds—whereas Gates is limned as "a sparrow that has flown in this place of muscle by mistake." But the cutesy comparison was restricted to the realm of the physical: there was no invidious comparison of Bosworth's intellectual capacities against Gates's. Instead, the reporter describes with undis-

guised delectation how Gates's gaze continually returned to Bosworth's attractive girlfriend.

34 More machine than human: Tom Brokaw's voiceover introduced Gates in this fashion: "Many believe he may be one of the smartest men of this century. Others think he might be part computer himself. . . ." "Tycoon," NBC Special With Tom Brokaw.

35 "Unused bandwidth": "Chairman Bill," *San Francisco Chronicle*, 12 May 1991.

35 Singularity of the intelligence: John Perry Barlow, "Another Side of Bill Gates," *Microtimes*, 26 November 1993, 53.

35 "Smart friends" and "smart strangers": Bill Gates, Executive Suite Talk, Seattle University, 25 October 1986.

35 Gates's "you've got to be very elitist": Bill Gates, oral history interview, with David Allison of the Smithsonian Institution, 30 November 1993.

35 Microsoft hires: The annual number of prospective job candidates was inflated because some résumés were duplicates, sent in by job applicants who thought that their chances of being hired were enhanced by sending the same résumé to different company outposts. Microsoft, in turn, began using automated résumé-scanning software, which culled duplicates and foiled such tactics. Still, the number of disappointed applicants remained high, considering that Microsoft, even growing at ripping speed, hired at most only 1500 to 2000 new employees each year.

35 Gates's "very young people": Bill Gates, Executive Suite Talk.

35 *Microsoft Employee Handbook*, online, noted March 1995.

36 Gates's "Young people more willing to learn": "Culture Club," *Newsweek*, 11 July 1994.

36 College graduates hired: In addition to hiring college graduates, Microsoft hired an additional 300–350 college students each year as student interns.

36 "Target schools": "Microsoft's William Gates Talks About the Age of 'Fingertip Information,'" *Washington Post*, 30 December 1990.

36 Gates's "not a single line of code": "Billg on Hiring," Microsoft Corporation, video, 1993.

36 Gates's "reasonably innate": "Billg on Hiring."

36 Gates on thinking in "real time" and perceiving connections: "Playboy Interview: Bill Gates," *Playboy*, July 1994.

36 Gates on understanding a long printout: Susan Lammers, *Programmers at Work* (Redmond, WA: Microsoft Press, 1986), 83.

36 Gates on thinking about programs even when driving or eating: Lammers, *Programmers at Work*, 75-76.

36 Gates on "smart" people and concentration: "Genius at Work," *Macleans*, 11 May 1992.

36 Gates on photographic recall of program code: Lammers, *Programmers at Work*, 81-82.

37 Gates's "bias towards intelligence": "Billg On Hiring."

37 Gates on mainframe programmers: "Managing Your Career: Bill Gates Reveals Secrets of Success—His and His Employees," *Wall Street Journal*, 8 November 1994.

37 Gates on hiring from the pure sciences: "Microsoft's William Gates Talks About the Age of 'Fingertip Information.' "

37 Gates's "are you stupid?": "People," *San Jose Mercury News*, 8 July 1994.

39 Gates's "it's pretty cast in concrete": Lammers, *Programmers at Work*, 81-82.

40 Where would Lotus be today: Coincidentally, Ray Ozzie, like Gates, was born in 1955.

40 Good programmers made it easier to attract others: Bill Gates, speech at Microsoft Annual Company Meeting, 1993.

40 Simonyi as "really bright guy": Videotape of Gates being interviewed by Seattle-based media, 4 August 1993. For a brief portrait of Simonyi and a discussion of Gates's more effective use of bright talent such as Simonyi compared to Steve Jobs's, see my previous book, *Steve Jobs and the NeXT Big Thing* (New York: Atheneum, 1993), 36-38.

41 Gates's "if you have somebody who's mediocre": "Billg on Hiring."

41 Gates on guarding against "100 people" doing what twenty should do: "How Bill Gates Keeps the Magic Going," *Fortune*, 18 June 1990.

41 "*N* minus one": Mike Murray, "Managing Microsoft People," Microsoft videotape, 23 March 1993.

41 Gates made himself available: Gates, Executive Suite Talk.

42 Microsoft's "Strike Team": "Strike Team in Recruiting," *MicroNews*, 10 March 1995.

42 Listed the fruits: Nathan Myhrvold, memo to Bill Gates, "1993 Year End Memo," 26 December 1993.

43 Agreement that Kahn and Gates had signed: "Opening of 'Windows' Shows How Bill Gates Succeeds in Software," *Wall Street Journal*, 21 May 1990.

44 Gates's last thing he did not understand: "Playboy Interview: Bill Gates."

44 Gaudette's "we're smarter": "Internal Challenges, Competition May Chip Away at Microsoft's Leading Edge," *Washington Post*, 15 March 1992.

44 Gates's "take our twenty best people away": "Bill Gates," *Forbes*, 7 December 1992.

44 Gates's "don't be so smart": "PC Industry Gets a Taste of the Real World," *Los Angeles Times*, 23 September 1992.

Chapter Three
The Model in Their Head

46 Rockefeller quotation: John K. Winkler, *John D.: A Portrait in Oils* (New York: Vanguard, 1929), 67. Winkler provides no date for the quotation.

46 Edison quotation: Matthew Josephson, *Edison* (New York: McGraw-Hill, 1959), 441.

46 Edison's wealth and popularity: Neil Baldwin, *Edison: Inventing the Century* (New York: Hyperion, 1995), 408–411. Edison's estate, at the time of his death in 1931, was worth $12 million.

47 Astor's son: Edwin T. Freedley, *Practical Treatise On Business, Or How To Get, Save, Spend, Give, and Bequeath Money* (Philadelphia: Lippincott, Grambo and Company, 1853), 193.

47 Gates's "if you're any good at math": "Unstoppable Bill Gates," *Upside*, April 1992, 74–75.

47 Gates's "mental cycles": "Playboy Interview: Bill Gates," *Playboy*, July 1994.

47 Gates's "oops": "Playboy Interview: Bill Gates."

47 Gates on "exponential phenomena": "Microsoft New Employee Orientation," Microsoft video, 1994.

48 Moore's original prediction: Gordon E. Moore, "Cramming More Components Onto Integrated Circuits," *Electronics*, 19 April 1965, 115.

48   Moore's revisiting his forecast: Gordon E. Moore, "Lithography and the Future of Moore's Law," in SPIE—The International Society of Optical Engineering, *Electron-Beam, EUV, and Ion-Beam Submicrometer Lithographies for Manufacturing: Proceedings* 5 (1995), 2–17.

In the past ten years, technology reporters can no more resist mentioning the Law than political commentators can resist slipping in a quotation from Tocqueville. But the time period that Moore predicted for the doubling effect frequently undergoes transmogrification in the retelling. Sometimes the doubling is said to occur every eighteen months (a figure arrived at perhaps by splitting the difference between Moore's 1965 and 1975 forecasts), or every three years, or other unauthorized variations. For an example of the "eighteen months" school, erroneously described as Moore's pre-1975 projection, see "The End of the Line," *The Economist*, 15 July 1995, 61. Bill Gates adopted the "every three years" characterization when describing Moore's Law to a group of college students in the 1980s: see Bill Gates, "The Future of Computing and the Direction of Microsoft," talk given to the Department of Computer Science, University of Washington, 22 October 1987.

48   Ten-million-fold decrease in price: Moore, "Lithography and the Future of Moore's Law."

48   Create opportunities aplenty in commercial software development: William H. Gates, "Next-Generation Software," typescript of speech given at the 1981 Rosen Research Personal Computer Forum.

48   Software only: References to Microsoft as a "software-only" company are for the sake of literary economy and are not strictly accurate. Some of Microsoft's non-software products have included mouse, keyboard, and its earliest hardware product, the SoftCard add-in board for Apple II computers. Still, the hardware products have never occupied a large enough percentage of the company's total revenue to change the company's character as a software company.

48   Gates had to convince Allen: Gates, Executive Suite Talk, Seattle University, 25 October 1986.

48   Gates's "lonely" position: Gates, Executive Suite Talk.

49   Without imminent fear of oversupply: "Mr. Software," *New York Times*, 25 August 1991.

49   Gates's charge of "ripping off" software: When Gates looked back on this period from the vantage point of 1993, he remembered that the problem of piracy was connected with the frustration that early pur-

chasers of Altair computer kits felt at the shoddy memory boards sold by MITS. Copying the BASIC software that ran on the machines, Gates said, was a way that some people thought they could retaliate against MITS. See Bill Gates, oral history interview, with David Allison of the Smithsonian Institution, 30 November 1993.

49 Warren praised Gary Kildall: Letter from Jim Warren, Jr., to unnamed recipients, 10 April 1976; on the copy held in the Microsoft Library, a handwritten salutation "Dear Bill" was scribbled on the photocopy and the document was signed "Jim W." but Warren's handwritten inscription to Gates has been blackened out.

50 Warren's sale of the West Coast Computer Faire: "Jim Warren: Tune In, Sign On, Fight the Feds," *San Jose Mercury News*, 20 February 1995.

50 Gates on "softness": William Gates, "A Trend Toward Softness," *Creative Computing*, November 1984, 121.

50 Gates on his "enthusiastic support": Bill Gates, "Software Column," *Personal Computing*, May/June 1977.

50 Gates on volume: Gates, "Next-Generation Software."

51 Million-to-one leverage: Nathan Myhrvold, Microsoft memo, "Telling It Like It Is," 1993.

51 Gates's oversight: "Microsoft Booms as Creators of New Computer Software," *Seattle Post-Intelligencer*, 21 March 1983.

51 Committee chairman to Edison: Matthew Josephson, *Edison* (New York: McGraw-Hill, 1959), 66.

52 Edison's "econotechnical" approach: Thomas P. Hughes, *Networks of Power: Electrification in Western Society, 1880–1930* (Baltimore: Johns Hopkins University Press, 1983), 28–29.

52 Edison's test: "Edison on College Men," *New York Times*, 6 May 1921. For list of 146 of the questions, with answers, see "Here Is Edison's 4-Column Sheaf of Knowledge," *New York Times*, 13 May 1921.

52 Edison's firing of workers: "Edison on College Men."

52 Edison on college students: "Edison on College Men." Edison also sought to place blame for the disappointing results on the inadequate educational methods employed by primary schools. See "Edison Condemns the Primary School," *New York Times*, 7 May 1921.

52 Reporters' testing of college students: "Can't Answer Edison," *New York Times*, 11 May 1921. See also "Edison's Questions Still Puzzle City," *New York Times*, 12 May 1921.

52 Einstein on the speed of sound: "Einstein Sees Boston; Fails on Edison Test," *New York Times*, 18 May 1921.

52 *New York Times* editorial: "No College Need Be Worried," *New York Times*, 11 May 1921.

53 Ballmer's delivery: An example of Ballmer's penchant for emphatic pounding is illustrated in a story told by a Microsoft employee who recalled, "The first time I met him, he came into my office and he said, 'Do you know what you need to know, Lisa? You need to think of only one thing: Windows, Windows, Windows!' And he started banging on the door so hard that chips started falling down from the ceiling." See "He's Bill Gates' Best Friend, and He Can't Sit Still," *Journal American*, 7 November 1993.

53 The sheet that the company used: No date and no title; in Box 2946 of Microsoft company archives.

53 *Fortune* chided: "Microsoft's Drive To Dominate Software," *Fortune*, 23 January 1984.

54 Gates on person "who builds this model": Gates, Executive Suite Talk.

54 Myhrvold on interest in origin of universe: Nathan Myhrvold, speech delivered at TED 6, 6 February 1995.

55 Group of hires: Cameron Myhrvold was described in a Silicon Valley magazine in 1995 as "real bright" and a FOB—Friend of Bill; David Weise was described by an unidentified Microsoft source as "one of the smartest guys I ever met." See "Fifteen Notable Microsofties," *Upside*, April 1995, 89.

56 Edison's simple solution: Josephson, *Edison*, 193.

56 Upton on framing questions: Thomas P. Hughes, *Networks of Power: Electrification in Western Society, 1880-1930* (Baltimore: Johns Hopkins University Press, 1983), 26. Hughes suggests that Upton was unduly self-deprecating; another Edison associate, Francis Jehl, wrote privately that it was Upton's "proficient and eruditive mind," not Edison's, that should receive the greater credit for applying science to the problems of designing the earliest electrical systems.

57 Gates on customers skipping early versions: "How Bill Gates Keeps the Magic Going," *Fortune*, 18 June 1990. For an early instance of Gates placing emphasis on the importance of learning from the company's own experience when developing software, see "Forum Looks to Future Software," *PC Week*, 8 May 1984.

58 Gates on GM's possession of the "right feedback loops": Bill Gates, "Reading Remains Effective Way To Convey Details," *Star Tribune*, 19 February 1995. Sloan himself did not share Gates's interest in feedback loops. He instead emphasized the delicate nature of balancing centralized and decentralized controls, and the superiority of decisions that come from groups rather than individual executives. See Alfred P. Sloan, Jr., *My Years With General Motors* (Garden City, NY: Doubleday, 1963), passim.

58 Ballmer told employees: Microsoft Annual Company Meeting, 5 August 1994.

59 Echoed the same sentiment: For examples of senior management encouraging employees to send upward bad news as well good, see Mike Maples in the internal Microsoft video, "Managing Microsoft People," March 1993, and Nathan Myhrvold, "The Audience Can Read: Tips and Techniques for Product Reviews & Presentations," Microsoft memo, 18 February 1996. Myhrvold's memo was addressed to Microsoft employees, whom he asked to remember the following two principles: "Nobody was ever fired at Microsoft for making an honest mistake" and "Nobody was ever promoted at Microsoft who didn't make a few prior mistakes." It was far better for staff members in their presentations to admit errors and show that they could "learn from them" than attempt to maintain an error-free past. Acquiring a reputation for "not being credible" was most damaging to one's career.

59 Myhrvold on empirical data: Nathan Myhrvold, Microsoft memo, "Notes on Application Development," 13 July 1988.

59 Each group "charged": See the comments of Rob Aney, Microsoft Product Support Services manager, in "How To Get Developers To Listen to Tech Support," *Soft•Letter,* 23 April 1994.

60 Myhrvold's "an enormously valuable thing": Myhrvold, "Notes on Application Development."

Chapter Four
Big Files

62 Bush quotation: Vannevar Bush, "As We May Think," *Atlantic Monthly*, July 1945, 102.

62 Machines as the handmaid of memory: For a discussion that directly traces the lineage of the Macintosh side of the personal computer family back to Bush's essay, see Steven Levy's *Insanely Great: The Life*

and Times of Macintosh, The Computer That Changed Everything (New York: Viking, 1994).

62 *Encyclopaedia Britannica* as size of matchbox: Bush, "As We May Think," 103.

63 Introduction of CD-ROM: "Optical-Disk Storage," *PC Week*, 17 June 1986.

63 Occupied one-fifth of the CD-ROM: Gary Kildall demonstration at First International Conference on CD-ROM.

63 Kildall's rivalry with Gates: Stewart Alsop, "Differing Visions: Gary Kildall and Bill Gates," *PC Magazine*, 10 June 1986.

64 Sponsoring conference: Gary Kildall claimed later that the idea of holding a conference for CD-ROM had been his and Kildall had mentioned his intentions to Gates in passing when Kildall visited Seattle; Kildall was aghast when he received the invitation to the Microsoft conference. Stephen Manes and Paul Andrews, *Gates: How Microsoft's Mogul Reinvented an Industry—And Made Himself the Richest Man in America* (New York: Doubleday, 1993), 336.

64 Kildall's work on optical technologies: Alsop, "Differing Visions." Alsop's 1986 observations of Kildall and Gates were acute: he characterized Kildall as possessing "20/20 vision," but Gates also had what Alsop called "peripheral vision" that allowed him not only to recognize important new technology but also how "to get that technology in the marketplace in a big way."

65 One-time event: Though the conference had been billed as "The First International Conference on CD-ROM, Sponsored by Microsoft Corporation," the ordinal reference was an expression of hope, not of concrete plans. No one at Microsoft seriously anticipated that there would actually be a second conference if the first one ran up several hundred thousand dollars in unrecoverable costs.

66 Lopez's appointment: "Microsoft Acquires a Compact Disk Firm," *Seattle Post-Intelligencer*, 22 January 1986.

67 Stork proposed: Carl Stork to Tom Lopez and Bill Gates, "6-in-6 Program," Microsoft memo, 21 October 1987.

68 Interview for *Metropolitan Home*: "The Met Grill," *Metropolitan Home*, July 1985, 21, 23.

68 Gates's prediction "you're going to be involved": Susan Lammers, *Programmers at Work* (Redmond, WA: Microsoft Press, 1986), 89.

68 Gates's "If a kid is addicted": Lammers, *Programmers at Work*, 89.

68 Gates's "ten years": Bill Gates, Executive Suite Talk, Seattle University, 25 October 1986.

69 Intentionally crippled CDs: Gates, Executive Suite Talk.

70 Gates on exponential improvements: Gates, Executive Suite Talk.

71 Seymour on "Thomas Wolfe": Jim Seymour, "Standard Enlivens CD-ROM With Sound, Video," *PC Week*, 1 April 1986, 30.

71 Newer product: The product that would use television sets was introduced as another pesky acronym: CD-I (Compact Disc-Interactive).

71 About to be rendered obsolete: Jerry Pournelle, "CD-ROMs Are Facing a Limited Life Span," *Infoworld*, 17 March 1986.

71 Did not become a potent threat: The much lower cost of a CD-ROM player that would work with a television set was a beguiling concept. In 1986 Gates himself was gulled into thinking that players connected to TVs would lead to proliferation of the CD-ROM along with the personal computer. He worried, however, that consumers would mistake the CD-ROM player for a computer: "It simply isn't one, any more than your VCR, dishwasher, and telephone are computers." Gates called for simultaneous development of CD-ROM for both the high end, the PC, and the low end, the TV-dependent viewer (which fizzled). See Gates's foreword to the volume published after the first CD-ROM conference: Steve Lambert and Suzanne Ropiequet, eds., *CD-ROM: The New Papyrus* (Redmond, WA: Microsoft Press, 1986), xi–xiii.

72 Price of drives in 1988: "CD-ROM Is Slow To Get on Track," *Seattle Post-Intelligencer*, 23 May 1988.

72 Estimate of 170,000 drives: From the Optical Publishing Association's second assessment report, quoted by Meta Nissley and Michael Schuyler, "Microsoft's CD-ROM Magicland: Two Conference Views," *CD-ROM Librarian*, September 1989. The report's author, Julie Schwerin, characterized 1988 as the "year of realization" for the CD-ROM publishing industry, but Schwerin's characterization seems a bit premature.

72 Ability to lead the industry: IBM was also smarting at this time for its MicroChannel disaster—an attempt to establish a new bus standard for personal computers, in which IBM had developed its own specification, picked up the flag, headed out to lead—and no one followed.

73 Headed for disaster: Glaser was more familiar with IBM's foibles than most of his colleagues at Microsoft because he had recently worked at the company during a summer while in college.

75 Earliest multimedia personal computers: Tandy brought out the first MPC (Multimedia Personal Computer) for the 1991 Christmas season; though Microsoft had turned to Tandy to lead the way toward a more affordable machine than the one IBM had been working on, even Tandy's underpowered machine with a 286 at its heart still ended up reaching the retail shelves at $3000, the same price that had appalled Microsoft when working with IBM. Pushing the price down would continue to prove difficult.

75 Apple dithered: Apple found it difficult to see the business possibilities in developing CD-ROM titles for the consumer market for a structural reason: its software title developers had been placed in a purposely separate group that was being readied for spin-off. Executive leadership at Apple was preoccupied with declining margins for its hardware business and other far afield issues. Microsoft was in a much better position to perceive and act on the opportunities in CD-ROM titles—chalk up still another benefit from the original decision to focus on software only.

75 Manzi's "big win": "Spreadsheet Rivalry Heats Up," *New York Times*, 17 January 1989.

76 "Rude" questions: " 'Rude' Questions—With Draft Answers," [Microsoft] Systems Multimedia Group, draft, 16 August 1990.

76 Gates on passive entertainment: Gates, Executive Suite Talk.

77 Nintendo: [Microsoft] Level 1 SWAT Team, "Multimedia Level 1: Project Plan," Microsoft memo, 3 February 1990.

Chapter Five
Britannica, Adieu

78 Whitelock quotation: Otto V. St. Whitelock, "On the Making and Survival of Encyclopedias," *Choice*, June 1967, 389. At the time, Whitelock was a senior editor in Xerox's Education Division.

78 Gates's "most popular encyclopedia": Gates noted that Microsoft's Encarta sold for much less per set than did World Book's CD-ROM encyclopedia, so World Book's revenues exceeded those of Encarta's.

79 Public service: The Encyclopaedia Britannica was operated as a business, but between 1980 and 1996, it was wholly owned by the Benton

Foundation, a nonprofit foundation established in 1980 whose sole beneficiary was the University of Chicago. In January 1996, the foundation sold the business to an investment group led by Swiss banker Jacob E. Safra. (Jacob Safra was the nephew of Edmund J. Safra, one of the world's richest men, and though the announcement of the sale included a disclaimer of a tie between nephew and uncle, it was a curious happenstance that the three most prestigious or best-selling encyclopedias—*Britannica, World Book*, and Encarta—would end up in the vicinity of, or the hands of, those who comprised a roster of the planet's wealthiest. See "Deal Is Set for Encyclopaedia Britannica," *New York Times*, 19 December 1995.) For a description of the Benton Foundation's relationship to the University of Chicago, see "Encyclopaedia Britannica's Stock to Go to the University of Chicago," *New York Times*, 2 October 1980.

80 Dire financial straits: "Britannica Looks for Cash Entry," *Chicago Tribune*, 5 April 1995. The *Tribune* story reported that "although financial data are not disclosed, the last time Britannica showed a profit was in 1990, when it earned $40 million after taxes on sales of $650 million." The next day, the *Tribune* printed a correction, in response to a statement issued by Britannica, that said that the company had "generated a profit before tax in every year since 1973, with the exception of 1993." Though the privately held company refused to supply specific numbers, it did not take issue with the *Tribune*'s report of drastically reduced sales.

82 Mature programs: In 1992, Microsoft's Word alone produced revenues of $750 million. Fred Moody, *I Sing the Body Electronic* (New York: Viking, 1995), 90.

82 Microsoft would keep an open mind: Susan Lammers to Nils von Veh et al., "World Book Meeting, June 4, 1989," Microsoft memo, 8 June 1989.

82 Answers ready: Min Yee and Susan Lammers to Peter Mollman, letter with attached proposal, "Multimedia Encyclopedia Proposal," Microsoft memo, 16 June 1989.

83 Proposal explained: "Multimedia Encyclopedia Proposal."

84 Internal strategy memo: Nils von Veh to Tom Corddry, "Merlin Business Case Backgrounder," Microsoft memo, 14 September 1989.

84 Yee's "Sexualus": Min Yee, "The Vanilla Top 20," Microsoft memo, 15 September 1985.

85 Quickie encyclopedia: Craig Bartholomew to Tom Ikeda, "The Case for Pursuing Bookshelf Encyclopedia for March '92 Ship," Microsoft memo, 19 February 1991. See also a refinement, Craig Bartholomew to Greg Riker, "Bookshelf Encyclopedia Proposal," Microsoft memo, 15 March 1991.

86 Bartholomew as program manager: For a portrait of Bartholomew and a nicely written account of the development of Microsoft's children's encyclopedia on CD-ROM, see Moody's *I Sing the Body Electronic*, passim.

86 "Inter-galactic space travel": Craig Bartholomew, "Encarta '93 Post-Mortem Analysis," Microsoft memo, 18 June 1993.

86 Glaser on paucity of titles: Glaser was the person responsible for developing the system software needed to provide multimedia capabilities in Intel-based PCs. Even with Windows 3.0, the operating system was blind to multimedia additions such as CD-ROM drives. Additional software "extensions" were needed to convert a PC into a multimedia-capable machine, and these extensions were installed by the computer's manufacturer, not by ordinary customers—hence the need to convince manufacturers about the delights of multimedia. Only with the release of Windows 3.1, in April 1992, were the extensions built into the operating system itself.

88 Buffett earned his investment back: Peter Mollman, "Some Thoughts on a Potential World Book Purchase or License," Microsoft memo, 2 September 1993.

90 "If you devoted": The "12 seconds" assumes a 1024 x 768 screen resolution and 16 bits per pixel of color (32,000 colors). Each frame would require about 1.57 megabytes of data, or about 47 megabytes per second. A lower resolution or fewer colors would enable the video clips to run longer. The hypothetical example in the text was provided only to illustrate how much space, comparatively speaking, video clips occupied. Full-screen video without compression was not a realistic option because the data transfer rate of standard-speed CD-ROMs was far, far too slow at only 150 kilobytes per second (when 47 megabytes—about 310 times as much data—would be required per second). Even six-speed drives, which move data at 900 kilobytes-per-second, would be far too slow. In any case, compression was required.

90 Mossberg pounced: Walter S. Mossberg, "Parental Guilt Sells Encyclopedias on CD-ROM, Too," *Wall Street Journal*, 29 April 1993.

92 Postman on Lincoln-Douglas debates: Neil Postman, *Amusing Ourselves to Death: Public Discourse in the Age of Show Business* (New York: Viking, 1985), 44.

92 Postman on the "Age of Exposition": *Amusing Ourselves to Death*, 63.

93 McHenry on the "dirty little secret": Robert Rossney, "Encyclopaedia Britannica Online?" *Wired*, August 1995, 80.

93 Belated transition: Britannica's initial foray into electronic encyclopedias was a text-only CD-ROM of its namesake encyclopedia, whose contents occupied a gigabyte of space and required two disks; this product, called the Britannica Instant Research System, was marketed to businesses, not to consumers.

Chapter Six
Pitching Consumers

94 Microsoft slogan: Bill Gates insists that this was the company's official slogan from the time of its founding in 1975, but there is no evidence of it in the company archives that I have found from the first ten years of the company's history, nor has the company archivist found documentary confirmation of it in those early years. The earliest appearance that we have run across is in 1986. Manes and Andrews, the authorative biographers of Microsoft's early history, also note that despite Gates's claims to the contrary, the slogan was not heard around the company until the mid-1980s. A company videotape shows that Gates did use the phrase in a talk given to Apple programmers that was probably, though not definitely, in 1984. See Stephen Manes and Paul Andrews, *Gates: How Microsoft's Mogul Reinvented an Industry— And Made Himself the Richest Man in America* (New York: Doubleday, 1993), 63, 251–252.

96 "Uncle Hayseed" and country bumpkin: Carolyn Marvin, *When Old Technologies Were New: Thinking About Electric Communication in the Late Nineteenth Century* (New York: Oxford University Press, 1988), 18–21. The 1889 example of the bumpkin who shouted into the phone without lifting the receiver would be the very picture of rationality in the future Gates envisioned in 1984 for the home in 1989, coincidentally a hundred years after the earlier example. For the home in 1989, Gates had predicted a bit prematurely that the voice recognition capability of computers wired throughout the house would enable one to say, wherever one was, "Hey, get me in touch with so and so," rather than picking up a telephone. See Gates's essay, "Microsoft," *Creative Computing*, March 1984, 70.

100 "Learning experience": Craig Bartholomew, "Encarta '93 Post-Mortem Analysis," Microsoft memo, 18 June 1993.

101 Gates "very irate": Bartholomew, "Encarta '93 Post-Mortem Analysis."

101 Arch-competitor Compton: Sonja Gustafson, "Encarta Marketing Backgrounder," Microsoft memo to Patty Stonesifer, 17 August 1993.

101 Riddled with bugs: Bartholomew, "Encarta '93 Post-Mortem Analysis."

101 Supermarket shopping cart: Gustafson, "Encarta Marketing Backgrounder."

102 Three percent market share: Gustafson, "Encarta Marketing Backgrounder."

102 "Reverse bundle": "Encyclopedia Business Plan," Microsoft memo, 5 April 1992.

105 Back-orders for another 60,000 units: Craig Bartholomew, "Home Ed Ref Product Unit Monthly Report," Microsoft memo, December 1993.

105 "Titles factory": Patty Stonesifer, "How Will Multimedia Change the Software Industry," Software Publishers Association, Spring 1994 Symposium, 15 March 1994.

106 Gates on consistency in design: Fred Moody, *I Sing the Body Electronic*, (New York: Viking, 1995), 88.

106 Stonesifer as Boeschen's successor: It is curious that Boeschen, a rare woman in the senior ranks of Microsoft, would be succeeded by another woman. Boeschen bristled when I asked about why the Consumer Division would be headed by two women in a row. She said she had been consulted when Gates was mulling over her successor and two of the three final candidates were men. She also pointed out that though Stonesifer, too, had children (in fact, put them on stage for the 1993 introduction in New York of the Microsoft Home brand), a sensitivity to family-oriented software was no more the province of a mother than it would be of a father.

Earlier, in 1991, an outside industry analyst, Jesse Berst, had credited Boeschen for helping Microsoft overcome what Berst saw as its two primary weaknesses: arrogance and "technocentrism." Berst praised Boeschen for founding the Usability Lab and heading up what was then still called the Entry Business Unit. Berst wrote, "At the risk of sounding like the One Minute Psychologist, I'd like to point out that arrogance and technocentrism are both male attitudes." See Berst, "Can a Gorilla Change Its Spots?" *Windows Watcher*, December 1991, 3.

107   Industrial era of P&G: Microsoft did not seek to distance itself from all things Procter & Gamble. In late 1994, for example, Microsoft recruited P&G's Bob Herbold as Microsoft's new executive vice-president and chief operating officer.

107   Dividends from its brand strategy: A leading software industry newsletter was extremely skeptical of Microsoft's decision in 1993, pointing with alarm at the departure from Procter & Gamble's established wisdom. At the same time, the newsletter presciently gave credit in advance for Microsoft's ability to learn from missteps: "Even if Microsoft stumbles a few times, the company is bound to end up learning more about the market than its more cautious competitors." See "Microsoft Unveils a New Consumer Strategy," *Soft•Letter*, 22 October 1993.

107   Other marketing programs: "Microsoft Home: Bringing Consumers the Power, Excitement and Fun of Home Computing," *Microsoft Backgrounder*, March 1995.

108   Took to heart lessons: My assertion may seem at odds with the portrait of wasted time and internecine strife found in the development of the CD-ROM children's encyclopedia Explorapedia, as closely observed in Fred Moody's *I Sing the Body Electronic*. Moody's account focused on the early portion of the project, when many false starts slowed its advance. A journalist, Moody had arranged a leave of absence from his newspaper to work on his book. Unfortunately his leave expired before the project came to a happy conclusion. Thus due weight was not given to the final stage of development when the pieces fell into place. Moreover, once a title is completed, the day-to-day vicissitudes of the developers' moods during the anguish of development fade in significance.

109   Four of the top ten places: Microsoft Corporation, *Annual Report to Stockholders,* 1993.

109   Lust for profits and power: Fred Moody observed Gates in a February 1993 meeting expressing his amazement that print publishers were not more aggressive in launching the development of their own CD-ROM titles. When a staff member told him that the other companies were privately held and uneasy about investing in development, Gates concluded aloud, "So they have finite greed." (Moody, *I Sing the Body Electronic*, 111.) For another example, see the early 1995 *Fortune* story, which noted that "the operative question these days has changed from 'What does Bill Gates want?' to 'Is there anything Bill Gates doesn't want?'" and asked Gates to be specific about his ambitions. See

"What Bill Gates Really Wants" and the accompanying sidebar, "What He Doesn't Want," in *Fortune*, 16 January 1995.

109 Did not pursue: In late 1995, the Consumer Division introduced Fury[3], a jet-fighter shoot-'em game that displays stunning visual effects but lacks an educational angle that its predecessors had. Not schlock, but not a candidate for a Parent's Choice award either. It will be interesting to see if this title proves to be a precursor to other kinds of titles that Microsoft's Consumer Division had deliberately shunned in the past.

Chapter Seven
David and Goliath

110 Franklin quotation: Benjamin Franklin, *The Works of Benjamin Franklin* (New York: G.P. Putnam's Sons, 1904), II:30.

110 Cook as "former fat salesman": "Intuit: An Installed Base Model for the 90s," *Soft•Letter*, 19 February 1993, 1.

110 Intuit's location: "Near Stanford University" means that Intuit's leased offices were first located in downtown Palo Alto, then in Menlo Park, and most recently in Mountain View.

110 Cook on "solutions": "Scott Cook: An Interview," *Upside*, April 1994, 34.

111 Cook on P&G's remaining "great for 100 years": "Microsoft Dominates the Vast Market for Computer Software," *Los Angeles Times*, 8 August 1993.

114 Financial temptation: Aside from seeking to retain the upgrade business for itself or giving it to its retailers, Intuit also could choose a third course that many software companies have used, contracting with an outside firm to handle order fulfillment. Intuit has experimented with this option, but it remains uncomfortable with the loss of control over the quality of service.

114 "Gripe Line": "When the Upgrade Offer Comes in the Mail, Your Best Bet May Be To Chuck It," *Infoworld*, 4 December 1995, 64.

119 Standard practice: The legality of copying the functionality of rival software programs has withstood challenges, the most notable and intellectually purest being Lotus's suit against Borland, filed in 1990, challenging the legality of Borland's imitation of Lotus's 1-2-3 menus in its own Quattro Pro. A federal judge in Boston initially ruled against Borland, but a federal appeals court overturned the decision and upheld Borland's position that menus and commands constituted a "method of operation" that was excluded from copyright protection.

In January 1996, the U.S. Supreme Court deadlocked 4–4 on the issue, thus affirming the appeals court's ruling in favor of Borland. Woe to every consumer if this legal protection were to be stripped away.

Related legal issues were raised when Apple unsuccessfully sued Microsoft and Hewlett-Packard for copying the "look and feel" of the Macintosh operating system, and Apple itself was sued, also unsuccessfully, by Xerox for copying the "look and feel" of the Mac's precursor, the Xerox Star. For a discussion of these cases that does not treat the plaintiffs in these shenanigans sympathetically, see Randall E. Stross, *Steve Jobs and the NeXT Big Thing* (New York: Atheneum, 1993), 42–44.

122 Cook's "mountain is being made": "Microsoft Dominates the Vast Market for Computer Software."

122 Cook's "the worst ad": "Scott Cook: An Interview."

123 Jesse Berst's worry: "Can Intuit Do It Again?" *Windows Watcher*, 8 August 1993, 11.

124 Cook on "fair pricing":"Scott Cook: An Interview."

Chapter Eight
Preparations

128 Hofstadter quotation: Richard Hofstadter, *Anti-Intellectualism in American Life* (New York: Alfred A. Knopf, 1966), 51.

128 Far greater portion: "Can Microsoft Blend Blue Jeans and Gray Flannel?" *PC Week*, 21 October 1986.

128 Greater efficiency in R&D: Michael K. Kwatinetz, "The PC Software Industry," *Market Forecast/Strategic Analysis*, published by Bernstein Research, 2 January 1991, 117.

129 History of personal computers: Nathan Myhrvold, "Microsoft Research Plan," Microsoft memo, 6 May 1991.

129 Gates's "Information at Your Fingertips": Microsoft reproduced the speech in a brochure that provided colorful graphics and screenshots of software. Worried apparently that some prospective customers would misunderstand, the company inserted a disclaimer at the back of the brochure, explaining that "the computer displays shown here illustrate potential software technology and do not necessarily represent existing products/or products in development."

129 Gates's "many of the changes": "Airing the 'Computer Papers,'" *Washington Post*, 23 June 1991.

131 "A product group": Myhrvold, "Microsoft Research Plan."

132 Gates's "had gotten away": "Gates Blasts IBM, OS/2 2.0," *PC Week*, 24 June 1991.

132 Alsop's "borrowing ideas": Stewart Alsop, "Microsoft's Research Arm Should Be Studied, Copied," *Infoworld*, 26 August 1991.

132 Employing Hitler's rocket scientists: Fred Davis, "New Microsoft Research Group Blasts Off to High Science," *PC Week*, 27 May 1991, 154.

133 Myhrvold envisioned: Myhrvold, "Microsoft Research Plan."

134 Myhrvold distinguished: "For $100 You Get Software That Cost $100 Million To Make," *Wired*, September 1995.

137 "Road Kill": When the memo was in draft form, Myhrvold had used a short working title of "Chicxlub," which was the name of the crater off the coast of Yucatan where the asteroid said to have killed the dinosaurs struck the earth. "Chicxlub" is modern Mayan that roughly translates as "the devil's asshole." Though not quite as salty, "Road Kill on the Information Highway," the title that Myhrvold devised before the memo went out, proved more readily recognizable to English-speaking readers, and the "Road Kill" phrase swiftly passed into the wider culture, even landing in cartoons. See Myhrvold's gloss in his "1993 Year End Memo" to Gates, 26 December 1993.

137 Myhrvold's "How radical can a revolution be": Nathan Myhrvold, "Road Kill on the Information Highway," Microsoft memo, 8 September 1993.

137 "Millionfold improvement": David Patterson, the University of California at Berkeley computer scientist who is one of the senior dons of microprocessor design, said in 1995 that if we looked at improvements in the microprocessor alone, it had improved 25,000 times since its invention 25 years earlier, which was more modest than the "millionfold" improvement claimed for semiconductors as a whole. But when Patterson compared microprocessors of 1995 with their "Neanderthal ancestors of the 1950s," he said that they were now 100,000 times faster, and when inflation is considered, they cost 1000 times less. In other words, the price/performance of microprocessors had improved a *hundred* million times since the 1950s. See David A. Patterson, "Microprocessors in 2020," *Scientific American*, September 1995, 62, 67.

139 Myhrvold on "non-capital-intensive": Nathan Myhrvold, "External Investments," Microsoft memo, 5 March 1994.

140 Gore claimed: "Colliding Clichés and Other Mishaps on Term Pike," *Wall Street Journal*, 1 February 1994.

140 Insisted on getting together: Myhrvold, "1993 Year End Memo."

140 Myhrvold on J. P. Morgan: Myhrvold, "External Investments."

142 Myhrvold's Hummer: A shortened version of Myhrvold's trip report appeared as "His Summer in a Hummer," *Fortune*, 2 October 1995.

Chapter Nine
PCs Versus TVs

143 Rotherie quotation: E. M. Rotherie, "Seeing Through the Telephone," *Telephony*, 12 August 1906, 96, quoted in Ithiel de Sola Pool, *Forecasting the Telephone: A Retrospective Technology Assessment* (Norwood, NJ: Ablex Publishing, 1983), 115–116.

143 Gates's "if a kid is addicted": Susan Lammers, *Programmers at Work* (Redmond, WA: Microsoft Press, 1986), 89.

144 Gates's "how can we make": "The Met Grill," *Metropolitan Home*, July 1985, 92.

144 Gates's more time "to read": "Playboy Interview: Bill Gates," *Playboy*, July 1994.

144 Time to read *The Economist*: "Mr. Software," *New York Times Magazine*, 25 August 1991.

145 Gates's "TV/PC": "Bill's Excellent Future," *Newsweek*, 11 October 1993.

145 Myhrvold's "Video PC": Nathan Myhrvold, "Visions for Consumer Computers," Microsoft memo, n.d. [September 1991].

146 Mundie's background: Mundie worked for Data General, the company that Tracy Kidder's classic, *A Soul of a New Machine* (Boston: Little, Brown, 1981), would immortalize. Chance placed Mundie on the design team that remained in the shadows of Kidder's narrative, as his group was the one sent to South Carolina, the internal competitors of the design group in Massachusetts that Kidder profiled.

146 Liked to get his hands dirty: Nathan Myhrvold, e-mail to Bill Gates et al., "Craig Mundie," 16 October 1992.

147 Gates's "I would hire": Bill Gates, "Dealing With Corporate Mistakes," *International Herald Tribune*, 27 April 1995.

148 "Microsoft's brave new world": "Microsoft Demonstrates Windows for TV," *Broadcasting & Cable*, 29 March 1993.

149 Gates's "I guarantee": "Bill Gates: An American Gladiator in the Digital Arena," *The Red Herring*, October 1993, 43.

150 Myhrvold's "interesting recruiting policy": Nathan Myhrvold, "Big Picture Conference," Microsoft memo, 28 March 1993.

150 Markey asked: "Watchdogs Wary of 'Cablesoft,' " *PC Week*, 19 July 1993.

151 Myhrvold's "500-card stud": Nathan Myhrvold, "500 Card Stud," Microsoft memo, 29 November 1993.

151 Microsoft at the back of the pack: "Oracle Tries To Outmaneuver Microsoft on Superhighway," *San Jose Mercury News*, 15 February 1994.

151 Myhrvold's "suggesting that it's all over": "Microsoft's Myhrvold Gives a Brief History of the Future," *Seattle Post-Intelligencer*, 2 March 1994.

152 At IBM's expense: "The Next Big Info Tech Battle," *Fortune*, 29 November 1993.

152 Ellison's family and educational background: "Can Larry Beat Bill?" *Business Week*, 15 May 1995.

153 Ellison needed no prompting: "Larry Ellison," *Forbes ASAP*, 7 June 1993.

153 Friends said of him: "Can Larry Beat Bill?"

153 Ellison's "will is more important": "Nerds, Not," *Forbes*, 19 October 1992.

154 Ellison's "it works": "Oracle Predicts Interactive Gear by Early 1994," *Wall Street Journal*, 10 November 1993.

154 Calling Microsoft a no-show: "Oracle Hopes to Steal a March on Microsoft," *New York Times*, 15 February 1994.

154 Ellison on Microsoft representing the present: "Oracle's Prognostication: Tomorrow Looks Terrific," *Business Week*, 20 September 1993.

154 Myhrvold reported to Gates: Myhrvold, "500 Card Stud."

155 Readerman's "as much as": " 'Tiger' May Put Teeth in Microsoft's Video Ventures," *Wall Street Journal*, 23 May 1994.

155 Gates himself was skeptical: Bill Gates, talk given at Edison Electric, 16 June 1994.

156 Sizable dividends: Code developed by Microsoft Research was incorporated in DOS, Windows 95, Office 95, and other Microsoft products. At the end of 1995, the *New York Times* took notice that Gates had "quietly assembled some of the industry's best and brightest computer researchers," including a powerhouse assemblage of pioneers in computer graphics research: Andrew Glassner (recruited from Xerox

PARC), Alvy Ray Smith (founder of Pixar, of *Toy Story* fame), Jim Blinn (from the NASA Jet Propulsion Laboratory), and Jim Kajiya (from Cal Tech). But the practical payoff for Microsoft's investment in research led the director of competitor Digital Equipment's research laboratory to sniff dismissively that Microsoft Research was engaged merely in "product development," not true research—as if to suggest that absence of practical application was the most desirable outcome. See "Microsoft Quietly Puts Together Computer Research Laboratory," *New York Times*, 11 December 1995.

157 Columnist pointed out: Stewart Alsop, "Microsoft's Tiger Beats the Stripes off Oracle's Server," *Infoworld*, 23 May 1994.

157 Oracle senior vice-president's [Jerry Held] "consumers like television": "Oracle Tries to Outmaneuver Microsoft on Superhighway," *San Jose Mercury News*, 15 February 1994. For an example of Ellison proclaiming an agnostic position on the question of PCs versus TVs, see Anthony B. Perkins, "We're Oracle, and You're Not," *The Red Herring*, Mune [May-June], 1994, 56.

157 Gates criticized: Bill Gates, remarks at Microsoft's Financial Analysts meeting, Redmond, Washington, 21 July 1994.

158 Ellison's "graceful scale-ability": "Oracle's Ellison Puts His Money on Massively Parallel Processing," *Washington Post*, 6 August 1993.

158 Time Warner and Bell Atlantic trials: "Dwindling Expectations," *New York Times*, 18 December 1995.

Chapter Ten
Toll Road

159 Greenberger quotation: Martin Greenberger, "The Computers of Tomorrow," *The Atlantic Monthly*, May 1964.

160 Ellison's "the idea of putting software bits": "Oracle Hopes To Steal a March on Microsoft," *New York Times*, 15 February 1994.

162 Several projects underway: Russell Siegelman, "On-Line Services Project Status," Microsoft memo to Bill Gates, 25 January 1993.

162 Siegelman on "product-oriented approach": Russell Siegelman, "On-Line Services: Initial Findings and Thoughts," Microsoft memo to Bill Gates, 28 January 1993.

162 Siegelman's "what business to enter": Russell Siegelman, "On Line Services Work Plan (Draft)," Microsoft memo to Bill Gates, 15 December 1992.

163 Siegelman's "multi-million-dollar opportunities": Russell Siegelman, "On-Line Services Project Status."

164 Gates's "enough confidence": Bill Gates, "On Line Services," Microsoft memo, n.d. [1993].

165 "AOL was the remaining possibility": Paul Allen, who, in addition to retaining major holdings in Microsoft, had also purchased a sizable portion of AOL on his own. He was not acting as an advance party for Microsoft. Quite the contrary, his actions made the contemplation of a Microsoft acquisition much more difficult. In May 1993, Siegelman pointed out to Gates that Allen "didn't understand our interest and has made our life much more difficult." See Russ Siegelman, "America Online Update and Thoughts," Microsoft memo to Bill Gates, 6 May 1993.

165 Some outside industry analysts: The analyst who sneered "Microsoft is going to have to stumble" was Mary Modahl of Forrester Research. Quoted in "A Physicist Is Propelling Microsoft into Cyberspace," *New York Times*, 26 February 1995.

167 Projected a modest beginning: Transparencies from "Marvel Review," Microsoft internal documents, February 1994.

167 America Online's subscription rolls: Responding to the criticism that AOL's claim of 3.5 million subscribers reflected an unknown percentage of people who were trying the service on a free trial basis, Lennert Leader, the chief financial officer of America Online, claimed in 1995 that AOL's users stay an average of 41 months. But the *Wall Street Journal* pointed out that only 5 percent of AOL's customers have actually done so, and Leader's claim was based on an "analytical model" whose details he refused to disclose. See "On-Line Services' User Counts Often Aren't What They Seem," *Wall Street Journal*, 6 October 1995.

168 Oldsters in their thirties: Among Gates's advisors, Rob Glaser made the biggest early bet on the Internet, but he did so outside Microsoft. In late 1993, after ten years, he left Microsoft as a full-time employee and temporarily continued on a part-time, contractual basis while he founded Progressive Networks, a start-up that he initially conceived as dedicated to "world improvement." In April 1995, the company released its first commercial product: RealAudio, personal computer software for playing audio received via the Internet in real time—that is, without a delay.

169 Tarter's "totally impassable": "A Physicist Is Propelling Microsoft into Cyberspace." Concern about the Internet's carrying capacity did not dissipate. Bob Metcalfe, the inventor of Ethernet and columnist for

Infoworld, sounded repeated alarms about the approaching "collapse" of the Internet. See, for example, Metcalfe's "Predicting the Internet's Catastrophic Collapse and Ghost Sites Galore in 1996," *Infoworld*, 4 December 1995, and "Coming Internet Collapse Spurring Shortsighted Proliferation of Intranets," *Infoworld*, 20 May 1996.

170 Siegelman's "public access channel": Russell Siegelman, "Update on MOS," Microsoft memo, 16 June 1994.

171 Caught by surprise: On Netscape and Java, see Lee Gomes's reminder about their early histories: "Solving the Riddle of the Internet," *San Jose Mercury News*, 18 December 1995.

171 Myhrvold on Minitel: Nathan Myhrvold, "A Look at Minitel," Microsoft memo, 28 December 1992.

172 Myhrvold's "transaction" model: Nathan Myhrvold, "Narrowband Platform Strategy," 20 August 1993.

172 Shopping mall landlord: "Interviews With Microsoft Executives," *Upside*, April 1995, 76.

173 Netscape oscillated: "Solving the Riddle of the Internet."

173 Gosling's "health of the Internet": "Staking Claim in Alternative Software on the Internet," *New York Times*, 25 September 1995.

174 Caruso's "after working so hard": Denise Caruso, "Digital Commerce," *New York Times*, 9 October 1995.

Chapter Eleven
The Last War Redux

176 Learned Hand quotation: Michael Rothschild, "Why Microsoft (Mostly) Shouldn't Be Stopped," *Upside*, April 1995.

176 Sherman Antitrust Act: Donald Dewey, *The Antitrust Experiment in America* (New York: Columbia University Press, 1990), 4.

177 Congress was pushed by public outrage: Comment by Lawrence Friedman in "Antitrust Laws Set Different Rules for Firms at Top," *San Jose Mercury News*, 27 February 1995.

177 Gates's "love to pursue opportunities": "Bill Gates," *Forbes*, 7 December 1992.

177 Gates's "these little boxes": Transcript of interview on ABC News's *20/20*, 22 November 1991.

178 Ballmer on "MARKET SHARE": "Microsoft Unplugged," Microsoft Annual Company Meeting, 1994.

178 Maples's "my job": Stuart Taylor, Jr., "What To Do With the Microsoft Monster," *American Lawyer*, November 1993.

180 McNealy on "Trabants": "What Bill Gates Really Wants," *Fortune*, 16 January 1996.

180 Kahn on "Nazi Germany": "Bill Gates's Baby Is on Top of the World: Can It Stay There?" *Business Week*, 24 February 1992.

180 Outlandishness of the comparison: "Playboy Interview: Bill Gates," *Playboy*, July 1994.

180 Myhrvold's "say what you want": "An Encore for Stage Fright," *San Jose Mercury News*, 10 March 1995.

180 Myhrvold confessed: "An Encore for Stage Fright."

181 Gates's "quickly educate the FTC": "Microsoft Founder Gates, In Memo, Warns of Attack and Defeat by Rivals," *Wall Street Journal*, 19 June 1991.

182 Terms discussed for Microsoft's purchase: "Going After Microsoft," *National Review*, 24 January 1994.

182 Purchase of WordPerfect: Revisiting Novell's March 1994 $1.4 billion acquisition of WordPerfect almost two years later, a *Wall Street Journal* story exposed the full extent of the sad disaster. See "Software Firm Fights To Remake Business After Ill-Fated Merger," *Wall Street Journal*, 12 January 1996.

182 Well into its twilight: When the government's investigation of Microsoft was being transferred from the FTC to the Department of Justice, Gates could call attention to the tardiness of the government's concern with DOS then, a decade after the competitive battles over it had been won. Gates asked, "Doing anything with MS-DOS is very strange . . . I mean, in 1993?" See "The New Rockefeller," *U.S. News and World Report*, 15 February 1993.

183 David's "prisoners of events long forgotten": Paul A. David, "Understanding the Economics of QWERTY: The Necessity of History," in William N. Parker, ed., *Economic History and the Modern Economist* (New York: Basil Blackwell, 1986), 34.

183 Government should handicap the leader: Paul A. David, "Some New Standards for the Economics of Standardization in the Information Age," in Partha Dasgupta and Paul Stoneman, eds., *Economic Policy and Technological Performance* (Cambridge: Cambridge University Press, 1987), 230–231.

183 Arthur on Chernobyl-like disasters: W. Brian Arthur, "Competing Technologies: An Overview," Working paper, Center for Economic Policy Research, Stanford University, July 1987, *CEPR Publication* No. 98, 12.

184 Neukom pointed: "Why Microsoft (Mostly) Shouldn't Be Stopped."

184 Gates's "if everybody at Lotus": "How Bill Gates Keeps the Magic Going," *Fortune*, 18 June 1990.

185 Gates on a "natural monopoly": William H. Gates, "Next-Generation Software," typescript of speech given at the 1981 Rosen Research Personal Computer Forum.

185 Gates's "direction of the leader": Bill Gates, Executive Suite Talk, Seattle University, 25 October 1986.

185 Arthur's "increasing returns to adoption": Arthur, "Competing Technologies."

187 Myhrvold's draft of an article: "Telling It Like It Is," Microsoft memo, n.d. [1993].

189 Market still seems to function well: The explanation for why prices have not climbed in the wake of Microsoft's domination of many sectors of the software industry must return to the nature of the industry. Unlike rail, petroleum, steel, or automobile empires of the past, the software industry is still characterized by relatively low barriers to entry for new entrants, making complacency unwise, even for those who dominate a market category. Even in the realm of operating systems, where necessary investments are quite high and where IBM's expensive bet on OS/2 had failed to make it a viable contender, countervailing examples of competition for DOS/Windows continued to pop up from the most modest and unlikely circumstances. Who would have guessed that the kernel of Linux, a clone of UNIX written for Intel-based personal computers that was placed in the public domain, could have been coded largely by a single person, Linus Torvalds—located in Helsinki, Finland, not in Redmond or Silicon Valley—and the supporting code that made Linux a complete operating system package was contributed by hundreds of volunteers scattered around the globe, connected via the Internet? Linux offered proof that even extremely ambitious projects in the software industry can be tackled without large supplies of capital. For Linux's origins, see "Checking Out Linux," *Unixworld*, March 1993.

190 Complaints of privileged information for Microsoft application developers: See, for example, Andrew Schulman, David Maxey, and Matt

Pietrek, *Undocumented Windows: A Programmer's Guide to Reserved Microsoft Windows API Functions*. (Reading, MA: Addison-Wesley, 1992), 40–46.

190 Ballmer on "church and state": "A Fierce Battle Brews Over the Simplest Software Yet," *Business Week*, 21 November 1983.

190 Microsoft demonstrated: "Microsoft Is Like an Elephant Rolling Around, Squashing Ants," *Business Week*, 30 October 1989.

190 Ballmer retreated: "Microsoft Is Like an Elephant."

190 Maples on "Chinese Wall": "Maples: No 'Chinese Wall' at Microsoft," *Infoworld*, 30 December 1991. Keep in mind that Microsoft hired Maples from IBM five years after Ballmer had made his remarks to the press about "church and state."

190 Gates never used the term "Chinese Wall": "Bill Gates," *Forbes*, 7 December 1992. When asked whether Microsoft should have a Chinese Wall separating systems and applications developers, Gates responded in an interesting way: "we would never, ever use the term" and "it is just one of those things that gets into the press and sort of perpetuates itself." By attributing the phrase's origin to some vague time when it "gets into the press," Gates seemed to suggest that the phrase was a journalist's invention, not Steve Ballmer's.

191 Stories of Lotus et al.: As recently as 1992, a respected software industry newsletter was still complacently predicting that the shift from DOS to Windows would not result in a change in the line-up of market leaders in the major application categories: "We suspect that when the dust settles, Lotus will dominate Windows spreadsheets, WordPerfect still will be top dog in word processing, and Borland will prevail in databases. In fact, it's hard to find a major category where Windows seems likely to create a radical realignment of the marketplace." See "The New Platform Myth," *Soft•Letter*, 23 March 1992, 4–5.

191 Gates's invitation to "name a Microsoft product": "Industry Hero or Villain? Microsoft's Gates Insists He's Neither One," *Infoworld*, 3 August 1992. The single exception to Gates's claim that all of its products have been critically acclaimed is, of course, Windows itself, but its commercial success derives from the increasing returns on its adoption. It need only be "good enough" to deliver increasing benefits to adoptees, which is a different basis for success than competition in the specific categories of software applications.

191 Eubanks on "person who can't dance": Gordon Eubanks, Jr., "Why Microsoft Is Not the Enemy," *Release 1.0*, January 1990. Transcript from 1990 PC Forum.

192 Unflattering book: James Wallace and Jim Erickson, *Hard Drive: Bill Gates and the Making of the Microsoft Empire* (New York: John Wiley & Sons, 1992).

192 Sporkin's "who knows": "Judge and Attorneys Duel Over Microsoft," *Wall Street Journal*, 23 January 1995.

192 Panel disqualified Sporkin: "Appeals Court Reinstates Microsoft Antitrust Settlement," *New York Times*, 17 June 1995.

192 New judge: "Judge Clears Antitrust Pact for Microsoft," *New York Times*, 22 August 1995.

Chapter Twelve
The Home Front

193 Hofstadter quotation: "What Happened to the Antitrust Movement?" (originally written in 1964) in Richard Hofstadter, *The Paranoid Style in American Politics and Other Essays* (New York: Vintage Books, 1967), 189.

193 Gates on "thank you": "Gates On:" *Computer Reseller News*, 27 May 1991.

193 Gates on "worst case": "Bill Gates's Baby Is on Top of the World: Can It Stay There?" *Business Week*, 24 February 1992.

194 Gates on "flying saucers": "Industry Hero or Villain? Microsoft's Gates Insists He's Neither One," *Infoworld*, 3 August 1992.

194 Evidence of the still healthy state of competition: Transcript of Toronto-based radio interview, "Bill Gates, on Fax: Internet and Interactive," 14 July 1994.

195 Gates's "wouldn't expect to find": "Bill Gates: The 1982 Interview," reprinted in *PC User*, 23 September 1992.

198 Gates's "get me into that": "Culture Club," *Newsweek*, 11 July 1994.

198 Head count: Microsoft's head count of 60 in the Money group was not exactly comparable to Intuit's because it excluded a hard-to-tally portion of Microsoft's general technical support team (PSS) that fielded calls for Money customers.

198 Cash reserves: "Brown Has Fun While Meeting Microsoft's New Financial Challenges," *MicroNews*, 22 April 1994, 3.

199 Gates had sought a merger with Lotus: "Gates Confirms Microsoft Once Sought Lotus Merger," *Wall Street Journal*, 13 October 1995.

200 Guidelines for reviewing horizontal mergers: "U.S. Department of Justice and Federal Trade Commission Horizontal Merger Guidelines," 2 April 1992.

202 These developers: While the merger was pending, Money's business development team found it all but impossible to keep its partners committed to Money. This complicated game of musical chairs involving the various players requires a scorecard. In the summer of 1994, while Microsoft and Intuit were negotiating, Microsoft had had the opportunity to buy National Payments Clearinghouse, Inc., the small bill-paying firm that it had turned to when Intuit had closed off Microsoft's access to Checkfree, its first choice as a partner. Instead of buying NPCI, Microsoft had decided it would not need its services once a new partnership it was arranging with Mastercard matured. But after Microsoft passed, Intuit bought NPCI in July. Microsoft seemed fortunate to soon reach an agreement to acquire Intuit. Otherwise, its principal competitor in this market segment would own the very company that Microsoft was, at least for the time being, technologically wholly dependent on for handling its customers' electronic bill payments. Once the merger was announced, Mastercard's commitment to Money evaporated. It did not want to face the combined Microsoft-Intuit colossus from the margins, trying to breathe life into Money as a hand-me-down at Novell.

203 Microsoft guaranteed: Anne K. Bingaman et al., United States Department of Justice, "Complaint for Injunctive Relief Against Combination in Violation of Section 7 of the Clayton Act," in a civil suit filed in U.S. District Court, Northern District of California, *United States of America* v. *Microsoft Corporation and Intuit, Inc.*, 27 April 1995.

203 Novell's CEO: "Microsoft, Justice Department Appeal Judge's Ruling on Antitrust Accord," *Wall Street Journal*, 8 March 1995. Note how Novell's behavior in this episode resembles a deliberate "head fake"— used by offensive players in football or basketball who deliberately move their head in one direction to deceive the defense when they actually are preparing to move in another—fully as much as when IBM applied the "head fake" label to Microsoft in the wake of Microsoft's withdrawal of its support for OS/2.

203 Gates talked:"What Bill Gates Really Wants," *Fortune*, 16 January 1995.

204 "I tried to tell him": Quoted in Bingaman et al., "Complaint for Injunctive Relief."

205 BankAmerica and NationsBank: "Banks Move Online With MECA Purchase," *Seattle Times*, 10 May 1995.

206 Its market value: "Intuit's Market Value on Rise," *Computer Reseller News*, 11 December 1995. Intuit's stock declined in the first five months of 1996, but even at a closing price of $50 a share on June 6, the company's market capitalization was still double what it had been in early October 1994, on the eve of the announcement of the proposed merger with Microsoft.

207 Mossberg expressed surprise: "Microsoft Starts To Catch Up to Intuit in Personal Finance," *Wall Street Journal*, 14 December 1995.

Chapter Thirteen
Preemptive Attack

209 DeLarmarter quotation: Richard Thomas DeLarmarter, *Big Blue: IBM's Use and Abuse of Power* (New York: Dodd, Mead & Company, 1986), xvii. DeLarmarter's book should not be confused with Paul Carroll's *Big Blues: The Unmaking of IBM* (New York: Crown, 1993), whose estimation of IBM could not be more different.

210 Government issued: Antitrust Division, U.S. Department of Justice, "The Department of Justice Issued the Following Statement Today Regarding Its Ongoing Investigation on Issues Surrounding Microsoft Windows," 8 August 1995.

211 Microsoft had hoped: "Advice Now in High-Tech: Be Selective," *New York Times*, 8 January 1996.

212 More damage to MSN: "MSN's Growing Pains," *P.C. Letter*, 10 August 1995, 4. The article was based on an evaluation of MSN during the beta period.

212 MSN as "Yugo": "On-Line Game Isn't So Easy for Microsoft," *San Jose Mercury News*, 1 October 1995.

212 500,000 subscribers: "Microsoft Passes Half Million Mark," *Seybold Report on Desktop Publishing*, 11 December 1995.

212 AOL gained: "America Online Claims 4.5M Users," *Financial Times*, 29 December 1995.

214   Proposed by Gordon Bell: Bell had been one of the principal architects of Digital Equipment Corporation's VAX minicomputer line. He had left Digital and from time to time worked as a consultant to Microsoft. Microsoft was interested in smarts of all ages, including those belonging to contrarian individuals like Bell who, as we shall see, did not necessarily subscribe to Microsoft orthodoxy.

215   Negroponte argued: Nicholas Negroponte, "Affordable Computing," *Wired*, July 1995, 192.

215   Myhrvold argued: Nathan Myhrvold, e-mail to Gordon Bell et al., 29 May 1995.

216   Glaser's "bad PC": Rob Glaser, e-mail to Gordon Bell et al., 21 May 1995.

217   Ellison's "PCs are old hat": "Oracle Plans To Sell Network Computer," *Wall Street Journal*, 6 October 1995.

217   Why should we expect: Nathan Myhrvold, "Where Are the Used Computers," e-mail, 6 December 1995. Myhrvold's position that consumers did not want less capable machines was held by others who were unconnected to Microsoft. For two of the earliest but best essays written by industry columnists on the subject, disparaging the idea of a storageless terminal, see Stewart Alsop, "Oracle, Sun, and IBM Are Trying To Replace the PC With *Dumb and Dumber," Infoworld,* 20 November 1995, 110; and John Dodge, "$500 Internet PCs: Where's the Beef?," *PC Week,* 20 November 1995, 3.

217   Microsoft's lengthening list: With the hiring of Gordon Bell and also that of Jim Gray, a leading database authority held in such high esteem that Gates made an exception and allowed him to remain in California, the press spoke of Microsoft's roster of eminent authorities as a "brain trust." See "Gordon Bell Is Latest High-Tech Star To Join Microsoft's Growing Brain Trust," *Wall Street Journal*, 16 August 1995.

217   Microsoft revived: "SIPC Systems To Rival Low-Cost NCs," *Infoworld*, 27 May 1996.

217   Oracle's Network Computer: An unidentified Oracle executive, when asked how the company had decided which parts of the standard PC to retain and which to discard, is reported to have replied, "There was no debate—we took out the Pentium and Windows." "Electric World," *Wired*, February 1996, 42.

217   Gates's "Sea Change": Bill Gates, "Sea Change Brings Opportunity," Microsoft memo, 6 October 1994.

217 Gates's "Tidal Wave": Bill Gates, "The Internet Tidal Wave," Microsoft memo, 26 May 1995. Gates blasted the state of Microsoft's own internal corporate network, on which navigation was more difficult than on the Web. But if Microsoft's internal system lagged, so too, he suggested, did the internal networks of corporate customers, and therein would be a new business opportunity for an Internet-savvy Microsoft.

219 Darling of Wall Street: "High Hopes Push Netscape into Stratosphere," *San Jose Mercury News*, October 26, 1995.

221 McNamee's "Why Microsoft and Intel Don't Matter Anymore": Summarized in Denise Caruso's "Digital Commerce" column, *New York Times*, 9 October 1995.

221 Berst pointed out: "Microsoft: Embrace. Extend. Exterminate." *PC Week*, 18 December 1995, 69.

221 Gates predicted: Bill Gates, "Internet Strategy Workshop Keynote," Microsoft conference, 7 December 1995.

222 Gates's "really gets us going": Bill Gates, Microsoft Company Meeting, 1995.

223 Smaller content providers: "Microsoft's Partners in On-Line Network Feel Brunt of Change," *Wall Street Journal*, 12 April 1996.

223 Content providers for CompuServe: "CompuServe To End Its Own Software, Move to Internet," *Wall Street Journal*, 21 May 1996.

223 Securing the support of AOL: "Microsoft Gets a Big Boost on Internet," *New York Times*, 13 March 1996.

223 Jobs's "this is really weird": "Microsoft Gives Demonstration of Its New Technologies," *New York Times*, 13 March 1996.

224 Myhrvold reasoned: Nathan Myhrvold, "Principles for Online Content & Brands," Microsoft memo, 16 July 1995.

225 Consumer Division's ability: "After Win95, What Do You Do for an Encore?" *Business Week*, 16 October 1995, 68.

225 February 1996 reorganization: "Internet Mandate Drives Microsoft to Reorganize," *Windows Watcher*, April 1996, 1, 10–16.

226 Less costly: The expensive box that was used in Encarta's debut year, which cost $13 each, had been selected when early planning had assumed the retail price would be $395. When Encarta's price was lowered to $99, $13 turned out to be outrageously high. The way that Microsoft in 1994 lowered its cost of goods for Encarta to

one-fourth what the costs had been and continued to pare costs subsequently, not just for Encarta but also for its other CD-ROM titles, illustrates one of the prosaic, little-noticed reasons for Microsoft's fabulous profits.

Afterword

228 Perkins quotation: Edward Chase Kirkland, *Dream and Thought in the Business Community, 1860-1900* (Ithaca, NY: Cornell University Press, 1956): 164–165.

228 Doerr quotation: Transcription of talk delivered to Intermedia Conference, 1994.

228 Emerson quotation: Ralph Waldo Emerson, *The Best of Ralph Waldo Emerson: Essays, Poems, Addresses* (New York: Walter J. Black, 1941), 161.

229 *Wealth and Biography*: Reprints of two early editions of *Wealth and Biography of the Wealthy Citizens of New York City*—the fifth, published in 1845, and the twelfth, published in 1855—are found in Moses Yale Beach, *The Wealthy Citizens of New York* (New York: Arno Press, 1973).

The census of the wealthiest expanded nationally in 1892, at a time when a high tariff was at the center of national political debate. The Farmer's Alliance had charged that no fewer than 31,000 businessmen had become millionaires by "robbery" in the form of charging higher prices due to the tariff. The *New York Tribune* set out to ascertain a precise list of those whose net worth had exceeded a million dollars. The resulting list consisted of 4047 names, far fewer than had been thought. See "The *Tribune* 4,047," *Forbes*, 24 October 1988.

229 Rockefeller's "bound to be rich": John K. Winkler, *John D.: A Portrait in Oils* (New York: Vanguard, 1929), 66–67. Peter Collier and David Horowitz in *The Rockefellers: An American Dynasty* (Holt, Rinehart and Winston: New York, 1976), 19, cite Winkler as their source for the "Bound to be rich" quotation, but they embellish the anecdote with details of uncertain provenance. In their account, unlike that of Winkler's, Rockefeller is not confiding to his partner but rather is alone in his office, unaware of a bystander at the door, when the tycoon jumps up in the air, clicks his heels, and repeats the phrase aloud as if it were a magical incantation.

230 Gates on "real wealth": "William Henry Gates III," *Forbes*, 27 October 1986, 173.

230 *Forbes* anointed: *Forbes*, 27 October 1986; 26 October 1987; 24 October 1988; 23 October 1989; 22 October 1990; 21 October 1991; 19 October 1992; 18 October 1993; 17 October 1994; 16 October 1995; the 1996 figure is an estimate as of May 29, when Microsoft shares closed at just above 117. According to the most recent available reports filed with the Securities and Exchange Commission, Gates owned a little more than 141 million Micosoft shares (just short of 24 percent of all outstanding shares).

230 Private metaphysics: To some extent Gates does have a point, even though the public has shown no interest in exploring this aspect. The widely reported net worth figure obscures the tax bite that he staves off as long as he holds on to the shares and the deflating effect on the share prices that his withdrawal from the company would undoubtedly occasion. To what degree prices would fall is hard to predict, so it is indeed hard to know what Gates would actually end up with if he were to actually try to cash out his Microsoft holdings.

230 Seattle reporter: Jack Broom, "Richest Guy in U.S. Could Lasso the Sun in Duct Tape," *Seattle Times*, 8 July 1994.

230 Gates still would have been worth: "Bill Gates' Next Challenge," *Fortune*, 28 December 1992.

230 Comparability is misleading: John Steele Gordon, "Numbers Game," *Forbes*, 19 October 1992. Gordon provided an inflation-corrected income equivalent of $42,000, which I have taken the liberty of adjusting upward to $45,000 to take into account inflation since the article appeared. See U.S. Bureau of the Census, *U.S. Statistical Abstract of the United States* (GPO: Washington, D.C., 1995), 491.

231 Friend's greeting: S. N. Behrman, "The Days of Duveen," *The New Yorker*, 9 November 1951, 56. Quoted in Kirkland, *Dream and Thought,* 3.

232 Experiences as a page: Bill Gates, oral history interview, with David Allison, of the Smithsonian Institution, 30 November 1993.

232 Same had held true: Kenneth Olsen, founder of Digital Equipment Corporation, would have been another member of the club, were it not for his having sold 77 percent of DEC's stock for $70,000 in the late 1950s. By 1987, if he had retained the stock, his net worth would have been about $5 billion. "The Computer Kings," *Fortune*, 12 October 1987.

232 Gates's family did not play: Even 20 years after its founding, Gates remains anxious to put to rest the story that the company was originally

funded with a trust fund. See his defensive declaration "from the start, Paul and I funded everything ourselves" in Bill Gates, with Nathan Myhrvold and Peter Rinearson, *The Road Ahead* (New York: Viking, 1995), 18. During an interview in 1990, he expressed exasperation at the way Philippe Kahn had glamorized Borland's school-of-hard-knocks origins. When the interviewer suggested that Kahn's Borland indeed had origins that better lent themselves to drama, Gates attempted to portray Microsoft's origins as similarly precarious: "Dropping out of school when there was no industry to go to MITS [the tiny company in Albuquerque that introduced the first personal computer kit, the Altair]? They have no money, they're a bankrupt company, they don't pay us, we're staying at the Sundowner Motel." During these tribulations, Gates said, Kahn was still a math student in France, Steve Jobs was off in India "trying to be cool," and Adobe's John Warnock was in "his cush laboratory at Xerox." See John Perry Barlow, "Another Side of Bill Gates," *Microtimes*, 26 November 1990, 62.

232 Gates's "just silly": "A Hard-Driving Program Is Key to Tycoon's Success," *Seattle Times*, 29 January 1984.

233 Abstract multiplication: "Playboy Interview: Bill Gates," *Playboy*, July 1994.

233 Gates's linguistic sophistry: Mark Stevens [Stephens], "Revenge of the Nerd," *M Inc.*, December 1990, 86. Did Gates learn his lesson? No, he did not. The very next year, in testifying in a civil case involving Microsoft, he was obviously so concerned with readying his it's-just-stock, it's-not-real-money soliloquy, that it was he who stumbled momentarily when cross-examined about his wealth by the plaintiff's attorney:

Q: Now Mr. Gates, you are the owner of approximately 57 million shares of Microsoft Corporation?

Gates: No.

Q: You deny that you are the owner of that?

Gates: That's right, since the last split, you are right. It is about 57. I forgot about the last split . . .

Each share was worth approximately $100, was it not, Mr. Gates? "I don't know," Gates replied. Everyone else might be fixated upon it, but Gates resisted acknowledging publicly the monstrous abstraction represented by the value of the stock. See transcript: *Alalamiah Electronics Company* v. *Microsoft Corporation*, U.S. District Court for the Western District of Washington at Seattle, volume 4-A, 26 December 1991, 620–621.

233 "Semi-public" conference: The fifth Technology, Education, Design Conference (TED 5); I refer to it as "semi-public" because tickets were expensive and scarce and press coverage was minimal. Hence it was a more relaxed gathering that did not require an always-on-the-record vigilance.

233 Lost $120 million: A federal jury assessed the judgment in February 1994, finding Microsoft guilty of infringing two patents pertaining to disk compression software held by Stac Electronics, a small software utilities company. The $120 million judgment against Microsoft was mitigated partially when the same jury found Stac guilty of appropriating some of Microsoft's trade secrets and awarded Microsoft $13.7 million in compensatory and punitive damages. The case dragged on when the judge ruled that Microsoft had to recall the software that infringed on Stac's patents and Microsoft appealed. But, before matters came to a head, the two companies announced an out-of-court settlement involving a broad cross-license agreement and Microsoft's purchase of a 15 percent stake in Stac. See "Doing What's Best for Business, Microsoft and Stac End Legal Tussling," *The Report on Microsoft*, 4 July 1994.

233 Gates's "bad day yesterday": Transcript, TED5, February 24–26, 1994. A few months later, when irritated by fatuous questions put to him by Connie Chung (sample: "Do you think you're successful?"), Gates was goaded beyond his threshhold of endurance by a question about the Stac case. He walked out of the interview in his office while the cameras rolled and Chung exulted at scoring what passes in her line of journalism as a coup. The incident would be retold at water coolers across the nation the next day with dramatic touches (*. . . and then Gates stormed out! . . .*). For readers who did not happen to see the broadcast but whose curiosity was piqued by the stories, here is what transpired at what turned out to be the end of the session:

[Clip of Stac Electronics' head, Gary Chow]

Chow: A lot of people make the analogy that competing with Bill Gates is like playing hardball. I'd say it's more like a knife fight.

[Jump to shot of Gates in his office, apparently having been asked to comment on Chow's statement]

Gates: I've never heard any of these things. You're saying like, knife fight? That's silliness, it's childish. I mean, why be the mouthpiece for that kind of silliness. Why doesn't he just say—anyway—because it has nothing to do with the patent lawsuit, it has to do with just craziness, a sort of David versus Goliath thing out of it.

[Gates turns to rear, to an off-camera person, with emphatic phrasing]

Well, I'm done.

Chung: Can I just ask you one more question?

Gates: No, I don't think so.

[Gates stands up, takes microphone off, walks slowly out of office]

Transcript of *Eye-To-Eye* broadcast, 19 May 1994.

234 Gates's "we never talk about money": "Playboy Interview: Bill Gates."

234 Would be volatile: "Gates Envisions Linked, Fast PCs," *Seattle Post-Intelligencer*, 13 October 1987. On his losses the day of the crash, see "PC Stock Prices Trampled on Market's 'Black Monday,'" *PC Week*, 27 October 1987.

234 Gates's uninflected reply: "$2 Bill Loss Leaves Gates With $13 Billion," *San Jose Mercury News*, 20 July 1995.

235 Gates's "just never grabbed me": Stevens [Stephens], "Revenge of the Nerd."

235 Gates as freakish figure: No one has worked harder to create a freakish image of Gates than reporter Mark Stephens (author of "Revenge of the Nerd" cited above) who published a book of computer industry gossip, *Accidental Empires*, under the pseudonym Robert X. Cringely. In it, he retailed a tale of Gates standing in a convenience store check-out line one night around midnight, fumbling for what he mumbled was a 50¢ coupon that he thought was somewhere in his pockets. Meanwhile his carton of ice cream was melting and the customers behind him were fuming. When the next person in line angrily slapped down two quarters, sarcastically telling Gates to pay him back "when you earn your first million," Gates, the penurious eccentric, scooped up the proffered quarters without quibble. The book became a bestseller, and that passage, which might have even shamed *The Simpsons's* Mr. Burns, was featured most prominently in excerpts and reviews. It was so irresistibly outrageous that to pause and inquire whether it was anything but urban-legend apocrypha would be the mark of a prim spoilsport.

Initially after *Accidental Empires's* publication, interviewers asked Gates about the story, and Gates naively thought that its preposterousness was self-apparent. Yeah, right, he sarcastically would answer when asked about it. But the story did not go away. Once conjured into existence, it would live on, not on the strength of any corroboration but simply because of the delicious comeuppance that its telling provided. Gates would never be able to put it to rest—even when he laid out logically the impossibility of such a story. In a subsequent interview, he wondered aloud, for example, whether 7–11's accepted coupons ("I should check that out, maybe I could prove that it is not true"). Meanwhile the interviewer was assembling evidence of an unflattering portrait unrelated to the contents of Gates's denial. Gates's voice rose in register "towards a high-pitched whine" and his credibility was further impugned when the reporter told of how Gates, "the richest man in America," only a few minutes later politely complained to a server at the airport snack concession about being charged $1.65 for a small Pepsi. For the original tale, see Robert X. Cringely, *Accidental Empires: How the Boys of Silicon Valley Make Their Millions, Battle Foreign Competition, and Still Can't Get a Date* (Reading, MA: Addison-Wesley, 1992), 93. On Stephens's avowal of the veracity of the story, which turned on Stephens's judgment that it "fit Gates's known behavior," see "Mr. X—Coupon King Bill Gates and Other High-Tech Tales," *Seattle Times*, 27 February 1992. (Stephens did not respond to any of my repeated inquiries about the particulars of the incident.) On the overpriced Pepsi, see "Genius at Work," *Maclean's*, 11 May 1992.

235   Sighted at a hotel bar: "Cringe's Agenda: Get Pammy Back, Fix NT Printing Problems, Acquire EDS," *Infoworld*, 27 September 1993, 118.

235   Being so rich: Joel Achenback, "Billionaire Bill Gates, Cult Hero, Cracks Open a Window on the Secret of His Success," *Washington Post*, 14 April 1993.

236   Underground garage: "Brain Drain Borland Style," *Windows Watcher*, September 1993, back page.

236   Winning architect: "Blending In—Jim Cutler's Designs Admit Up Front That We Are Visitors on This Planet," *Seattle Times*, 8 July 1990.

236   "Injustice of concentrated wealth": Gifford Pinchot, *Breaking New Ground* (New York: Harcourt, Brace, 1947), 48, quoted in Kirkland, *Dream and Thought*, 42. Pinchot was employed on the Vanderbilt's Biltmore estate, on which had been built a feudal castle, which Pinchot felt "did not belong" in the United States, among the one-room cabins of the Appalachians.

236   Wealthy benefactor: Originally quoted in H.F. May, *Protestant Churches and Industrial America* (New York: Harper, 1949), 192. Cited in Kirkland, *Dream and Thought*, 37.

237   Gates's architect "do penance": "Blending In."

237   Gates's "indulgent": "Playboy Interview: Bill Gates."

237 Partial justification: "Gifted Houses," *Forbes*, 22 October 1990; also see Stevens [Stephens], "Revenge of the Nerd," for an early attempt by Gates to argue that the large house was needed to have "big gatherings of employees over for dinner."

237 Unlike Hearst's estate: Gates, *The Road Ahead*, 215–216. On 27 November 1995, in the course of public appearances to promote the book, Gates encountered David Letterman's insistent questions about the house's outsized scale:

Letterman: How many square feet is this [new house]?

Gates: Well, it's fairly big.

Letterman: What are we talking about?

Gates: Oh, more than 50,000 square feet. [Loud "Ooh" from audience]

Letterman: 50,000 square feet? This *theater* is not that big, Bill. [Audience laughter]

237 Assailed by Ida Tarbell: "John D. Rockefeller: A Character Study," *McClure's Magazine*, July-August 1905, 249, 387. Cited in Kirkland, *Dream and Thought*, 38.

238 Gates's "I like": ABC News, *20/20*, 22 November 1991.

238 Future spouse: "A Marriage Made at Microsoft: Gates To Wed an Insider," *Wall Street Journal*, 24 March 1993.

239 Press badgered: G. Pascal Zachary, "The Once and Future Microsoft," *Upside*, April 1995, 16, 18.

239 Witnessed an increase: The estimates were given in a talk, not presented in a published article, so the methodology used to arrive at these suspiciously even figures—both market capitalization and revenues happened to be an even $100 billion?—was not divulged. Perhaps the figures should not be read literally but instead interpreted as an adjectival phrase meaning "really big."

241 I am not convinced: As a skeptic of the notion that PCs and the Net have had, are having, or even will have a revolutionary positive impact on society, I am glad to have all the company I can, including Steve Jobs. Readers who are familiar with my previous book know that, in the past, I have been rather hard on Mr. Jobs and his revolutionary proclamations. So I was surprised to see a different Steve Jobs in 1996 from the one I had lambasted. When an eager *Wired* reporter sought Jobs's blessing for the idea that the Web would be the "great democratizer," Jobs replied, "The Web is not going to change the world, certainly not

in the next 10 years.... The problem is I'm older now, I'm 40 years old, and this stuff doesn't change the world. It really doesn't." See "Steve Jobs: The Next Insanely Great Thing," *Wired* (February 1996), 106.

242 Cumulative voting: Nathan Myhrvold, "Road Kill on the Information Highway," Microsoft memo, 8 September 1993.

242 Major change was ahead: Bill Gates, oral history interview, 1 December 1993.

242 Highway will help us: For trivial examples of benefits, see Gates, *The Road Ahead*, 9, 10, 66, 76, 80, 87, 115, 129, 165, 211, 213.

243 Offers as sop: Gates, *The Road Ahead*, 6. This theme was advanced by Gates earlier, too:

> The things we do that use a lot of resources and time can be done more efficiently. So people wonder, Will there be jobs? Will there be things to do? Until we're educating every kid in a fantastic way, until every inner city is cleaned up, there is no shortage of things to do. And as society gets richer, we can choose to allocate the resources in a way that gives people the incentive to go out and do those unfinished jobs.

That phrase "we can choose ..." is essential. Suppose society does *not* choose to increase the allocation of resources to these other tasks? What then? See "Playboy Interview: Bill Gates."

244 Puts on the robes: The one instance when Gates does bring up his personal finances in *The Road Ahead* is when he offhandedly mentions (p. 260) that he paid more than $100 million in taxes in 1994. He said he was not complaining, and he mentioned the figure only to illustrate a point about variation in "prices" for services—and also, clearly to make a tacit point that he pays his fair share, too. But he did not disclose his total income from that year. So, based on what he chose to tell us, it's impossible to form a judgment about "fair share." And mention of the $100 million figure could backfire when readers speculate just how much income is required for him to face a tax bill of such magnitude. For the curious who compared his net worth in 1995 at the time of *Forbes's* annual survey of the 400 wealthiest Americans with the number in 1994 and did the math, the average increase works out to $450 million each month for an entire year!

244 Gates "confident and optimistic": Gates, *The Road Ahead*, 11.

244 Gates's "wonderful time to be alive": Gates, *The Road Ahead*, 276.

245 Gates on "dynasty": "Mr. Software," *New York Times*, 25 August 1991.

245 Planned to give away: "Playboy Interview: Bill Gates."

245 Gifts had totaled: "Noblesse Oblige . . . With Strings," *New York Times*, 30 April 1995.

245 To Stanford: When presenting the gift to Stanford, Gates did not say outright that he had an ulterior motive in helping Microsoft recruit promising computer science students, but he did exuberantly say that he wanted to invest in "the future of the industry" and "Stanford is one of the five best computer science schools in the country." See "Microsoft's Gates Donates $6 Million to Stanford," *Wall Street Journal*, 27 August 1992.

245 "Bill Gates—Save Us": "Microsoft's Unlikely Millionaires," *New York Times*, 28 June 1992.

245 Campus newspaper complained: "Gates' Gift Good News, But . . ." *The Daily* [UW], 9 October 1991.

246 Gates's "degree Microsoft can do well": "Mr. Software."

246 Ford was still nattering: Henry Ford, in collaboration with Samuel Crowther, *My Life and Work* (Garden City, NY: Doubleday, Page & Company, 1922), 206-207.

246 Sought to prevent: Robert Lacey, *Ford: The Men and the Machine* (Boston, Little, Brown: 1986) 450-451.

246 Let's imagine: The estimates of how long Gates's net worth would last if applied to existing federal programs are based on 1995 estimates provided in U.S. Bureau of the Census, *U.S. Statistical Abstract of the United States* (GPO: Washington, D.C., 1995), 337-338.

247 Forty years later: David L. Lewis, *The Public Image of Henry Ford: An American Hero and His Company* (Detroit: Wayne State University Press, 1976), 70.

248 Historians do not agree: Lewis, *The Public Image of Henry Ford*, 69. For an account that portrays the figure of $5 as the outcome of a series of dares, see Nevins, *Ford*, 533.

248 Neither "charity nor wages": Nevins, *Ford*, 534.

248 Had to demonstrate: Lewis, *Public Image of Henry Ford*, 70.

248 *Cleveland Plain Dealer* and other newspaper coverage: Lewis, *Public Image of Henry Ford*, 70-71.

249 *New York Times* and *Wall Street Journal*: Lewis, *Public Image of Henry Ford*, 71.

249 Actual cost: Lewis, *Public Image of Henry Ford*, 72.

249 Americans polled: "$5 a Day," *Automotive News*, 2 January 1989.

250 These events introduced: Nevins, *Ford*, 551.

252 Ford launched: Lewis, *Public Image of Henry Ford*, 76, 78.

252 Gates's "not a politician": "Gates' Way to Success," *PC User*, 11 September 1991.

252 Gates preposterously proposed: Gates, *The Road Ahead*, 156.

Index